THE WORLD
IS TURNING

" '9/11' ",
THE MOVEMENT FOR JUSTICE,
AND RECLAIMING AMERICA FOR THE WORLD

DON PAUL

About the author of *The World Is Turning* ...

'Don Paul's work reaches the core of the crime of 9/11/01, follows it beyond US boundaries to its global roots, and is one of the rare efforts that also moves the case forward as a serious criminal investigation. Paul's books also are inspiring, touching on social movements and figures that point toward solutions to benefit all.'
VICTORIA ASHLEY

'Don Paul continues to offer hope and inspire others. It is an honor to stand alongside such a passionate, caring man.'
GREGORY W. JOHNSON, Houston, TX 9/11 Truth group

'In Houston, my appreciation for Paul's immense multi-talents as a writer, musician, and an advocate for change grew.'
MARK WINITZ, *California Track and Running News* profile, 2006

'Don Paul's <u>Good</u> <u>Intentions</u> proposes and explores the only kind of revolution that that seems possible in North America.'
LAWRENCE FERLINGHETTI, first Poet Laureate of San Francisco

'Read these poems and listen for the music that is there.'
MATT GONZALEZ, former President of the San Francisco Board of Supervisors, in his Introduction to the collection <u>Flares</u> (2002)

'DON PAUL HAS GIVEN FREELY HIS MONEY, HIS TIME AND HIS FULL EFFORT FOR THE RECOVERY OF NEW ORLEANS. I KNOW OF NO OTHER PERSON IN MY LIFE THAT IS SO DEDICATED TO THE WELFARE AND HEALTH OF PEOPLE.'
DAVID PEARLMAN (POPPA NEUTRINO), subject of Alec Wilkinson's <u>The</u> <u>Happiest</u> <u>Man</u> <u>in</u> <u>the</u> <u>World</u> (Random House, 2007)

Still from video by O.C. Draughan, July 2007, at rebuildgreen.org

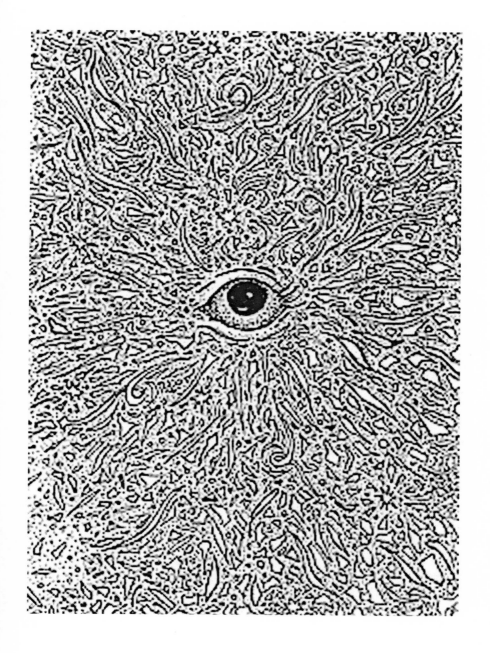

The columns for the *San Francisco Bay View* that make up **What a Plot!** were first published between September 12 and December 12, 2001.

The chapters from **" '9/11' "** / <u>**Facing**</u> <u>**Our**</u> <u>**Fascist**</u> <u>**State**</u> entitled **Forward!**, **The Airliners and Their " 'Hijackers' "**, **The Air-Defenses and Their " 'Failures' "**, and **The Buildings and Their Victims** were first published in the *San Francisco Call* on-line between September 29 and October 20, 2002. The book itself was published in December 2002.

The **American Crusade 2001+ Trading Card** images in ... <u>Fascist</u> <u>State</u> were created by **Ted McManus** and are published as free downloads by The Infinite Jest at http://yorick.infinitejest.org:81/1/cards.html .

The interview by **Marie Harrison** was printed on December 18, 2002 in the *San Francisco Bay View*.

The interview by **Bob Feldman** from June 2003 was posted at **New York Indymedia** and available online at **Jim Hoffman's** site **911review.com--** http://911review.com/articles/dp/DPInterview.htm .

The piece for the online publication *Garlic & Grass*, 'The Best Evidence Available on the 9/11 Conspiracy', came out in June 2005.

The review of **Jack Hirschman's** <u>**Front**</u> <u>**Lines:**</u> <u>**Selected**</u> <u>**Poem**</u>s came out in the online *S. F. Call* of March 10, 2003.
The review of **Lawrence Ferlinghetti's** <u>**Americus**</u> <u>**1**</u> came out in the online *Beyond Chron* of January 20, 2005.

The book <u>**To**</u> <u>**Prevent**</u> <u>**the**</u> <u>**Next**</u> **" '9/11' "** / <u>**Abandoning the**</u> **'New World** <u>**Order'**</u> <u>**of**</u> <u>**Financiers'**</u> <u>**Corporate**</u> <u>**State**</u> was published in August 2005.

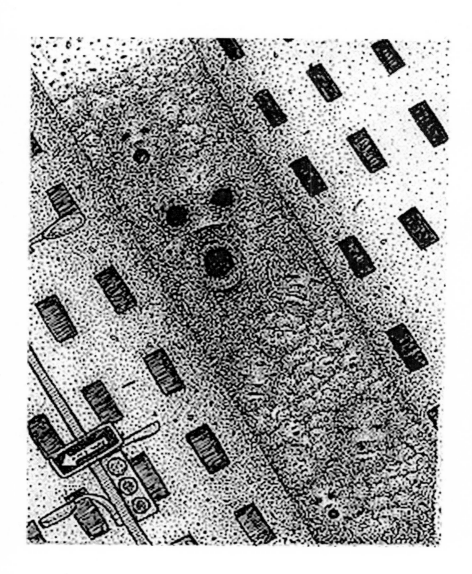

The interview by **Bob Feldman** from September 2006 was posted online at the ***Toward Freedom*** site and is available at http://towardfreedom.com/home/content/view/905/69/ ,

The **Chief Prosecutor's Findings for the San Diego Citizens' Grand Jury on the Crimes of September 11, 2001 in New York City** is from April 2007 and is posted online at the Scholars for 9/11 Truth and Justice site-- http://stj911.org/paul/CPFindings_SDCGJCharges.html . The **'Wanted Poster'** is also available at this site (thanks to **Rob Leslie** for the poster)-- http://stj911.org/paul/SDGJWantedPoster.pdf

The introduction by **Kevin Ryan** is from November 2008.

Back-cover shadow-art art and other drawings of the 9/11/01 experience in New York City are by **Mac McGill** and are posted online at a **Library of Congress** site-- http://www.loc.gov/exhibits/911/911-comics.html .

Special thanks to **Jerry Anomie** and **Shiu Hung** for fundling the first edition of **" '9/11' "** / **Facing Our Fascist State** .

IRRESISTIBLE/REVOLUTIONARY
POB 74-1365, New Orleans, LA 70114
www.wireonfire.com/donpaul
www.rebuildgreen.org

For my daughter PALOMA,
for my nephews KEENAN and AIDAN,
and for their mothers,
my mother,
and her mother

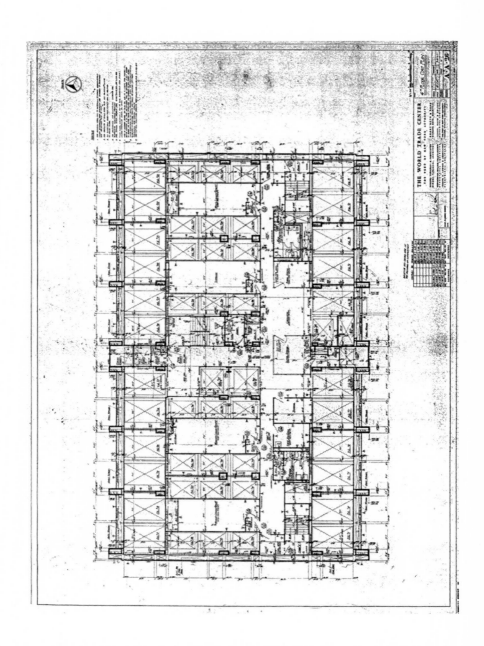

BLUEPRINT FOR NORTH TOWER 4TH FLOOR ELEVATORS

CONTENTS

INTRODUCTION by KEVIN RYAN
3

'WHAT A PLOT!'
(Columns from September 12, 2001 to December 12, 2001
for the *San Francisco Bay View* weekly newspaper)

" '9/11' " / FACING OUR FASCIST STATE
(Completed on September 14, 2002)

JOURNALISM

POETRY BREAK

TO PREVENT THE NEXT " '9/11' ' /
ABANDONING 'THE NEW WORLD ORDER'
OF FINANCIERS' CORPORATE STATE
(Published in August 2005)

JOURNALISM

CHIEF PROSECUTOR'S RECORD
OF FINDINGS, INDICTMENTS AND PRESENTMENTS
FROM THE *SAN DIEGO CITIZENS' GRAND JURY*
ON THE CRIMES OF SEPTEMBER 11, 2001
IN NEW YORK CITY

WANTED
FOR CONSPIRACY TO COMMIT MASS MURDER

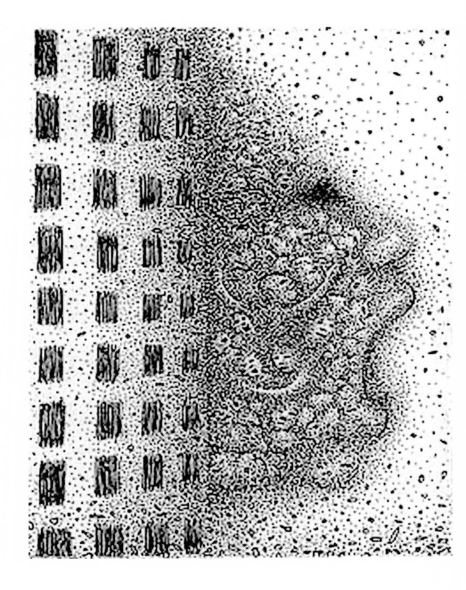

INTRODUCTION
by KEVIN RYAN

The World Is Turning: " '9/11' ", the Movement for Justice, and Reclaiming America for the World combines two earlier books by Don Paul and much other material into a single volume. This book of books, including pieces that expose 2008's bail-out of commercial and investment Banks, altogether takes us on a crucially revealing journey into realities and lies that shape our present.

Each of the two earlier books by Don Paul uses an odd orthography in its title: " '9/11' " / Facing Our Fascist State from 2002 and To Prevent the Next " '9/11' " / Abandoning the 'New World Order' of Financiers' Corporate State from 2005. Paul explains in FOFS that 'the double quotes' around 9/11 are meant 'to represent the echo-effect of Government officials and Corporate media on public consciousness. 'The information thus repeated in our dominant media-scape makes up one big echo-chamber or mirror for Corporate Government.'

A large part of what we gain from the two books--and from the three interviews that are also included in this volume--is knowledge that those responsible for our multi-national 'Corporate Government' are most likely responsible for at least the cover-up of the crimes we've come to know as 9/11. Most importantly, this record of seven years' work gives us tools to penetrate layers of deceit, to perceive guilt, to arrive at justice, and to free ourselves.

Don Paul quickly sensed that something was amiss in the Official Story for our 21st-century Day of Infamy.

He wrote in a September, 19, 2001 column for the *San Francisco Bay View* weekly: 'I think the best protection we have now, the best antidote we have to vengeful hysteria among a sadly underinformed public, is to consider and investigate as fully as we can the possibility that at least one part of the U. S. Government at least allowed the attacks of September 11.'

One year later his FOFS reiterated 'the undeniable proofs' for 'three defining facts' that disproved the Official Story. The last of these 'facts' became of special, life-changing interest to me and many others who were later able to offer compelling physical evidence in support of the basic assertion that Don Paul put forth in 2002: '... the World Trade Center's 110-story Twin Towers and 47-

story Building 7 COULD NOT have fallen as they did unless they were demolished by explosives set off within their structures.'

Now, recognition of that 'fact' of the three Buildings' demolition on 9/11/01, a 'fact' multiply substantiated over the past few years, may itself be so traumatic, challenging and daunting, that its reality must be denied, unless the recognition is accompanied by an analysis that allows one to make sense of that very provable fact's causal forces and to thereby fight back against those forces.

What do we do with such a shattering, staggering fact and its implications?

The gift of this single volume is that it lets us see how one person's understanding went forward. Interviewed by Bob Feldman in 2003, Don Paul pointed to 'a skein of conspiracies that have benefited a tiny superelite within the U.S. over at least the past 40 years--from "Dallas" to "9/11" and beyond.... These conspiracies' endgame, I believe, is a "New World Order" that will rob everyday people of their rights and powers to resist the superelites' accelerating degradation of once natural environments.'

In 2005 Paul began to write an introduction to a planned second edition of FOFS. The writing grew beyond its expected bounds and became the subsequently published To Prevent the Next " '9/11' " / Abandoning the 'New World Order' of Financiers' Corporate State. Here we see what Paul has learned (an education partly conveyed in the 2004 book that he co-authored with 911research.wtc7.net creator Jim Hoffman, Waking Up from Our Nightmare / The 9/11/01 Crimes in New York City) about roots of our post-9/11 predicament during years of deepening United States' occupations of Afghanistan and Iraq.

He goes far and wide in this book that was meant to augment FOFS.

The first section of To Prevent is called 'The Ruling Few on We Masses' and it starts with a lengthy quotation from a letter written by the Rothschild Brothers investment-bankers of London, England to an associate firm on New York's Wall Street during the U. S. Civil War.

The June 23, 1863 letter from the Rothschild Brothers in London cites a U. S. Senator, 'a Mr. John Sherman' of Ohio, as speaking in support of the 'profits that may be made in the National Banking business under a recent act of your Congress', an act 'Apparently ... drawn upon the plan formulated here last Summer by the British

Bankers Association' and an act that 'would prove highly profitable to the banking fraternity throughout the world.'

The Rothschild Brothers letter quotes Sherman thus: 'The few who can understand the system,' he says, 'will either be so interested in its profits, or so dependent on its favors, that there will be no opposition from that class, while on the other hand, the great body of people, mentally incapable of comprehending the tremendous advantages that capital derives from the system, will bear its burdens without complaint and perhaps without even suspecting that the system is inimical (adverse) to their interests.'

The quoted excerpt lets us see what Paul means by his posed perception of 'The Ruling Few on We Masses'.

He's ranged so far as to begin a 2005 book that's titled To Prevent the Next " '9/11' " with a 142-year-old quote from private bankers in England about how the enactment of the third central bank in the United States' history (Thomas Jefferson, John Adams and James Madison vehemently opposed the first such Bank and Andrew Jackson "killed" the second) 'would prove highly profitable to the banking fraternity throughout the world.'

Most telling toward the deep view that Paul wishes to communicate, however, is the attitude of dismissal ascribed to Senator Sherman (later author of the Anti-Trust Act) in the letter between the bankers. The 'few who can understand the system' will be compliant to profit from it, while 'the great body of people, mentally incapable ... will bear its [the system's] burdens without complaint and perhaps without even suspecting that the system is inimical (adverse) to their interests.'

In To Prevent ... Don Paul helps us to comprehend how this system of debt-based servitude and rule by financiers over Governments has come to dominate " 'the developed world' " and to ruthlessly exploit resources of " 'the underdeveloped world ' " from the Colonial to Neo-liberal eras.

He shows how mass-media lies since 2003 have served as post-9/11 traumas, further duping and demoralizing our nation's public. He makes clear, too, that 'the enemy is us', whether we bear our increasing 'burdens' without complaint, or whether we're 'so interested' in the 'profits' or 'so dependent' on the 'favors' of an inimical system that we choose not to oppose it.

A few years ago, I found myself in a position to speak out about one event in what I came to identify as continuing, increasing efforts for deception and domiance by a Ruling Few. I had come across information that allowed me to bring attention to the absolute discrepancy between evidence and findings by my employer, Underwriter Laboratories, about the fire-resistant capacities of structural steel within the Twin Towers. Through the Internet and through the cooperation of far-flung allies, the discrepancy that I brought up, one which made the National Institute of Standards and Technology's ultimate treatment of the evidence seem like surreal nonsense, received millions of readings. It was, I suppose, another step on our collective journey toward arriving at accountability for the crimes of 9/11/01.

In April of 2007, two years after <u>To Prevent</u> ... and one year after the "9/11Guilt" DVD that he co-produced with Jim Hoffman and Celestine Star, Don Paul served as Chief Prosecutor for the *San Diego Citizens' Grand Jury on the Crimes of September 11, 2001 in New York City*. Jim Hoffman was that one-day inquiry's Chief Investigator. Architect Richard Gage and former commercial-pilot Ted Muga were in-person Expert Witnesses and Steven Jones and I were presented on video-tape. 23 U. S. Citizens from southern California volunteered to be the Grand Jury and almost the same number attended the proceedings at San Diego State University as Alternate Jurors. The 'Chief Prosecutor's Record of Findings, Charges, Indictments and Presentments from the *San Diego Citizens' Grand Jury on the Crimes of September 11, 2001 in New York City*' makes for a fitting conclusion to this book's narrative of pursuing realities and justice.

The detail and depth of this Record exceed a rejection of the Official Story for 9/11. The Findings, Charges, Indictments and Presentments move boldly through politicians, Generals, Attorney Generals, F.B.I. Agents and Directors, and come--in the 'Indictments and Presentments for Conspiracy to Commit Mass Murder'--to several businessmen who have sat at the head of the United States' most powerful Banks and secretive groups. These businessmen were heavily invested in the New York City's World Trade Center, their connections more or less direct, and they shared in more or less ways from the tremendous profits that ensued from the " 'Attack on America' ", the destruction in Lower Manhattan, and the invasions and occupations of Afghanistan and Iraq.

That the *San Diego Citizens' Grand Jury*--We Masses--stepped up with such an enlarged map of crimes and such a roster of possible criminals was exhilarating.

The courage shown in San Diego is a sign that we, the long-deceived public of the U. S. and elsewhere, may be ready to 'refuse denial, abandon illusions, shake off the traumas that have been visited upon us, throw off repression, and pursue remedial justice that includes everyone in our society', as Don Paul supposes toward the close of <u>To</u> <u>Prevent</u> .<u>the</u> <u>Next</u> " '9/11' ". Once we know them, the true atrocities of international terrorism may move us to both rebellion and cooperation, the liberating 'all-be world America' that Paul imagines as alternative to elitists' and plutocrats' 'New World Order.'

How will we choose to live? Will we finally throw off our fears and throw off the vampires to our fears? Will we finally see that helping others to develop most helps ourselves--that 'One for all does one most good', as Paul wrote in his novel, <u>Good</u> <u>Intentions?</u>

I think that we may finally achieve such a transformation. I think that the global growth of our movement for truth and justice foretokens a brighter though difficult future.

We can't go on as we have been. We must change. That 'We Masses' remain prey to crimes of 'the Ruling Few' is crystal-clear in 2008's bail-outs of major 'bettor/debtor' financiers of the Western world (some of them key beneficiaries of the 9/11/01 demolitions), as Paul stresses in his recent 'Getting Rid of the "Fed", ...' and 'Five Steps to Freedom and Solvency.'

The 21st-century world is indeed turning. Choices are especially demanded of us in the United States. As crucial parts of the interdependent, increasingly conscious system that is our life on Earth, we may proceed as Don Paul urges-- 'from courage with compassion.' We may thus come to the humbling but empowering realization to which he arrives: 'There is no Other.'

The journey contained within this book speaks for our moving toward justice and for our thus choosing freedom.

Kevin Ryan
November 2008

(Kevin Ryan is co-editor with Dr. Steven Jones and Dr. Frank Legge of the Journal of 9/11 Studies *(journalof911studies.com). He contributed to the 2006 book <u>9/11</u> <u>&</u> <u>American</u> <u>Empire:</u> <u>Intellectuals</u> <u>Speak</u> <u>Out</u>, edited by David Ray Griffin and Peter Dale Scott, and to the 2006 book <u>The</u> <u>Hidden</u> <u>History</u> <u>of</u> <u>9/11</u>, edited by Paul Zarembka His latest publications are available at Scholars for 9/11 Truth and Justice (stj911.org) and an extensive list of his contributions is available at ultruth.com/ .)*

WHAT A PLOT!

Being 6 columns for the San Francisco Bay View
('National Black Newspaper of the Year'),
from the Fall of 2001,
including an early prayer for George W. Bush
& arriving at the 'most enormous and evil scam
in U.S. ruling-class history'

These columns--like this book--trace the evolution of my understanding of how the world works.

On September 11, 2001 I believed that Muslim hijackers must have carried out the attacks of that day in the United States, as I believed that they had obvious reasons for retaliation against this nation and the faith to suicide themselves, Such was the basis for my first San Francisco Bay View *column on the attacks.*

The next day, 9/12/01, I saw the then 34-minutes-long gap in the timeline between the second hit to a Twin Tower and the hit to the Pentagon. This gap (Why was American Airlines 77 not intercepted?) caused my doubts about our Government's and mass media's portrayal of the day's events to leap upward. I began to pursue alternative explanations.

The Bay View *columns document a day-by-day gathering and gleaning. They're reprinted because their information might still be valuable and their findings might still register with others who are pursuing truth about " '9/11' ".*

Since concluding them, however, I've come to see that forces less obvious than nations or a greedy hunger for pipelines and oil direct modern history. I've come to see that a much larger plot, a plot that goes back more than two centuries, a plot whose consistent aims are orchestrated from generation to generation by financiers and their central Banks, a plot relying on acts of terror to provoke wars which maximally advance financiers' profits and control, is most responsible for events whose implausibility and interrelationships (handfuls of vastly outnumbered terrorists command airliners with box-cutters, the U. S. Military fails to intercept hijacked airliners over more than an hour, skyscrapers collapse into their footprints at nearly free-fall speed, and the Western world's mass-media is as one in failing to ask enormously obvious questions) are otherwise difficult to explain.

First, however, to my/our days and weeks of shock and seeking in the Fall of 2001.

THE ONLY REAL SOLUTION IS JUSTICE WITH COMPASSION
(published Sept. 12, 2001)

Again, this day that could lead to a truly new world order, Tuesday, September, 11, 2001, thousands of innocent people have died due to attacks from the air--thousands and perhaps tens of thousands of hard-working, family-loving civilians, none of them witting or willing combatants in war--all of them dead in single moments of terror that together encompassed less than two hours.

Again, the world looks on with stunned horror at the enormity and suddenness of devastation and loss.

Again, relatives of the dead and dying--wives, husbands, daughters, sons, mothers, fathers, ...--wonder how they will ever recover from this nightmare of news, this wrenching rip to their innards and futures, knowing that they can never replace the ones lost.

The difference today is that the victims, the ones lost, did not live in Palestine or Israel or Iraq or Yugoslavia or Somalia or Afghanistan or Sudan or Japan--or in Bayview Hunters Point. Instead, they lived and worked in the commercial and military hearts of the United States.

Few who died in the World Trade Center and the Pentagon and four American and United airliners today knew the desperation, the long and brutal history, the generations of futile struggle and false hopes, that moved their killers.

As of now, Tuesday afternoon in San Francisco, September 11, the Popular Democratic Front for the Liberation of Palestine is reported to have claimed responsibility for the attacks. The hijackers of the crashed airliners, however, might have come from dozens of groups that are aggrieved by policies of the United States Government. In 1993 more than 60 entities said that they'd set off the bombs that almost toppled the World Trade Center towers.

Few here receive information other than through Corporate media. Thus, few here know how Palestinians have been betrayed in the eight years since the 'Oslo Peace Accords.' Few know how Israeli settlements have bitten from Palestinean territory. Few know how Israel and its current head-of-state, Ariel Sharon, provoked the current uprising or intifada. Few know how Palestinean's official leadership has implored the United States to broker terms of a peace that could last--one that would relieve the de facto apartheid that Israel has imposed on Palestineans since at least 1967. Few know how often Israel has resorted to missile attacks on Palestinean civilians in the past two months. Few know that more than seven times more Palestineans than Israelis have died in the uprising that began last September. Few here even know that Israel receives more than 5 billion in aid from the U.S. each year.

Few here will have heard the judgment of Madeline Albright, Secretary of State for the Clinton Administration, that the deaths of

500,000 Iraqi children due to U.S.-led sanctions since 1991 was a "reasonable" price to pay.

Few here know that the U. S. missile attack on China's Consulate in Yugoslavia during the War in Kosovo, an attack that killed three civilians, was a deliberate and brazen warning.

Few here notice the anniversaries of the U.S. atomic bombs' holocausts of Hiroshima and Nagasaki, holocausts that each killed about100,000.

Changing Our Course

What happened today changes everything in terms of the material balance of forces in the world.

No object that the U.S. Government holds sacred can ever again be seen as secure. A dozen well-trained people, ready to sacrifice themselves, can do untold damage.

Modern, technological society is most vulnerable.

What remains to be seen is whether the United States Government will now change its moral course.

Today even Network anchors have to acknowledge the "anger" and "bitterness" that much of the world feels toward our Government. Arab spiritual leaders speak of "the oppression, exploitation and injustice" that the United States has perpetrated.

We must now do the right thing.

If we have the clarity and strength to see that our own Government's forms of mass murder--both international and domestic--have produced the terrible, desperate and unprecedented response of today, we have the chance to go forward to a solution.

The military retaliation that our Government's leaders are already threatening ("Make no mistake ... We will pass this test ... Our military stands ready ... We will hunt down and punish the terrorists") can only escalate warfare. More boundaries will be violated, more means will be found, and thousands and perhaps hundreds of thousands more of innocent people will be killed. A woman down the street where I live worries about "germ warfare-- from us and from them."

Our only real safeguard, our only way out of the minefield that belligerent arrogance has made of the world, is to stand with justice, to fight for justice, and to let "Help the poor" be our watchword.

TRUTH IS THE WAY TO PEACE ... DON'T BELIEVE THE
HYPE ... AND A PRAYER FOR GEORGE W. BUSH
(published Sept. 19, 2001)

How can we really begin to solve the problems that led to last Tuesday's attacks?

How can we really prevent more of the warfare that kills thousands of innocent people in the U.S. and elsewhere?

In 1967 Dr. Martin Luther King nominated the Buddhist poet and monk Thich Nhat Han, exiled from his home country of Vietnam the previous year, a year of increasing war, for the Nobel Peace Prize that Dr. King had won in 1964.

Thich Nhat Han, now 75, continues to speak around the world.

He says that only through suffering can a person gain understanding and compassion.

Thich Nhat Han urges the practice of "deep listening, compassionate listening, and loving speech" to penetrate the blocks of bitterness and hatred between people who have long opposed each other. Practice of his teaching has brought Israelis and Palestineans to work together for peace.

Thich Nhat Han also urges us to seek truth as the foundation for solving problems. He urges us to use each day as a step toward finding clarity, courage and compassion.

With such teaching in mind, teaching that's like that of Christ and Muhammed as well as the Buddha and many others, let's look at the terrible events of last Tuesday, September 11, events that have forced us to repeatedly view TV-fed horrors, and try to find truth, clarity, courage and compassion.

We'll have to ask hard questions. Our questions will have to go beyond the headlines and broadcasts that drum 'WAR' and "War" in Corporate media.

The longer that I look at events of Tuesday, September 11, the more that global information reveals to me about them, the more doubtful the stories told by NBC (owned by General Electric), CBS (owned by Westinghouse), and ABC (owned by Capital Cities/Disney) seem to me.

Check out these questions.

Is it credible that 18 or more men could have escaped detection in boarding four airliners at three major U.S. Airports with knives and other weapons within one hour?

Is it credible that the planning for such precise and multiple attacks, preparation that even Network TV "experts" estimate must have taken months, could have escaped detection by U. S. and all Western intelligence-agencies? Wouldn't students with Arab surnames at flight-schools in Florida be an alert to U.S. intelligence?

Then there's the sequence of crashes.

How could American Airlines Flight #77 lumber into the Pentagon, uncontested, 35 minutes after the second crash by an airliner into the World Trade Center (9:38 a.m. EST versus 9:03 a.m.)? Wouldn't the nation's air defenses be on Red Alert no later than 9:03? Shouldn't F-16s have scrambled to defend the nation's capital no later than one minute after 9:03?

Then there's Corporate media's immediate coverage. Why did CNN report for hours that the Popular Democratic Front for the Liberation of Palestine had claimed responsibility for the attacks, when CNN's only basis for the report was one phone-call from Abu Dhabi?

Why such a rush to judgment by Corporate media?

The cumulative weight of these questions, facts and coincidences reminds me of the assassination of John F. Kennedy and the cover-up of probable truths about that killing.

More than half a dozen people have separately said to me since last Wednesday: "There's something fishy in all of this."

I think the best protection we have now, the best antidote we have to vengeful hysteria among a sadly underinformed public, is to consider and investigate as fully as we can the possibility that at least one part of the U.S. Government at least allowed the attacks of September 11.

Who and What Stand to Gain from "The Terror"?

Let's look now at who and what stand to most benefit from effects after the attacks. "Follow the money," said "Deep Throat" during Watergate. Nikolai Lenin said the same thing as to causes of World War I.

Big Oil and fascistic repression in this nation stand to gain a great deal now.

The price of a barrel of crude oil has already jumped more than $5 on world markets. We know that George W. Bush's Cabinet is thick with ties to oil-and-gas Corporations.

Other economic interests are relieved of pressures by the attacks. Strategic metals were in a tailspin due to the downturn in production of computers--now their main exchange, COMEX, is gone with World Trade Center.

In fact, the entire prospect of blaming Republicans for a Recession/Depression is now gone from from the news.

At the same time, protest against the Corporate neo-colonialism that's called "globalization" is now sidetracked. Unions in the AFL-CIO have dropped their participation in protests against the IMF/World Bank that were scheduled for the last week of September in Washington, DC. Any dissent is imperiled by the "necessary" repression of civil liberties for which Government officials, led by the President, are now calling.

George W. Bush's approval rating has jumped to 89% in Corporate polls. Congress has given him $40 billion and more war-making power than any President has wielded since Franklin D. Roosevelt.

We should therefore recall prior pretexts for 'WAR' by the United States. We should indeed "Remember Pearl Harbor"--and remember our Government's foreknowledge of Japanese attacks (see the books Infamy and Day of Deceit). We should remember the sinking of the *Maine* in 1898 that let Hearst newspapers demand the Spanish-American War. We should remember the sinking of the *Lusitania* that got the U.S. into World War I and thus protected J.P. Morgan from tens of millions of German debts. We should remember that the illusory " 'Gulf of Tonkin Incident' " in 1964 let the U.S. go full-bore into Vietnam.

We should, in short, be very careful about what we believe.

We should be watchful about defending our own hard-won freedoms and rights.

In the middle 1980s Oliver North and others in the U.S. Government, many of them confidants of then Vice-President George Bush, planned 'Operation Rex.' 'Operation Rex' would have swept 400,000 potential 'dissidents' in the U.S. into concentration-camps.

Dissident now means me. It may also mean you.

Justice and Peace

George W. Bush has told the nation that we must "hunt down, find and whip terrorism" in order to "do future generations a favor" and "rid the world of evil."

What would the military campaign that George W. Bush promises mean to us in the U.S. and to the rest of the world?

Would it mean bombing Afghanistan, the presumed refuge of Osama bin Laden, the Saudi exile who's the presumed "mastermind" of a "terror network" that's presumed responsible for the September 11 attacks (though Afghanistan and bin Laden deny any connection to the attacks).

Would it mean invading Afghanistan?

The campaign that George W. Bush promises would kill thousands or tens of thousands or hundred of thousands more of innocent civilians. It would subject the U.S. public to further terror. Supplies of water, oil, gas and even air here are vulnerable to attacks far easier to accomplish than the crashing of an airliner into the Pentagon. Around the world outrage at massive U.S. bombing-- outrage not only from followers of Islam--would surge up to topple Governments. All but a few of us would suffer unimaginably.

Injustice is the source of terrorism, whether terror is used to enforce injustice (the bombing of Lebanon, the bombing of M.O.V.E.) or to resist injustice (Israelis against Britain, Palestineans against Israelis). Efforts to replace basises of injustice with basises for justice are therefore the only possible "end" to terrorism.

Equity is the only worthy basis for peace.

Justice can be the only lasting solution.

We need to ask further questions about our immediate peril. Our questions must be hard and material. Should the U.S. re-engage in the "peace process" between Israel and Palestine? Should Israel return the West Bank to Palestineans? Should Arab nations guarantee Israel sovereignty in a Treaty that the United States backs? Should the U.S. recommit to the Kyoto Protocols to reduce global warming? Should it continue to honor, not renege on, 1972's ABM Treaty? Do African-Americans deserve just compensation (reparations) for their ancestors' 300 or more years of slavery that enriched owners and traders in much of the Western Hemisphere? Do Native Americans deserve equitable compensation?

Answering such questions could lead to a truly new world order.

We must hope that George W. Bush is strong enough to ask and answer such questions.

We may know that he came to the Presidency through tactics that particularly took the vote from African-Americans and Jewish-Americans. We may know that he's always profited from privilege. We may see him as insecure from being overshadowed by his father and younger brother. We may know that he's worried about passing tests. We may find his world-view simplistic at best.

We must nevertheless listen deeply to what there is in George W. Bush, I suggest, even as we ask hard questions about him. If we can see what moves him--what capabilities and incapacities, what conceptions and misconceptions, drive him--we may better understand how we came to September 11 and its aftermath.

Last night I woke up with worries around 4:00 a.m. You may have too. A line came to me that felt like a gift from the Creator.

Truth is the way to peace, it said. Truth is the way to peace within each one of us and truth is the way to satisfaction between ourselves, I heard. Truth is the way to peace between States.

Let us hope that George W. Bush pauses and looks for truth: Truths about himself, this nation and the world. At the same time, let us do everything we can to bring the greatest material power on Earth to courage, clarity and compassion.

Thus we can respect the lives lost so pitiably last Tuesday--imagine being smashed and smothered under rubble--lives perhaps given so that we may face realities--and the many more lives lost before last Tuesday.

(Don Paul works with Marie Harrison, Malik Rahim, Alma Lark, Duc Nim and others in *Housing Is a Human Right*. He thanks you all for the e-mails.)

FIGHT AGAINST, NOT FOR, ANOTHER RICH MAN'S WAR
(published Sept. 26, 2001)

Can't Fool The Youth

Hey, "thug life." Hey, you, stuck in "the game" or inescapably close to it--all of you, brave and able brothers who must hang out on street-corners with nothing but something criminal to do for your survival--who must live in Developments whose buildings might change but whose opportunities don't ("Buildings don't commit crimes," says Malik Rahim)--let me speak directly to you.

Is your anger being played by TV? Are you being led into a 'WAR' that can't possibly benefit you?

Since September 11 images of destruction and suffering in New York City have shown relentlessly on network TV. How many times have we seen the World Trade Center towers collapse? How many weeping faces have we seen? How often have we been told that a far-off, diabolical "terror network", led by a bearded, brown-skinned someone named Osama bin Laden, is responsible for the " 'Attack on America' "?

Dont' believe the hype--if you were at all inclined to believing such hype--relentless as it is.

Images promoted by General Electric (NBC), Westinghouse (CBS), Capital Cities/Disney (ABC) and Rupert Murdoch (Fox Networks) show to the exclusion of realities that are actually more horrific.

They show instead of sick and starving Iraqi children--more than 500,000 of whom have died in the past 10 year due to sanctions set by the United States, according to the United Nations. They show instead of two generations of Palestinean refugee-camps. They show instead of the 17,000 civilian corpses left by Israel's 1982 invasion of Lebanon. They show instead of the desolate housing in Sunnydale and on the Shipyard side of the Hunters Point hill.

There is a major, revealing difference between the sets of images that network TV shows and does not show. This difference is crucial to us all.

After two weeks the U.S.Government and Corporate media still can't specify an organizing source for the September 11 attacks. They can't even identify for sure who the hijackers were, much less connect Osama bin Laden to them. Regarding the horrors that are not shown, however, foreign and domestic, there are

indisputable, obvious sources. These sources are policies of the
United States Government.

When God Means Oil

Over the past two weeks this column has urged justice as the only
solution to inequities that produce mass violence.

It's urged George W. Bush to find courage, clarity and compassion
in himself so that he might effect a true peace. At the same time it's
pointed out huge holes in the official stories told by our Government
and its echoing media.

Now it's clear that George W. Bush intends war. His Address to
more than 500 clapping Congresspersons last Thursday promised "a
lengthy campaign unlike any other we have seen." George W. Bush
said: "From this day forward, any nation that continues to harbor or
support terrorism will be regarded by the United States as a hostile
regime." He said: "The advance of human freedom, the great
achievement of our time and the great hope of every time, now
depends on us."

The second Bush President of the United States said all such stuff
even as the United States remains the overwhelming leader in State
terror worldwide, sponsoring dictatorships in every Hemisphere. He
said such stuff in the same speech as he suggested new, sweeping
measures to curtail civil liberties here.

He said all such stuff after ordering the executions of more
people--most of them people of color--than any Governor of any
State in the United States' history.

He said all such stuff after stealing the Presidency through
denying African-Americans and Jewish-Americans their votes and
twisting the U. S. Supreme Court to value his interests above the
nation's laws.

The 9/11/01 attacks have been a boon to the second Bush
Administration. They've rescued it from a position of fundamental
illegitimacy, from global protests, and from a recession that had
already cost 1 million U. S. jobs in the first eight months of 2001.

The second Bush Administration now has a green light to go
anywhere and do anything it wants in the service of its 'lengthy
campaign' against any 'terror' it chooses to name. With the
September 11 attacks George W. Bush and his father have gotten the

war that his Cabinet can be seen as designed to serve. Big Oil and military-industrial contractors will be the long-term beneficiaries of this open-ended "new Cold War." $180 billion is set as the sum for immediate expenditures. Everyday people's needs, freedoms, perceptions and our shared environment will be the ongoing victims.

Afghanistan is named as the first target of the GWB Ad.'s "war on terrorism".

Why Afghanistan? Afghanistan is said by Corporate media to 'harbor' Osama bin Laden, September 11's supposed 'mastermind', though the only evidence so far offered of Osama bin Laden's connection to the shifting gallery of supposed hijackers is someone shaking hands with someone in Kuala Lumpur.

Why else Afghanistan? Afghanistan is the route for a potential pipeline from Turkmenistan and the Caspian Sea's oil riches--riches estimated to be worth as much as $4 trillion--that will go through Pakistan and thus to the Arabian Sea. Western oil-corporations have long pushed for such a pipeline, one that would avoid routes through Iran or Russia. To U.S.-oil-corporation interests (Unocal is the principal one in Turkmenistan), typical, flunky rulers in Afghanistan would be preferable to the current Taliban.

You can see the picture.

Youth especially can see the picture.

The first play is Afghanistan. George W. Bush's "war", one for which he too says God is only on "our" side, serves the same interests as his father's Gulf War. As in 1967 ("The United States is the greatest purveyor of violence in the world"--Dr. Martin Luther King) and as in 1999 ("The biggest gangsta in the world is the United States"--Minister Louis Farrakhan), so goes 2001.

Speak to Millions

Next Saturday's Town Hall meeting at Milton Meyer gym (195 Kiska Road), 3:00 TO 6:00 p.m., will be broadcast on KPFA, 94.1 f.m. KPFA's 59,000 watts and its affiliated stations reach millions in northern and central California. Its programming is carried worldwide via the Internet.

This Town Hall is a great chance for the community to be heard.

In particular the U. S. Navy's record of neglect since it abandoned its Hunters Point Naval Shipyard in 1974 needs to be told.

You probably know that the 1990s saw a subversion of grassroots efforts at self-help (Ujamaa and other such efforts on the Hunters Point hill) that set off bitterness and bloodshed between neighboring 'Developments' which remain unresolved.

So come on out, young people, 'thug life' and others, and let the world hear what you know, what you're thinking, and how you're feeling.

"I want to rule my destiny"--

Buju Banton, "Destiny", <u>Inna Heights</u>.

WATCH OUT FOR THE SECOND WAVE OF 'TERROR'
(published Oct. 10)

In September this column pointed out who and what stand to benefit from the 9/11 atrocities that killed thousands of everyday people at the World Trade Center and elsewhere in the U. S.

Big Oil and State repression appear to be the immediate and long-term beneficiaries of those atrocities.

Now, on this first day of B-2 bombers and Tomahawk missiles striking Afghanistan (October 7, 2001), I recall warnings by United States Attorney General John Ashcroft and Secretary of Defense Donald Rumsfeld over the prior 10 days.

Ashcroft and Rumsfeld said that we here should expect a second wave of 'terrorist attacks' inside the United States. They said that our Government was particulary worried about biochemical warfare.

Last December--just after the Supreme Court allowed George W. Bush to become the United States' President--Vice-President Dick Cheney said that the Administration faced three major threats: 1) a recession; 2) terrorist attacks on domestic targets; and 3 biochemical warfare. We are, we know, already suffering from the first two of Cheney's predictions.

Now, I think, we must ask who and what could possibly benefit from loosing lethal biochemcial agents on civilians in the U.S. Who could benefit from using any number of scenarios to gas to death hundreds or thousands of innocent people--from mass murder that might be far more outrageous than the atrocities of September 11, 2001.

One group who would benefit from the ensuing hysteria would be those who want to increase our post-9/11 'Homeland Security'. They who would benefit would be those who want to stifle the questions and dissent that have begun to arise among us here since 9/11/01.

Who would benefit would be those who want no opposition to a long and costly war--a "new Cold War"--that profits the purveyors of weapons <u>and</u> of oil to the world.

Who would benefit would be those who want to themselves use biochemical weapons in Afghanistan's forbidding terrain.

Who and what would benefit would be the Bush Administration and many of the Corporations that principally fund the Republican and Democrat Parties.

But who could be capable of such horrible and cynical mass murder?

Who could stomach the faces and cries of victims' surviving families? Who could be so cold? Could they be followers of a religion that bans the killing of anyone except in battle? Or could they be those who brought us Contragate, Watergate, and Wars in Vietnam and elsewhere? Could they be descendants of those imperialists whose contest for profits brought us the killing of tens of millions in World War I and World War II?

Some of these tens of millions of victims, we may remember, were also gassed to death in trenches.

<u>Bush War II: Blood for Oil Redux</u>

Since September 11 we've learned a great deal that contradicts the stories that the Big 6 U. S. Networks tell.

We know now that from mid-August onward many warnings were delivered to the CIA about imminent attacks on huge targets in New York City and D.C. We read now that executives of supranational financial firms with many floors of offices in the World Trade Center (Goldman, Sachs and Morgan, Stanley for two) were warned. We read that ordinary protections by Air Controllers and NORAD went awry on September 11, allowing the crashes to happen. We read that the U.S. shut down 500 Arab Websites on the day before September 11.

We have more grounds for doubts about the credibility of reports about events of that shocking day.

We've also learned more about Afghanistan, the country that the U.S. and Great Britain have just begun to bomb.

We the Public are told that the West's campaign is to "rid the world of terrorism" by capturing Osama bin Laden, "dead or alive", and punishing Afghanistan's Taliban Government-- though both bin Laden and the Taliban were funded allies of the U.S. not later than two years ago and no proof has yet been shown to We the Public that ties Osama bin Laden or the Taliban to the 9/11 attacks.

Why should this one person and this one poor country deserve so much firepower? Why do the U. S. and Great Britain savagely bomb Afghanistan when the destruction visited on Afghanistan will inflame Muslims around the world to further hatred and retaliation?

Why? Well, we now know that Afghanistan contains prizes that could be worth trillions of dollars to two of the biggest businesses on Earth: Those that deal in fossil fuels (oil and gas) and those that deal in opiate narcotics (heroin).

According to the Statistical Review of World Energy, Central Asia and the Middle East have reserves of 800 billion barrels of crude petroleum and its equivalent in natural gas (versus the 160 billion barrels that are estimated to remain in the rest of the world). These regions are strongholds of Islamic fundamentalism.

Reserves in the Caspian Sea and nearby are the major new find of the past 10 years in oil-exploration. Western Corporations want a pipeline east, one that avoids Russia, Iran and the Bosporus, one that offers a short route to sales in Asia that are expected to increase by 10 billion barrels per year (versus a 1 billion-per-year increase in Europe, according to the United States Department of Energy).

Unocal (Union 76) was the chief partner in the Central Asian Oil Pipeline and the Central Asian Gas Pipeline. Both of these Pipelines were to run east through Turkmenistan, one nation that borders the Caspian Sea, then south through Afghanistan and Pakistan to the Arabian Sea. In December 1998, four months after U.S. missiles first struck Afghanistan in pursuit of Osama bin Laden, Unocal pulled out of both projects, citing 'instability' in Afghanistan due to the Taliban.

As to opium, the source of heroin, Central Asia produces 3/4 of the world's supply. Central Asia's 4600 metric tons per year of opium is worth $100 billion to $200 billion, about 1/3 of the $500 billion that's the annual profit from narcotics in the world, according to an excellent article by Michael Chossudovsky, Professor of Economics at the University of Ottawa and at the Centre for Reseach of Globalization. Chossudovsky's piece was posted on the Internet on September 12, 2001.

On October 6 of the past week an article by Ranjit Devrah in the Hong Kong-based *Asia Times* began with this paragraph: 'Just as the Gulf War in 1991 was all about oil, the new conflict in South and Central Asia is no less about access to the region's abundant petroleum resources, according to Indian analysts.'

The *Asia Times* article continued: ' "US influence and military presence in Afghanistan and the Central Asian states, not unlike that over the oil-rich Gulf states, would be a major strategic gain," said V R Raghavan, a strategic analyst and former general in the Indian army.'

From the information we know now, information not likely to soon broadcast on Big 6 Network TV, we can also see a great deal more to beware and to resist about this second Bush War.

Go well.

FOURTH REICH RISING:
BOMBS, OIL, DRUGS, STOCKS AND BANKS
(published Oct. 24)

That Corporations now rule Governments is felt by many people.

Since the last *Across the White Divides* column, two weeks ago, we've seen many more U. S. bombs, made by and for Corporations, blow up helpless civilians in faraway places.

We can now see more clearly the reality that Governments serve Corporations. We can better see the underlying reality that the national U. S. Government and its Armed Forces serve the interests of Chevron around the Caspian Sea--just as local Governments serve Chevron in the San Francisco Bay Area.

Some people think that this is how things <u>should</u> be.

They make statements such as: "The business of America is business."

They favor completion of the "New World Order" that the first President Bush promised us more than 10 years ago.

Benito Mussolini, an outright fascist, was one person with such thinking. The proudly Fascist dictator of Italy and ally of Adolf Hitler during the 1930s thought so much of businesses' dominance that he called his nation 'the Corporate State.'

TIME Magazine, NBC radio, and Henry Ford all praised Mussolini's and Hitler's new model of a Nation-State. Even during World War II General Motors, General Electric, Standard Oil, the Chase Bank, International Telephone and Telegraph, and the investment-bank of Brown Brothers, Harriman partnered with businesses in Fascist Germany and Italy. I. G.Farben, maker of Bayer commercial products, was among the largest of such German businesses.

These U.S. Corporate and Nazi/Fascist partners helped to kill tens of millions in World War II.

Now the United States and its Western allies are entering into a new war. They're devastating the nation of Afghanistan, forcing the flight of thousands of refugees, enraging millions of Muslims by bombing those they purport to save. This new war is purported by Corporate media to be against the "terrorist" Osama bin Laden and the Taliban Government that "harbors" Osama bin Laden

Propaganda unprecedented in my lifetime surrounds us.

Every Network's screen shows the Stars-and-Stripes like a logo..'America Strikes Back'is the slogan of the day and night. James Brown, Paul McCartney, Michael Jackson, Clint Black and Faith Hill perform to benefit victims of September 11. At the same time, four everyday workers in the U. S. already are dead from exposure to anthrax spores that were delivered via letter.

Citizens' fears and calls for patriotism increase together.

One certainty also grows clear, however, from observing the complex of connections now. Scan events from the 1930s onward that have led to horrific profiteering by a relative few, note those few whose privileges and machinations go back generations, and you too will see: This new war is an old one.

This war on Afghanistan is not for freedom.

This war is not not for justice.

This war is for the rich and fear-mongering. This war is for Corporate interests. This war is for the stuff of modern, hidden fascists' dreams--the dreams of George W. Bush, his father, both their Cabinets, and their supporters in and outside Government.

Those Darn Coincidences

Bear with me through some history, please.

You will remember Brown Brothers, Harriman from the collaborators with Nazi Germany that are listed above. A Senior Partner in this investment-bank was Prescott Bush, father of George Herbert Walker Bush and grandfather of somebody's President. After World War II Prescott Bush and Banker's Trust helped I. G. Farben executives (see above) and other Nazis retain their assets. Worldwide cartels in aluminum (Alcoa one partner), oil and synthetic rubber (Standard Oil of New Jersey one partner), and pharmaceuticals were thus protected.

Now, October of 2001, we learn that Bayer of Germany, an I. G. Farben subsidiary, somehow controls U. S. rights to the only vaccine for inhalation of anthrax spores that's approved for sale in the U. S.

Bayer's drug, Cipro, costs $690 for two months' supply of it here. Generic equivalents from India would cost us $20 for the same supply.

We also know now that BioPort, a Michigan firm headed by former Admiral William J. Crowe, Chairman of the Joint Chiefs of Staff under Ronald Reagan, in 1998 somehow gained control of U.S. rights to the only vaccine against skin-contact with anthrax that's approved for sale in the U.S. till 2003.

(Please also know that many Doctors believe varieties of readily available penicillin to be equally effective, much cheaper antidotes to anthrax.)

George W. Bush has ordered National Guard units to protect BioPort's plant.

A major stockholder in BioPort is the Carlyle Group, a Washington, DC firm that manages more than $12 billion for investors (including $425 million from the California Public Employees' Retirement fund). Former Secretary of State James Baker III is among the Carlyle Group's staff. His former boss, George H.W. Bush, also visits heads of state on behalf of the Group, paid a fee of $80,000 to $100,000 per speech.

Oil is also big with the Carlyle Group. Baker III, the elder George Bush, and the current U.S. Vice-President, Dick Cheney, have all negotiated with Governments that surround the Caspian Sea about how Corporations can profit from oil there. Pipelines are their particular interest. The Group's Chairman, Frank Carlucci, has a resume of multiple, related interests. Carlucci was Secretary of Defense under Ronald Reagan, Deputy Director of the CIA under Jimmy Carter, Undersecretary of HUD under Richard Nixon, and a classmate at Princeton with Donald Rumsfeld, the current Secretary of Defense and this Bush Administration's chief cheerleader for bombing Afghanistan.

Back to BioPort. Another major stockholder in this sole patent-holder for a vaccine against anthrax in the U.S. is--brace yourselves--the bin Laden family of Saudi Arabia.

George H. W. Bush also acts as a consultant for the bin Laden family. The "terrorist" Osama, you will remember, is the most famous son of this family.

Then there are stocks. Bush family connections also figure in the suspicious purchase of a wildly high volume of "short" stocks in United and American Airlines just before September 11. To "short" a stock is to bet it will fall--your profit will then be the amount of that stock's drop when you sell it minus your broker's commission. On September 6 and 7 "short" orders were taken for United Airlines at rates over 1000% the norm at Chicago's Board of Options Exchange, according to Michael Ruppert in his newsletter *From the Wilderness*. The same was true for American Airlines on September 10. The CIA monitors such transactions for signs of trouble afoot. Somehow, however, the extraordinary spikes of "shorts" against United and American didn't prompt the CIA to warn anyone we know of danger. The source of much of these "short" stock transactions was Deutsche Bank in Germany and its new subsidiary in the U. S., Banker's Trust (see above), a firm for which the current Executive Director of the CIA, A.B. "Buzzy" Krongard, served as Vice-Chairman till 1999.

Back to oil. On September 7 Chevron and Texaco merged, creating a Corporation with more than $100 billion in assets. Among those assets are a 45% interest in the Tengiz oil-field of Kazakhstan. Exxon Mobil owns 25% of this field that's estimated to hold nine billion barrels of oil (multiply nine billion by $20 or $30 for revenues). Dick Cheney was on the Kazakhstan Oil Advisory Board while head of Halliburton, an oil-field supplier, before his selection as U. S. Vice-President.

On September 7, too, Jeb Bush, the younger brother or son or grand-son, signed an Executive Order in Florida that readied the National Guard for martial law there.

You may be seeing a pattern from the complex of connections and coincidences immediately above.

That pattern may in turn form a picture in your thoughtful mind.

To me, the pattern is of privileged insider after insider profiting from events on or around September 11 while they--through the agency of the U. S. Government--also take steps to both suppress dissent and to reap further profits from much greater violence and expropriation in the future.

That is, the pattern that I see is one of covert fascism.

On to the Taliban.

The Taliban means "students." Thus in Afghanistan there is currently a "Government of students." Although military novices, the Taliban took power in 1996 from seven factions of warlords who had fought over Afghanistan after the Soviet withdrawal of 1989. The Taliban have since rebuilt schools and hospitals and eliminated (according to a year 2000 United Nations Drug Control Program study) opium cultivation in their territory. They have barred the selling of women as chattels. In fact, acccording to a speech by their roving Ambassador, Sayyid Rahmatullah Hashemi, at the University of Southern California on March 10, 2001, women work in the Taliban's Ministries of Health, of Education, of the Interior, of Social Affairs, and more women than men attend the schools of Medical Science that the Taliban had re-opened in all of Afghanistan's major cities.

Such, however, of course, is not the representation that Corporate media makes of the Taliban here.

Nor is the Taliban's and Unocal's failure to agree on a pipeline through Afghanistan much mentioned here.

Contrary information doesn't suit the Corporate State.

Real journalism reveals contradictions that upset thought-control.

We must therefore find out as much as we can of independent information.

We must resist the programming that would rob us of judgment and compassion.

The U. S. Government--not <u>our</u> government--is again bombing
Hospitals, convoys of refugees, and Red Cross food-centers even as
celebrities on TV appeal for donations to "aid the victims of terror"
in New York City through the American Red Cross. How is any
civilian casualty--mother, father or child--worth more than another?
How does pitting Northern Alliance warlords against the Taliban in
order to return a King--a King!--help?

How is the Corporate Government accomplishing any of the goals
it tries to sell us?

(Compassion is more alien to the Corporate Government than
sweat is to a stone.)

How is such a Government deserving of any respect? How can it
be honored if it chooses to use its power so selfishly and cruelly and
for ends so brutal and stupid as money for oil?

The Corporate Government wants us to buy for it and die for it
and that is all.

So, folks, knowing what we do, we must go on working and
fighting for justice and peace, here and everywhere.

THE MOST ENORMOUS AND EVIL SCAM
IN U.S. RULING-CLASS HISTORY
(OH SAY CAN YOU SEE RED-WHITE-AND-BLUE S.U.V.'S)
(published Dec. 12, 2001)

*During the conversation in which he agreed to publish this column
in the* San Francisco Bay View *newspaper Willie Ratcliff said: "You
better find you a good place to hide when it comes out."*

*Now, however, what this column has to tell seems to me only part of
of a centuries-old, supranational 'enormous and evil scam'. It seems
substantially short of the larger realities about financiers' supranational
empire that are related in* <u>To</u> <u>Prevent</u> <u>the</u> <u>Next</u> *" '9/11' ".*

What remains unchanged is that only We Masses can save ourseloves.

The leading Corporate-sponsored News these days is all about the
U.S.-led war in Afghanistan.

We can't avoid such News. It affects us even if we ignore it. It
reaches all the way to the cars we drive along 3rd Street.

Stories are told daily in newspapers and on TV. They come under the headings of 'America Responds' , 'America Fights Back', 'The War on Terrorism', and so on.

None of such News much examines why the U.S. is in Afghanistan. None of it much investigates likely aims and ends of the war there, nor probes the huge holes in Official accounts of the war there and of the crimes of 9/11/01.

None of it dares to suggest that a multinational plot of jaw-dropping scope and cruelty, a kind of global coup, is hijacking our futures, robbing our freedoms, and hurting poor people most of all.

Since September 11 this column has tried to explore what's really going on.

Its early, inescapable conclusion (September 19) was that at least part of the U.S. Government at least allowed the attacks on the World Trade Center and the Pentagon. More investigation (September 26, October 10) revealed that the Bush Adminstration and its prime Corporate sponsors were the main, economic and political beneficiaries of outcomes from the September 11 horror.

Oil--that is, billions and trillions of dollars from oil and gas nearby the Caspian Sea and from the pipelines that would carry said oil and gas--was revealed as a key objective behind the U.S. campaign to wipe out the Taliban government in Afghanistan.

Repression of dissent, cuts to civil rights, and a new legitimacy for the Bush Administration were the big, immediate domestic gains of Government for Corporations. Finally ('Fourth Reich Rising', October 24) this column pointed out the generations-old connections (from Nazi Germany forward) between the U.S. Corporate Establishment and openly fascist partners. It showed that profits with Bush-family ties extend even to the U.S. Patents for vaccines against anthrax.

Evidence that has since emerged since my last column points to a plot more sinister and brutal than decent people can imagine.

The evidence's sources are themselves multinational and mostly Establishment. They include MS-NBC, *Le Figaro* in France, *the Guardian* and BBC in England, dailies in India, Pakistan and Spain, and a new book titled <u>Bin</u> <u>Laden:</u> <u>The</u> <u>Hidden</u> <u>Truth</u>. Many are cited in Michael Ruppert's e-mail newsletter 'From the Wilderness' and on the globalcircle.net and Irish Times Websites.

Here is a timeline of facts. See what pictures they form for you.

A Carpet of Gold ... or a Carpet of Bombs

*February-April 2001. Negotiations began between U.S. Government and Taliban representatives to revive construction of pipelines that Unocal (Union 76) had proposed 6 years earlier. The pipelines would carry oil and gas through Turkmenistan, Afghanisan and Pakistan to the Arabian Sea, the shortest possible route to lucrative markets in the Far East.

Last March, Laila Helms, Afghan neice of Richard Helms, he a former Director of the CIA and a former U.S. Ambassador to Pakistan, assisted an aide of Taliban leader Mullah Muhammed Omar, Sayed Rahmatullah Hashimi, in meetings with the CIA in Washington. In April Secretary of State Colin Powell announced aid of $43 million to the Taliban. (*The Irish Times*, 11/19/01.)

*In May 2001 U..S Central Intelligence Agency (CIA) Director George Tenet met with Pakistan's President General Pervez Musharraf in Islamabad, Pakistan. The meeting was reported to be 'unusually long.' It presumably included Tenet's counterpart, Lt. General Mahmud Ahmad, head of the ISI, Pakistan's equivalent of the CIA. (The Indian SAPRA news agency, 5/22/01)

*In July 2001 Thomas Simons (former U.S. Ambassador to Pakistan), Karl Inderfurth (former Assistant Secretary of State for South Asian affairs) and Lee Coldren (former State Department expert on South Asia) met in Berlin with negotiators from the Taliban, Russia and six oil-rich nations that neighbor Afghanistan. (*The Guardian*, 9/22/01; the BBC, 9/18/01.)

*According to Jean-Charles Brisard, co-author of <u>Bin Laden: The Hidden Truth</u>: "At one moment during the negotiations, the U.S. representatives told the Taliban, 'either you accept our offer of a carpet of gold, or we bury you under a carpet of bombs'."

Naif Naik, former Pakistani Minister for Foreign Affairs, was also present. He recalled that the discussions turned around "the formation of a government of national unity. If the Taliban had accepted this coalition, they would have immediately received international economic aid.... And the pipelines from Kazakhstan and Uzbekistan would have come." Naik also recalled 'that Tom Simons, the U.S. representative at these meetings, openly threatened the Taliban and Pakistan. Simons said, 'either the Taliban behave as they ought to, or Pakistan convinces them to do so, or we will use another option'. The words Simons used were 'a military operation'," Naik claimed.' (Inter Press Service, 11/15.01.)

*On July 14, 2001 Osama bin Laden, reputed "mastermind of the al-Qaeda terror network", was in his private suite at a hospital in Dubai, United Arab Emirates, for treatment of chronic kidney infection. He met there with 'a top CIA official.' Although bin Laden was subject to 'execution' by the U.S. for his presumed role in the 1998 bombing of Embassies in Kenya and Tanzania, his private jet left Dubai without interception by U. S. Navy planes. (*Le Figaro*, 10/31/01).

*July 2001. Pakistan's ISI Chief Lt. General Mahmud Ahmad had an aide wire-transfer $100,000 to Mohammed Atta, the pilot who later became infamous as presumed leader of the September 11 hijackings/atrocities. In October 2001 Mahmud Ahmad resigned from the ISI after the FBI confirmed this crucial wire-transfer. (*The Times of India*, 10/11/01.)

*August 2, 2001. Christina Rocca, the State Department's Director of Asian Affairs, met with the Taliban's Ambassador to Pakistan in Islamabad, the last direct contact between U.S. Government and Taliban representatives (*The Irish Times*, 11/19/01.)

*August 2001. Russian President Vladimir Putin ordered operatives to warn the U.S. Government "in the strongest possible terms" of imminent attacks on airports and government buildings (MS-NBC interview with Putin, 9/15/01)

*August 2001. The New York Stock Exchange dropped more than 900 points in three weeks, prompting predictions of a Depression-like crash of the Market.

*End of August, 2001. Economic bulletins noted the 1,120,000 jobs lost in the U.S. since January and the precipitous falls of growth in all Western economies (Spanish newspaper *Cinco Días*, 9/5/02; speech by Cuban President Fidel Castro, 11/2/01)

*September 3, 2001: Pakistan launched the independent Interstate Gas Company Limited (IGCL) to pursue 'regional pipeline options' from Iran, Qatar, Turkmenistan and the United Arab Emirates (*The Dawn*, 9/3/01).

*September 4-13, 2001. Pakistani ISI Chief Lt. General Mahmud Ahmad, benefactor of Mohammed Atta, met with U. S. State Department and CIA officials in Washington, DC. On September 13

Pakistan agreed to cooperate with the U.S. war on Afghanistan. (MS-NBC, Oct. 7, 2001)

*September 11, 2001. At 8:15 a.m. the first of four hijacked U.S. airliners diverged sharply from its flight-plan. 75 minutes later--and 45 minutes after the first airliner crashed into the World Trade Center--the National Command Authority scrambled jets to defend U.S. air-space. [Sources: CNN, ABC, MS-NBC, more.)

*October 9, 2001. Wendy Chamberlain, U.S. Ambassdor, visited Pakistan's Minister of Oil. The pipelines desired by Unocal and other Western Corporations are reported to be "back on the table." (*The Frontier Post* of Pakistan, 10/10/01).

We Can Fight or We Can Lose

What do you see from the above timeline of facts?

I see a plot with many twists. I see one blind and brutal aim: pipelines through Afghanistan. The Bush Administration, acting for Corporations that derive their wealth from oil, tried to make the Taliban ' "behave as they ought to" ' through inducements and threats. Their ultimate threat was the U. S. ruling-class's tried-and-true ' "military operation" ', offered last July by Thomas Simons.

Lt. General Mahmud Ahmad, former Chief of Pakistan's ISI, is a more uncertain element. Either he was working with the presumed 'ISI/Taliban/bin Laden axis', or he was setting up Afghanistan for a possible U.S.-led war from a time not later than that of CIA Director George Tenet's visit to Afghanistan last May. His dispatch of $100,000 to Mohammed Atta would fit either role. Or Mahmud Ahmad may have changed sides under extreme pressure just after the attacks of September 11.

Any of the logical scenarios that can be deduced from the evidence before us now, however, are 100% contrary to the rhetoric delivered by George W. Bush and the 'goals' that his Adminstratrion uses to support 'America Responds ...The War on Terrorism.'

The plot that I now see arouses in me sadness, scorn, disgust and anger.

I feel sad for the victims first. Survivors of the more than 4000 who died--the current, reduced estimate--in New York City and Washington, DC and rural Pennsylvania are living victims. They must persist without loved ones for the rest of their lives. I also feel sad for the dead who passed without the least knowledge of why they were perishing. I feel sad, too, for the the millions more who will die from U.S.-led bombing of Afghanistan and the ensuing consequences there.

Scorn is what I feel for the plot's crudity and obviousnes. Did its operatives not expect the public to connect threats with actions and actions with consequences?

Disgust is the least that's deserved for the hyprocrisy and ruthlessness of the plot's evident perpetrators: the Corporate Government of the United States.

Anger is my final and most unshakeable feeling. Seeing to the bottom of this rich man's war sets my jaw against it.

This whole show--with its tens of thousands of deaths already--is first for possible profits from gas and oil.

Now we may all know the true enormity and evil of events on and around last September 11. Our first duty is to spread the word.

The Bush Administration is not stopping. In the past six weeks it's seen its USA PATRIOT Act pass in the Senate and Congress, letting the Government eavesdrop on e-mail and other forms of private communication whenever it wishes. It's put forth a Bill to give $100 billion more to U. S. Corporations ($1 billion to Ford, $833 million to General Motors, $671 million to General Electric, and so forth) through repeal of the Alternative Minimum Tax; another $21 billion of the giveaway would be through legalization of offshore tax-havens in the Bahamas and elsewhere).

And the Bush Administration now declares the need for 'secret military tribunals' outside the rule and reach of any other law, the tribunals' defendants to be decided by the Government, all evidence hidden. Nazis and Fascists never asked for more judicial power.

We're headed, in short, toward outright fascism: A Corporate State outright.

We're headed, I suppose, toward red-white-and-blue S.U.V.'s.

Or, to be more inclusive and domestic: Red-white-and-blue dog-collars. Let Rex show the flag.

We may want to add music to this patriotic display. Press red on our patriotic Rex's collar for "The Stars and Stripes Forever."

Blue for "America the Beautiful. "

White for "God Bless America."

Also, I suppose, we should drop any pretense of representative democracy in our Government.

We should let CEOs of Corporations directly make up the United States' Cabinet. Let them directly set the Federal Budget. Let Dick Cheney go back to Halliburton. Let Secretary of the Defense Donald Rumsfeld go back to Searle Pharmaceuticals. Let Secretary of the Treasury Paul O'Neill go back to Alcoa Aluminumn. Let George W. Bush go back to Harken Energy and the Texas Rangers.

And yet ... And yet ... I hope and believe that another turn will soon be taken.

I hope that we'll resist the robbery of hard-won freedoms.

We know too much to have our futures hijacked by a cabal of fascist Corporate gangsters.

Our own communication, through the Internet and word-of-mouth, has helped to expose this latest attempt at a global coup.

We know what's urgent and necessary and we'll do ourselves whatever is necessary.

The majority of us believe not a bit in hacks of either Corporate Party, Republicrat or Democan.

We see and feel and breathe the real terrors that invade our lives every day. Mothers of the Bayview and Hunters Point--and of Richmond, Martinez, and, yes, Walnut Creek--all wake up to their children coughing.

We on the poisoned ground know who suffers most from norms that are themselves crimes.

We know who and what are responsible for the everyday and exceptional (September 11, 2001) crimes.

We have only to act--act now for our children's future--from what we know in our hearts.

" '9/11' "
FACING OUR
FASCIST STATE

Being a study of the infamous day's crimes
& how and why the U. S. ruling elite
have committed other atrocities
that have so benefited them
for more than a century
& how and why
we can still win
a livable future for our children

PRECEDENT FOR A 'PRETEXT'
(SEE PAGES 128-29)

~~TOP SECRET SPECIAL HANDLING NOFORN~~

THE JOINT CHIEFS OF STAFF
WASHINGTON 25, D.C.

UNCLASSIFIED   13 March 1962

MEMORANDUM FOR THE SECRETARY OF DEFENSE

Subject: Justification for US Military Intervention
in Cuba (TS)

1. The Joint Chiefs of Staff have considered the attached
Memorandum for the Chief of Operations, Cuba Project, which
responds to a request of that office for brief but precise
description of pretexts which would provide justification
for US military intervention in Cuba.

2. The Joint Chiefs of Staff recommend that the
proposed memorandum be forwarded as a preliminary submission
suitable for planning purposes. It is assumed that there
will be similar submissions from other agencies and that
these inputs will be used as a basis for developing a
time-phased plan. Individual projects can then be
considered on a case-by-case basis.

3. Further, it is assumed that a single agency will be
given the primary responsibility for developing military
and para-military aspects of the basic plan. It is
recommended that this responsibility for both overt and
covert military operations be assigned the Joint Chiefs of
Staff.

For the Joint Chiefs of Staff:

SYSTEMATICALLY REVIEWED
BY JCS ON ___ 9 May 84
CLASSIFICATION CONTINUED

L. L. LEMNITZER
Chairman
Joint Chiefs of Staff

1 Enclosure
Memo for Chief of Operations, Cuba Project   EXCLUDED FROM GDS

EXCLUDED FROM AUTOMATIC
REGRADING; DOD DIR 5200.10
DOES NOT APPLY

~~TOP SECRET SPECIAL HANDLING NOFORN~~

WHAT THEY SAY:
"LAW" ... "LOVE" ... AND "A NEW WORLD ORDER"

John D. Rockefeller, Jr. speaks in a radio broadcast
for the United States' National War Fund on July 8, 1941:

"I believe in the supreme worth of the individual and in his right to life, liberty and the pursuit of happiness....

I believe that law was made for man and not man for the law; that government is the servant of the people and not their master.

I believe in the dignity of labor, whether with head or hand; that the world owes no man a living but that it owes every man the opportunity to make a living....

I believe that truth and justice are fundamental to an enduring social order....

I believe that love is the greatest thing in the world, that it alone can overcome hate; that right can and will triumph over might.'

(John D. Rockefeller, Jr., the only son of the United States' first billionaire and father of David and Nelson Rockefeller, spoke for the National War Fund five months before " 'Pearl Harbor' " and at the same time as the Rockefeller, Bush, Dupont, Ford, Harriman, Hearst, Warburg and other ruling-class families continued to profit from Nazi Germany and Fascist Italy through Standard Oil and other Corporations.

George H. W. Bush speaks to the
U. S. Congress on September 11, 1990:

"We stand today at a unique and extraordinary moment. The crisis in the Persian Gulf, as grave as it is, also offers a rare opportunity to move toward an historic period of cooperation. Out of these troubled times, our fifth objective--a new world order--can emerge."

(George Herbert Walker Bush, 41st President of the United States, was the first son of Prescott Samuel Bush, an investment-banker who partnered with W. Averill Harriman in using slave-labor from Auschwitz for their Silesian-American Corporation during World War II and who later became a U. S. Senator from Connecticut.)

FORWARD!

"... They will do anything/
To materialize their every wish"
Bob Marley, "Guiltiness", <u>Exodus</u>

<u>*To Solve the Crime, to Name Our Enemy,*</u>
<u>*Facts May Be a Good Place to Start*</u>

This short book, " '9/11' " / <u>Facing Our Fascist State</u>, will be
published around one year after the horrors of September 11, 2001
struck the United States.

The attacks of that day--American Airlines Flight #11 and United
Airlines #175 crashing into Towers of the World Trade Center,
American Airlines #77 apparently driving into the Pentagon, and
United Airlines #193 disintegrating in western Pennsylvania--have
been called " 'The Crime of the Century.' "

Government officials and Corporate media--whose word, we'll see,
is often one and the same, forming a kind of Corporate Government--
at once compared last September 11's attacks to those on Pearl
Harbor, the " 'Day of Infamy' " that launched the U. S. into World
War II. According to his Press Secretary, Andrew Card, President
George Walker Bush said in Florida on the morning of 9/11/01,
responding to news of the second airliner's crash into the World
Trade Center's South Tower: ' "We're at war." '

What's happened since then? The events of " '9/11' " have led to
slaughter of more thousands of innocent people outside the United
States and to drastic cuts of civil liberties within this nation.

The " 'War on Terror' " has thus furthered control of populations
and resources by an unelected and intimately related elite. These few
appear to care more for oil and gas and profits than they do for
people. Their methods--and their history, we'll soon see--are aligned
with fascism of the 1930s' " 'Corporate State.' "

What I hope to show you first in this book are facts and likelihoods
that disprove the fundamental stories told by Government officials
and Corporate media about " '9/11.' "

Almost one year after that day, no *FORTUNE*-500 Network or
publication has done anything like a thorough investigation of its

events. Corporate media's neglect or cover-up is more extensive than that which protected " 'the Magic Bullet Theory' " after the assassination of JFK.

The only skeptical investigators and true journalists toward " '9/11' " have been independent and Internet-distributed. I've drawn from many of their Websites. Please keyword, if you can, Michael C. Ruppert and the 'From The Wilderness' site, Michel Chossudovsky and the 'Global Research' site, Jared Israel and the 'Emperors Clothes' site, Brian Salter and the questionsquestions site, Catherine Austin Fitts and the 'Solari' site, Larry Chin and Bev Conover and the *Online Journal* site, Kellia Ramares, Bonnie Faulker and the Rise4News site, Robert Lederman and Baltech.org, David McGowan and the davesweb site, the Serendipity and Rense.com sites, Carol A. Valentine and the Public Action site, Michael Rivero and the whatreallyhappened site.

A few of these sites have prejudices that I think are ungrounded, but all have crucial information that's yet to be touched by *TIME*, *NEWSWEEK*, *NBC*, et cetera.

To me, three key facts expose the likelihood that far more than " 'Arab terrorists' " were involved in the plot which carried out " '9/11.' "

FACT #1) All of the airliners that crashed on September 11 COULD NOT have completed their courses without interception by U.S. military aircraft IF officials at the Federal Aviation Agency (the FAA) or North American Aerospace Command (NORAD) or the National Military Command Center (the NMCC) had followed their own Rules and ordinary procedures of response to a flight that should be engaged as an 'emergency.'

If the FAA had responded as promptly on 9/11/01 as it did on 10/25/99, when an F-16 fighter-jet from Eglin Air Force Base in Florida intercepted the 6-passenger Learjet that was carrying golfer Payne Stewart, the World Trade Center's Twin Towers and the Pentagon would have been protected.

FACT #2) At least one of the Flights that crashed on 9/11, that which struck the Pentagon, American Airlines 77, COULD NOT have been flown by the young Arab, Hami Hanjour, whom Government officials and Corporate Media still identify as its pilot.

Most probably, we'll see, none of the other Arabs who are supposed to be pilots of the other hijacked airliners on 9/11 flew those planes. More probably, we'll see, these jets were flown by remote control through technologies developed by the U.S. Government, technologies named Home Run or Global Hawk.

FACT #3) The 110-story North and South Towers and the 47-story Building 7 of the World Trade Center COULD NOT have fallen due to the causes that Government officials and Corporate media stories have presented for their " 'pancake' " collapse.

Neither jet fuel's fire nor anything else that was in the Towers that morning burns hot enough (1022 degrees Fahrenheit), we'll see, to deform steel.

Also, to not topple sideways, but to instead fall straight-down within their foundations, the 110-story Towers had to be imploded by explosives set off against their load-bearing columns and beams.

That is, we'll see, the Towers and WTC 7, all owned by Silverstein Properties, had to be demolished.

" '9/11' " was the mnemonically perfect pretext (9/11 synonymous with life-threatening emergency) for frightening and outraging people within this nation and for allowing U. S. Government officials to rush into place sweeping cuts to civil liberties.

We'll soon see that the entire pretext for these officials' acts and legitimacy is a lie--the 'Big Lie' favored by totalitarian regimes.

We'll see how " 'the War in Afghanistan' " has benefitted the interests of major oil Corporations around the Caspian Sea. The Turkmenistan-Afghanistan-Pakistan pipelines that these Corporations wanted before the ouster of the Taliban are now under way.

We'll see how opium from that " 'War' " is likely to generate far more in immediate profits than oil will. Farmers in Afghanistan have raised a crop of 3500 metric tons of opium in 2002, worth between $100-150 billion, after the Taliban removed poppy fields within their territory in 2000-2001.

We'll see through former investment-banker Catherine Austin Fitts how such a crop of illegal narcotics will likely be worth $2 to $4 trillion--one trillion is one thousand times one billion--as its revenue is laundered through Banks, Stock Markets and other financial institutions.

We'll see how and why Banks need "smack" (heroin) as well as Crack.

We'll see long-time players behind the global crimes that affect our neighborhoods. We'll see their many conspiracies.

We'll see the same families, a tiny but dominant ruling elite, profiting from the current " 'Endless War' " just as they profited from collaborating with Nazi Germany before and/or during World War II--the Rockefeller, Bush, Harriman, Dupont, Hearst, Ford, Warburg, ... families.

We'll see that many of these elite few's rule dates from feudal times. Al Gore and George W. Bush are distant cousins, both descended from Charlemagne, Emperor of the Holy Roman Empire.

We'll see how David Rockefeller's drive built the WTC Towers that were destroyed 30 years after their completion for probably great profit due to insurance-moneys.

We'll see how Zbignew Brzezinski (National Security Advisor to President Jimmy Carter and among the main strategists on the Trilateral Commission and the Council on Foreign Relations, both bodies funded by Rockefellers' money) set forth reasons for the United States to dominate Central Asia in his 1997 book The Grand Chessboard.

Four years before " '9/11' " Brzezinski wrote that the U. S. should command Central Asia to counter Russia and China and to maintain the rest of the world as its 'vassals.'

Brzezinski wrote, too, that 'the pursuit of power is not a goal that commands popular passion, except in conditions of a sudden threat or challenge to the public's sense of domestic well-being.... Democracy is inimical to imperial mobilization.... The public supported America's engagement in World War II largely because of the shock effect of the Japanese attack on Pearl Harbor.'

About Pearl Harbor, we'll see that the then U. S. President, FDR, had foreknowledge of that day's infamy.

We'll see, too, at close of this book, how short is the time we have to change our collective courses.

We'll see systems of fraud, exploitation and speculation collapsing (Enron, Worldcom) and teetering near collapse (Citigroup, J.P. Morgan, and the Chase Bank).

We'll see that if we in the modern North go on as we are now, consuming times more than our share, we'll need two other planets to live on no later than the year 2050.

Still, we'll see hope. We'll see hope in the hundreds unto millions

unto billions around the Earth who reject our old lords' would-be
" 'New World Order.' "

We'll see that we have the power to change everything through
simple and direct choices. We'll see that we can compel any turn we
want through tactics we apply. We can use the power of protracted
boycotts and other refusals. We'll see that we can win back America--
an America of Americas that honors numberless un-Americas
worldwide, a world of limitless potentials and accomplishments--in
the next and truly new revolutions.

By the way, you may be wondering what those double
quotes (like, say, " 'Bluto did it' ") are supposed to mean. I mean
them to represent the echo-effect of Government officials and
Corporate media on public consciousness. The latter reinforces the
former.

The information thus repeated in our dominant media-scape makes
up one big echo-chamber or mirror for Corporate Government. And
so great masses of normal, intelligent and compassionate people are
grievously misled.

'The lie can be maintained only for such time as the State
can shield the people from the political, economic and/or
military consequences of the lie. It thus becomes vitally
important for the State to use all of its powers to repress
dissent, for the truth is the mortal enemy of the lie, and
thus by extension, the truth becomes the greatest enemy of the
State.'
    Dr. Joseph M. Goebbels, Minister for People's
    Enlightenment and Propaganda in Germany's National
    Socialist Government.

    "There's too many people/ Tellin' too many lies"
    The Staples Singers, beginning the song "City In
    The Sky" by Charlie Chalmers, Sondra Rhodes
    and Donna Rhodes, 1974.

THE AIRLINERS AND THEIR " 'HIJACKERS' "

'Instructors at the school told Bernard that after
three times in the air, they still felt he was unable
to fly solo and that Hanjour seemed disappointed ...'
Prince George's Journal, Bowie, Maryland 9/18/01

The Pilot Who Couldn't Fly

Hami Hanjour, age 25 and a citizen of Saudi Arabia, is still
identified by Government officials and Corporate media as the pilot
of the American Airlines Boeing 757, Flight 77, that struck the
Pentagon last September 11.

On April 10, 2002 the Associated Press' John Solomon reported
that the manager, Peggy Chevrette, of the flight-school in Phoenix,
Arizona, JetTech, where Hanjour studied in January and February of
2001, doubted that Hanjour could legitimately possess the commercial
pilot's license that he claimed.

Peggy Chevrette said: ' "I couldn't believe he had a commercial
license of any kind with the skills that he had." '

In early 2001 Peggy Chevrette had told a Federal Aviation
Administration inspector, John Anthony, of her concerns about
Hanjour, but Anthony, then attending one class at JetTech with the
young Arab, declined to flag Hanjour out of training.

The Associated Press' John Solomon continues: 'Chevrette said she
contacted Anthony twice more when Hanjour began ground training
for Boeing 737 jetliners and it became clear he didn't have the skills
for the commercial pilot's license.

"I don't truly believe he should have had it and I questioned that. I
questioned that all along," she said." '

Seven months later, in August 2001, one month before
" '9/11' ", Hami Hanjour tried three times to demonstrate to
instructors at the Freeway Airport in Bowie, Maryland that he could
be trusted to fly solo in a single-engine plane.

A local Maryland newspaper, the *Prince George's Journal*, quotes
the Airport's Chief Flight Instructor, Marcel Bernard, in its September
18, 2001 edition about Hanjour's attempts to reliably fly a Cessna
172.

'Instructors at the school told Bernard that after three times in the air, they still felt he was unable to fly solo and that Hanjour seemed disappointed ...' Now let's look at the acrobatics of American Airlines 77 just before it hit the Pentagon one month later.

The expert handling of this Boeing 757, an airliner with a wing-span of 124 feet and controls much more complex than a Cessna 172's, impressed commentators.

On September 12 CBS News' Bob Orr recounted AA 77's final maneuvers. "The plane flew several miles south of the restricted airspace around the White House," Orr said. "At 9:33 it crossed the Capital Beltway, flying at more than 400 mph ... The hijacker pilots were then forced to execute a difficult, high-speed, descending turn. Radar shows that Flight 77 did a downward spiral, turning almost a complete circle and dropping the last 7,000 feet in two-and-half-minutes. The steep turn was so smooth, the sources say, it's clear there was no fight for control going on. And the complex maneuver suggests the hijacker had better flying skills than many investigators first believed."

Orr continued: "The jetliner disappeared from radar at 9:37 and less than a minute later it clipped the tops of streetlights and plowed into the Pentagon at 480 miles per hour."

Then, as now, U. S. Government and Corporate media name Hami Hanjour--he who could not be trusted to fly a Cessna 172 one month earlier--as the last pilot of AA 77.

What about other alleged pilots of hijacked airliners on September 11?

The *Washington Post* of September 19, 2001 reported that Mohammad Atta, Atta the supposed " 'ringleader' " of the " '19 terrorists' " and the supposed pilot of American Airlines Flight 11, the first airliner to fly into a World Trade Center Tower, and Marwanal-Al-Shehhi, Shehhi the supposed pilot of United Airlines Flight 175, the airliner that flew into the W T C's South Tower, did in fact take hundreds of hours of lessons at Huffman Aviation, a flight school in Venice, Florida, and also took lessons at Jones Aviation Flying Service Inc., a business which operates out of the Sarasota-Bradenton International Airport in Florida.

However, an instructor at Jones Flying Service said that 'neither man was able to pass a Stage I rating test to track and intercept', and that they left their instructors with bitter words.

What about other Arabs supposed to be aboard the the American Airlines 757 that struck the Pentagon?

The *Washington Post* of September 24, 2001 recounts how Nawaq Alhazmi and Khaid Al-Midhar fared at another flight-school. This young pair went to Sorbi's Flying Club at Montgomery Field, a community airport nearby San Diego, CA. They received two lessons at Sorbi's before instructors there advised them to quit.

One instructor is quoted by the *Post*. ' "Their English was horrible, and their mechanical skills were even worse. It was like they had hardly even ever driven a car.... They seemed like nice guys, but in the plane, they were dumb and dumber." '

Home Run and Global Hawk

If the supposed pilots are impossible or unlikely prospects for flying a Boeing 757 or 767 through sharp turns and complex manuevers, how COULD those airliners otherwise have been flown?

In an interview with the German newspaper *Tagesspeigel* on January 13, 2002, Andreas von Buelow, Minister of Technology for the united Germany in the early 1990s, a person who first worked in West Germany's Secretary of Defense 30 years ago, told about a technology by which airliners can be commanded through remote control.

The former Minister of Technology said: ' "The Americans had developed a method in the 1970s, whereby they could rescue hijacked planes by intervening into the computer piloting." '

Andreas von Buelow said that this technology was named Home Run.

The German went on to give his *Tagesspeigel* interviewer his overall perspective of the 9/11/01 attacks: ' "I can state: the planning of the attacks was technically and organizationally a master achievement. To hijack four huge airplanes within a few minutes and within one hour, to drive them into their targets, with complicated flight maneuvers! This is unthinkable, without years-long support from secret apparatuses of the state and industry.... I have real difficulties, however, to imagine that all this all sprang out of the mind of an evil man in his cave." '

.

Another technology devised by the U. S. military for remote control of huge airplanes is named Global Hawk.

On April 24, 2001, four months before " '9/11' ", Britain's International Television News reported: "A robot plane has made aviation history by becoming the first unmanned aircraft to fly across the Pacific Ocean...."

Britain's ITN continued: "The Global Hawk, a jet-powered aircraft with a wingspan equivalent to a Boeing 737, flew from Edwards Air Force Base in California and landed late on Monday at the Royal Australian Air Force base at Edinburgh, in South Australia state. . . . It flies along a pre-programmed flight path, but a pilot monitors the aircraft during its flight via a sensor suite which provides infra-red and visual images."

According to the Australian Global Hawk manager Rod Smith: ' "The aircraft essentially flies itself, right from takeoff, right through to landing, and even taxiing off the runway." '

Now, who or what would you trust for aerial missions as demanding as those of " '9/11' " (or trust to fly an airliner from one airfield in California to another in Australia): The Arab students who are described above, or the Global Hawk or Home Run technologies?

The Indestructible Passport

Just after last September 11, telltales identifying " 'the hijackers' " were obvious as Autumn's falling leaves.

Andreas von Buelow said that the supposed culprits left ' "tracks behind them like a herd of stampeding elephants." '

Von Buelow listed these tracks: ' "They made payments with credit cards with their own names; they reported to their flight instructors with their own names. They left behind rented cars with flight manuals in Arabic for jumbo jets. They took with them, on their suicide trip, wills and farewell letters, which fall into the hands of the FBI, because they were stored in the wrong place and wrongly addressed." '

The FBI found Mohammad Atta's suitcase in his rental car at Boston's Logan Airport. From said suitcase the FBI also produced a Koran and a " 'suicide note' " written in Arabic. A similar " 'suicide note' " was also announced as found nearby the curiously scattered wreckage of United Airlines Flight 93 in western Pennsylvania. Said note somehow survived this airliner's crash. Most improbably, a passport identifying one of " 'the hijackers' " was declared by New York City Police Commissioner Bernard Kerik, then by U.S. Attorney General John Ashcroft, as found a few blocks from the smoldering World Trade Center Towers. Said passport somehow survived fire-temperatures in excess of 600 degrees Fahrenheit and the collapse of more than 200,000 tons of steel and concrete.

Here's how the Cable Network News (CNN) reported the finding last September 16: "In New York, several blocks from the ruins of the World Trade Center, a passport authorities said belonged to one of the hijackers was discovered a few days ago, according to City Police Commissioner Bernard Kerik."

H'mm!

The incriminating passport was uncovered, but neither of the supposedly indestructible "black-box" flight-recorders (bright-orange, shoebox-sized, and pulsing flight-recorders) aboard American Airlines 11 and United Airlines 175 have yet been found in Manhattan or elsewhere.

Ted Lopatkiewicz, spokesman for the National Transportation Safety Board, told *USA TODAY* on September 24, 2001: ' "It's extremely rare that we don't get the recorders back. I can't recall another domestic case in which we did not recover the recorders." '

Maybe if those black-boxes had passports attached to them....

On April 19, 2002 the Director of the United States' Federal Bureau of Investigation, Robert S. Mueller III, addressed the Commonwealth Club in San Francisco.

Robert S. Mueller III said: "In our investigation, we have not uncovered a single piece of paper--either here in the United States or in the treasure trove of information that has turned up in Afghanistan and elsewhere--that mentioned any aspect of the Sept. 11 plot."

The FBI's Director attributed this total lack of any further finding to the Al Queda network's sophistication and secrecy--a sophistication and secrecy not be seen in the elephantine '' "tracks" ' that the FBI brought forth in the few weeks after
" '9/11.' "

' "I have a feeling that in a democracy you don't get a
government that is much better than a reflection of
the people. A dictatorship can get an unusual person." '
   Nelson Rockefeller, a little before his death on January
   26, 1979, three years after he left a Vice-Presidency
   in which assassinations of the then President, Gerald
   Ford, were attempted at least three times.

'"If this were a dictatorship, it'd be a heck of a lot
easier... just as long as I'm the dictator..."
   George W. Bush on Dec 18, 2000, during his first trip
   to Washington, DC after the U.S. Supreme Court
   decided to make him the 43rd President of the United
   States.

THE AIR-DEFENSES AND THEIR " 'FAILURES' "

'Consider that an aircraft emergency exists ... when:
...There is unexpected loss of radar contact and radio
communications with any ...aircraft.'
Federal Aviation Agency Order 7110.65M 10-2-5

Learjet Lost over Florida!

Let's look now at the air-controls and air-defenses that should have
protected the World Trade Center and Pentagon on 9/11/01.

The basic question for me here is: Why weren't any of the airliners
that struck the World Trade Center or Pentagon intercepted by U.S.
fighter-jets?

Two entities share responsibility for monitoring air-space over U.S.
cities: the Federal Aviation Agency (FAA) and the U.S./Canadian
North American Aerospace Command (NORAD). Given that both
have been entrusted with protecting against any kind of aerial attack
since the Cold War, their guidelines for immediate response allow
little room for discretion or error.

The FAA requires that flight-controllers call military aircraft to
intercept any plane that deviates from points (or 'fixes') on its flight-
path by more than 15 degrees (about 2 miles) and then fails to
respond to Air Traffic Control.

Such regulation is sensible due to the busyness of air-traffic over the
U.S (in particular over the northeast U.S.) and as a safeguard against
hijacking or aerial attack.

On September 11, 2001 American Airlines' flight 11 took off from
Boston's Logan Airport for Los Angeles at 7:59 Eastern Daylight
Time, carrying eighty-one passengers, two pilots and nine flight-
attendants. At 8:15 this Boeing 767 first went off-course, swinging
north.

The *New York Times* story of September 13, 2001 about Flight 11
had this picturesque heading: 'A Plane Left Boston and Skimmed
Over River and Mountain in a Deadly Detour.'

The *NY Times* story proceeded: 'Five minutes later, at 8:20, Flight
11 failed to follow an instruction to climb to its cruising altitude of
31,00 feet. It was at this point that air controllers suspected something
was wrong. And just about then the plane's transponder, a piece of
equipment that broadcast its location, went out.'

Please keep that transponder in mind. The disabling of transponders as reason for losing track of the airliners is a key part of Government/ Corporate stories about " '9/11.' "

At 8:20 a.m., then, Air Traffic Control and the FAA should have alerted NORAD that neaby military aircraft needed to intercept Flight 11 at once.

FAA Order 7110.65M 10-2-5 states: 'Consider that an aircraft emergency exists ... when: ...There is unexpected loss of radar contact and radio communications with any ...aircraft.'

FAA Order 7110.65M 10-1-1 tells monitors to act rather than wait in the event of any possible emergency: "If ... you are in doubt that a situation constitutes an emergency or potential emergency, handle it as though it were an emergency.'

There is a well-known, recent precedent for fulfilling the FAA's need-to-intercept regulation.

On October 25, 1999 a Sunjet Aviation Learjet carrying golfer Payne Stewart, three of his friends, and two Sunjet pilots took off from Orlando, FL for Dallas, TX at 9:19 Eastern Daylight Time.

14 minutes later this plane, registered as N47BA, lost contact with the Air Routes Traffic Control Center in Jacksonville, FL.

The following is taken from the U.S. National Transportation Safety Board's account of the flight. 'At 0933:38 EDT (6 minutes and 20 seconds after N47BA acknowledged the previous clearance), the controller instructed N47BA to change radio frequencies and contact another Jacksonville ARTCC controller. The controller received no response from N47BA. The controller called the flight five more times over the next 4 1/2 minutes but received no response. About 0952 CDT, a USAF F-16 test pilot from the 40th Flight Test Squadron at Eglin Air Force Base (AFB), Florida, was vectored to within 8 nm (nautical miles) of N47BA. About 0954 CDT, at a range of 2,000 feet from the accident airplane and an altitude of about 46,400 feet, the test pilot made two radio calls to N47BA but did not receive a response.'

The important information to me here is that an Air Force F-16 was dispatched and ready to intercept this plane--a six-passenger Learjet flying over sparsely populated Florida--within 19 minutes of this flight's appearing to be off-course.

On September 12, 2002 MSNBC said about the recent precedent: 'When golfer Payne Stewart's incapacitated Learjet missed a turn at a fix, heading north instead of west to Texas, F-16 interceptors were quickly dispatched.'

No such quick dispatch was done by any ATC or the FAA on the morning of September 11--even after two enormous commercial airliners flew into Towers of the World Trade Center and Networks repeated their galvanizing news that America was "under attack."

On the " '9/11' " morning American Airlines Flight 11 continued off-course, turning sharply southeast.

At 8:38 EDT, 23 minutes after this Boeing 767 first missed a 'fix' on its flight-path and 18 minutes after it failed to follow ATC instruction to achieve its cruising altitude, the FAA alerted NORAD that Flight 11 was a confirmed hijacking. NORAD then dispatched two F-15 jets from Otis Air Force Base on Cape Cod, Massachusetts.

On September 18 NORAD announced that it had scrambled jets from Otis AFB 6 minutes after the FAA's alert--that is, at 8:44 EDT. Flying at their top speed of 1875 miles per hour, the F-15s could have reached Manhattan in less than 10 minutes: too late to stop Flight 11 from crashing into the North Tower, but several minutes before United Airlines 175 struck the South Tower.

Yet, according to NORAD and Corporate media, the F-15s were 70 miles northeast of Manhattan when United Airlines #175 hit the South Tower.

Let's look back now at the airliners' transponders. Their disabling has been supposed to have let hijackers avoid tracking by the FAA and NORAD.

However, regarding NORAD's responsibilities and capabilities, here's what the Canadian Defense website says under 'Canada-United States Defense Regulations': 'NORAD uses a network of ground-based radars, sensors and fighter jets to detect, intercept and, if necessary, engage any threats to the continent.'

That is, the United States' and Canadian Governments are sensibly equipped to detect attacks that don't feature transponders --attacks that don't want to call attention to themselves, you know--attacks by other nations' armed forces such as have been anticipated for more than 50 years. The U. S. and Canadian Governments are equipped to then defend against such attacks.

In short, NORAD sensibly relies on radar that doesn't need transponders for NORAD to track aircraft.

Radar serving the United States' highest military leaders, in fact, tracked the flight that ultimately killed Payne Stewart and his five companions. On October 26, 1999, one day after that fatal crash, CNN reported: "Officers on the Joint Chiefs were monitoring the Learjet on radar screens inside the Pentagon's National Military Command Center."

At 8:14 EDT the Boeing 767 that was United Airlines Flight 175 took off from Boston's Logan Airport for LAX in Los Angeles, carrying fifty-six passengers, two pilots and seven flight-attendants.

Less than 15 minutes later this airliner first missed a 'fix' on its course, veering southward over Connecticut. United Airlines 175 continued south, almost intersecting with American Airlines Flight 11 above the Hudson River, as if both 767s were intended to strike the World Trade Center simultaneously, and reached airspace over middle New Jersey (Trenton the nearest city) before it angled northeast on a beeline for Manhattan.

Again Air Traffic Control and the Federal Aviation Agency failed to take prescribed steps.

At 8:43 EDT--nearly 15 minutes after UA 175 first went off-course and 28 minutes after American Airllnes 11 first missed a 'fix'--the FAA informed NORAD that the second divergent airliner also required interception.

At 9:06 EDT UA 175 exploded into one corner of the World Trade Center's South Tower around the 80th floor.

53 minutes later the South Tower--the Tower hit second and hit much less directly--was the first to fall from what commentators termed a " 'pancake' " collapse.

The Squadrons Who Stayed Home

As faulty as FAA/NORAD behavior was in regard to the off-course airliners that struck WTC Buildings 1 and 2, it's with American Airlines Flight 77, the jet blamed for devastating one wedge-block of the Pentagon, that the holes in Government officials' and Corporate media's stories become gaping and in fact sickening.

AA 77 was the Boeing 757 (a plane a little smaller than the 767, its

wingspan of 124 feet against the 767's 156 feet) that left Dulles
Airport in Washington, DC at 8:21 EDT for LAX in Los Angeles.

Like its doomed predecessors that morning, AA 77 was about one/
quarter full, carrying fifty-six passengers, two pilots and four flight-
attendants.

By 8:55 EDT, just after crossing the Ohio border above
Parkersburg, West Virginia, AA 77 had lost contact with Air Traffic
Control due to the disabling of its transponder.

You know from the above-quoted FAA Orders that such loss of
contact means an 'emergency.'

You also know that an 'emergency' means that the ATC/FAA must
call at once for NORAD or other military interception of the out-of-
contact aircraft.

You also know that aircraft in flight do not need an active
transponder in order to be tracked by radar.

Around 9:00 EDT, AA 77 turned 180 degrees and headed back
toward the nation's capital.

About 6 minutes after this airliner made its 180-degree
wrong turn the Boeing 767 that was United Airlines 175 burst into
flames as it struck the World Trade Center's South Tower, its impact
shadowed by the already smoking 110-story Tower beside it.

You, watching at home, might have considered this
second airliner's strike to be sign of one of the greatest
emergencies you'd ever seen. You might have expected the
Controllers and Officers who are charged with maintaining the United
States' safety and security to ready defense of air-space over
Washington, DC--the nation's capital--home to President, Pentagon
and Congress--even without the threat represented by a third
commercial airliner, American Airlines 77, reversing its course to
head straight for the capital.

Officials in Washington were, in fact, watching AA 77 fly at them.

In the September 15 *New York Times* Matthew Wald wrote: 'During
the hour or so that American Airlines Flight 77 was under the control
of hijackers, up to the moment it struck the west side of the Pentagon,
military officials in a command center on the east side of the building
were urgently talking to law enforcement and air traffic control
officials about what to do.'

What to do? What to do!

You--who are likely a lay person who must first rely on common sense for your judgement--might think that the urgent thing to do was: Scramble jets from the nearest possible U.S. airfield to defend the nation's capital.

Not till 9:24, however, almost one half-hour after AA 77's transponder shut off, did the FAA tell NORAD what NORAD's own tracking would have already known: This third airliner/missile had to be intercepted.

Still, you might be glad and relieved to know now that a U. S. Air Force Base sits only 10 miles from Washington D.C. You might also be glad to know that it, Andrews AFB, is especially prepared with aircraft to defend the nation's capital.

Andrews AFB is, in fact, home to two Flight Squadrons.

The 121st Fighter Squadron (FS-121) of the 113th Fighter Wing (FW-113), flies F-16 fighters.

The 321st Marine Fighter Attack Squadron (VMFA-321) of the 49th Marine Air Group, Detachment A (MAG-49 Det-A), flies F/A-18 fighters.

Hundreds of personnel serve in these Squadrons.

The specific missions of each Squadron is spelled out by www.dcmilitary.com, a private Website that's authorized by the military to provide information for members of the armed forces.

Regarding the 121st Fighter Squadron of the 113th Fighter Wing, dcmilitary.com states: '...as part of its dual mission, the 113th provides capable and ready response forces for the District of Columbia in the event of a natural disaster or civil emergency. Members also assist local and federal law enforcement agencies in combating drug trafficking in the District of Colombia. [They] are full partners with the active Air Force.'

Regarding the 321st Marine Fighter Attack Squadron, dcmilitary.com states: 'In the best tradition of the Marine Corps, a 'few good men and women' support two combat-ready reserve units at Andrews AFB.... Marine Fighter Attack Squadron (VMFA) 321, a Marine Corps Reserve squadron, flies the sophisticated F/A-18 Hornet. Marine Aviation Logistics Squadron necessary to maintain a force in readiness.'

Somehow, however, neither NORAD nor the National Military Command Center in the Pentagon called for fighter-jets to be scrambled from the two 'combat-ready' Squadrons at this Air Force Base 10 miles from the White House.

49, Detachment A, provides maintenance and supply functions Instead, three F-16s from Langley Air Force Base in southern Virginia, 129 miles away from the NMCC, were scrambled.

Still--and yet--perplexed as you may be by the decision to call for jets from Langley and not Andrews--you might be glad and relieved to know that F-16s can fly 1500 mph. According to NORAD's press-release of 9/18/02, three F-16s from Langley were aloft by 9:30 EDT. Each was capable of jetting to air-space over the White House and Pentagon within 7 minutes.

Further, you, as a normal, intelligent and compassionate person, would be glad and relieved to also know that Pentagon employees regularly practice to evacuate their building in less than 5 minutes if threatened by an attack. Your worries about these employees' safety would be further allayed by the surface-to-air missiles that are among the Pentagon's sensible anti-aircraft defenses.

Meanwhile, as some jets went up and some stayed down, AA 77 continued straight back at the White House and Pentagon.

The *Washington Post* of September 12 reiterated the breathtaking last turns of this 757, the expertise that was later credited to flight-school failure Hami Hanjour: 'But just as the plane seemed to be on a suicide mission into the White House, the unidentified pilot executed a pivot so tight that it reminded observers of a fighter jet maneuver.'

The airliner thus turned away from the Command Center and the office where Secretary of Defense Donald Rumsfeld sat in the the Pentagon's east wedge. Instead it apparently drove into the west block, exploding among relatively low-level personnel at 9:43 EDT.

Your final perplexity about events relating to American Airlines Flight 77 might be that none of the Pentagon's personnel were evacuated, nor were any of its alarms or air-defenses activated, prior to the crash.

123 people in the Pentagon and all 62 aboard AA 77 died.

The jets from Langley arrived over Washington, DC around 10:00 that morning, having been flown for some reason flown at 1/5 of their top speed.

H'mm! H'mm--H'mm--H'mn--and woe!

Who Knew?

What to do? What to do!

As a normal, intelligent and compassionate person, watching with shock and alarm events of the 9/11 morning repeat on Networks' TV, you likely were moved to find out all that you could, to do whatever you could, in terms of aid for the victims and prevention for society-- even if you weren't this country's President or the United States' highest-ranking Air Force General.

So: What did our selected President, George W. Bush, and U. S. Air Force General Richard B. Myers, his service's representative among the Joint Chiefs of Staff on 9/11/01, do between 8:45 and 9:30 EDT, the first 45 minutes of the " 'Attack on America' "?

They went on with their scheduled appointments.

General Richard B. Myers met on Capitol Hill with Senator Max Cleland of Georgia, a Democrat member of the Senate Armed Services Committee, while the two World Trade Center Towers burned after they were struck by airliners and American Airlines 77 reversed its course and headed back at Washington, DC.

On September 11 General Myers told the American Forces Radio and Television Service: "When we came out, somebody said the Pentagon had been hit."

Two days later General Myers had a confirmation-hearing before the Senate Armed Services Committee. He told the Committee's Chairman, Carl Levin, Democrat of Michigan, that he didn't know when NORAD had scrambled jets.

The General explained to the Senators: "At the time of the first impact on the World Trade Center, we stood up our crisis action team. That was done immediately. So we stood it up. And we started talking to the federal agencies. The time I do not know is when NORAD responded with fighter aircraft. I don't know that time."

H'mm!

Two days after " '9/11' ", a span in which the FAA's and NORAD's logs were certainly available to him, the ranking Officer in the United States Air Force claimed to still not know when jets were scrambled over New York City and Washington, DC.

On October 1, 2001 the U.S. Senate confirmed General Myers as Chairman of the Joint Chiefs of Staff.

On the " '9/11' " morning this nation's President, George W. Bush, was in Sarasota, Florida for a session at the Emma E. Booker Elementary School to promote education
    ABC correspondent John Cochran told anchor-person Peter Jennings that reporters saw White House Chief of Staff Andrew Card whisper into the President's ear as GWB left his hotel for the motorcade to the Booker School just before 9:00 a.m. EDT. Cochran related: "The reporter said to the President, 'Do you know what's going on in New York?' He said he did, and he said he will have something about it later. His first event is about half an hour at an elementary school ..."
    During the next half-hour--as the Towers smoked, as AA 77 targeted Washington, DC, and as more than 50 other airliners remained in unpredictable flight over the mainland United States--President George W. Bush read and heard the story of a goat with 3rd-Graders at the Emma E. Booker Elementary School.
    The Secret Service's primary mission is to protect the United States' President. The Booker School is 5 miles from the Sarasota-Bradenton International Airport (home to one of the flight-schools that Mohammed Atta and Marwanal-Al-Shehhi are reported to have used). During the latter 1990s the Secret Service has particularly prepared to protect and remove the President from the threat of hijacked aircraft.
    The Secret Service certainly knew of the hijacked airliners, crashes and dangers of the 9/11 morning.
    On Sunday, September 16, 2001, the United States Vice-President, Dick Cheney told NBC correspondent Tim Russert on --Meet the Press-- that the Secret Service and the FAA had "open lines" on the 9/11 morning. Before breaking off as if he'd revealed too much, Cheney said: "The Secret Service has an arrangement with the F.A.A. They had open lines after the World Trade Center was..."
    Despite their "open lines" the Secret Service and President George W. Bush left themselves 5 miles--or less then 30 seconds--from attack by another airplane.
    They were somehow unconcerned.

The story of the goat proceeded. White House Chief of Staff
Andrew Card again stepped near the President and whispered into
GWB's ear. Card told Bush that a second hijacked airliner had
flown into the World Trade Center and a third was headed
straight for Washington, D. C.

Network tapes show the President's response. George W. Bush
nods as if he's been told about an appointment changing from
10:15 to 10:30--that is, as if the news is of little surprise or
concern to him--that is, as if such unprecedented disasters and
dangers appear to be no shock or sorrow to him.

Card steps away without waiting for word from the nation's
Commander-in-Chief.

Tambien, photos from the next few days after " '9/11' " show
President Bush and his father, George Herbert Walker
Bush (George Herbert Walker Bush fourth in a line of Bush
patriarchs, we should remember here, who have profited from
the United States' international wars since World War I, GWHB
the former United States President and Vice-President and
Director of the Central Intelligence Agency, GWHB the former
boss of former Secretary of Defense Dick Cheney, GWHB the
veteran of the Watergate and Iran-Contra and Iraq-gate scandals,
and GWHB the current consultant for the Carlyle Group, a firm
that has lately made billions of dollars from and with Department
of Defense contractors), smiling and laughing.

"David Rockefeller is the most conspicuous representative today of the ruling class, a multinational fraternity of men who shape the global economy and manage the flow of its capital. Rockefeller was born to it, and he has made the most of it.... Rockefeller sits at the hub of a vast network of financiers, industrialists, and politicians whose reach encircles the globe.... But what some critics see as a vast international conspiracy, he considers a circumstance of life and just another day's work."

Bill Moyers in --Bill Moyers Journal, 'The World of
David Rockefeller'--first broadcast in April 1980

'The West thinks in terms of bringing advance and opportunity to such a place. In actuality, we bring a cultural bankruptcy which will last for many years. The Asmat, like every other corner of the world, is being sucked into a world economy and a world culture which inists on economic plenty as a primary ideal.'

Michael Rockefeller, age 22, third son of then-Governor Nelson
Rockefeller, writing in a letter to his family from his studies
among the Kurelu and Papaguan peoples of New Guinea, just
before his sudden death in 1961.

THE BUILDINGS AND THEIR VICTIMS

' "I was taking firefighters up in the elevator to the
24th floor to get in position to evacuate workers. On
the last trip up a bomb went off. We think there were
bombs set in the building." '
Louie Caachioli, New York Fire Department, about
the WTC's South Tower, *People Weekly* 9/24/01

'It also may end up being a good investment. In the
end, Mr. Silverstein may wind up controlling 11
million square feet of attractive, lower-rise modern
space instead of 11 million square feet of 30-year-old
space in New York's tallest and most conspicuous
buildings.' *Real Estate Journal* 11/5/01

1, 2, 7--All Fall Down

Here the going becomes most disturbing to me.

Here the horrors that facts suggest become most difficult for
normal, compassionate people to imagine, I think.

In examining the World Trade Center Buildings that fell on
September 11--Buildings 1 and 2 the WTC's Twin Towers, Building
7 the 47 stories of offices completed by Silverstein Properties in
1986--and in examining how they fell, we must at least register as
individuals the thousands of people who died on the WTC site that
day. We must enter into their experience if we're to gather what
happened. We must look at who died and who did not.

I wrote earlier that the WTC North and South Towers COULD NOT
have fallen due to the causes (primary among these causes: fire so hot
it deformed steel) that Corporate Government and Media stories have
presented for the Towers' " 'pancake' " collapse.

You likely remember the depiction-cum-explanation that Networks
and newspapers repeated soon after " '9/11.' "

It went like this. As the 767s struck their targets--AA 11 driving
into the North Tower's 90th floor and UA 175 hitting the South
Tower toward one corner around the 80th floor--each airliner
exploded. The ensuing flames of jet-fuel created a white-hot inferno
inside each 110-story building. Fire blasted up <u>and</u> down elevator
shafts.

Fire's increasing, unprecedented heat then turned to "licorice" the structural steel beams and columns that stood as core and outer and lateral supports of the Towers.

Thus weakened, the steel supports buckled, carrying concrete down with them. One floor of each Tower fell into the next below. Then both fell through the next floor below. Then the three floors ....

And so all of each Tower's floors collapsed in a "pancake effect" of terrible, increasing impact. Each Tower's 100,000 tons of concrete, steel, plastic, wiring, and marble dropped like an unpleating facade or straight-down Slinky, their weight pulverizing into their foundations.

The British Broadcasting Company story of September 13 is typical of this immediate depiction/explanation.

It's titled 'How the World Trade Center Fell.'

The BBC quotes 'structural engineer' Chris Wise: ' "It was the fire that killed the buildings. There's nothing on earth that could survive those temperatures with that amount of fuel burning.... The columns would have melted, the floors would have melted and eventually they would have collapsed one on top of each other." '

Another BBC-quoted expert then echoes Chris Wise.

'The buildings' construction manager, Hyman Brown, agrees that nothing could have saved them from the inferno.

"The buildings would have stood had a plane or a force caused by a plane smashed into it," he said.

"But steel melts, and 24,000 gallons (91,000 litres) of aviation fluid melted the steel. Nothing is designed or will be designed to withstand that fire." '

So there you have it. Two experts say two days after " '9/11' " that the Towers' beams and columns did more than buckle--their structural steel ' "melted." '

How hot must steel be heated in order to melt?

Steel is 99% iron. According to chemcialelements.com, temperatures of at least 2795.0 degrees Fahrenheit are needed to 'melt' iron. Even hotter temperatures would be needed to 'melt' the more fire-resistant structural steel of the WTC Towers.

How hot, then, must steel be made in order for it to soften and warp toward producing the " 'pancake collapse' " that Networks and newspapers have described? Temperatures of 1022 degrees F. are needed to to begin to deform structural steel. As to the steel in the WTC Towers, a report from the University of Sydney's Department of Civil Engineering in Australia says: 'Fireproofed steel is rated to resist 1,500 to 1,600° F.'

The basic question then becomes: How hot can fire from jet fuel make structural steel?

Corus Construction is a maker of car-parks in Europe. In order to be sure its structures could withstand collapse from multiple gas-tanks exploding into flames inside a car-park, Corus tested steel against fires from kerosene. (Jet fuel and kerosene are interchangably alike in their capacities for fueling and burning.)

Corus exposed steel to fire from kerosene over periods as long as one hour in 'Full scale fire tests' in the United States, United Kingdom Japan and Australia. The highest temperatures these tests registered were 644 degrees Fahrenheit for beams (Australia) and 680 degrees F. for columns (United Kingdom).

The tests show us more exactly why the Towers COULD NOT have collapsed due to jet-fuel's fire.

Several other facts counter Corporate media's widespread depiction/explanation of the " 'pancake collapse.' "

*The South Tower was hit second and hit obliquely by the Boeing 767 that was United Airlines 175. Much of that airliner's half-full load of fuel ignited outside the building, The South Tower consequently suffered far less fire within its structures.

And yet the South Tower fell in almost half the time after impact (53 minutes: 9:05 EDT to 9:58 EDT) as the North (101 minutes: 8:46 EDT to 10:29 EDT).

If fire's deforming steel was the cause of the two buildings' collapse, the North Tower should have fallen first and in less time.

*Each Tower should have tilted sideways if its fall were undirected. In particular the South Tower--hit around its 80th floor, about 10 stories lower than the North Tower--should have toppled toward the corner where it was hit.

If they'd toppled sideways the Towers--each almost 1/4-mile tall-- would have ruined much surrounding real estate. The Towers' collapse within their foundations--per a perfect demolition--saved billions of dollars of property from devastation.

*Networks' coverage of both burning Towers that morning shows the smoke of fires turning from white to gray to darker shades as minutes pass.

Such a change in the smoke of a fire indicates that the fire is cooling, producing more carbon, because it's exhausting oxygen.

So: We see that the Towers' structural steel was cooling, contracting less heat, at the time when each collapsed.

At the head of this section you've read one New York City firefighter's recollection, less than two weeks after last September 11, of ' "a bomb" ' that went off in the South Tower. Louie Caachioli, 51, was among the first firefighters to enter that building as it burned overhead.

Caachiolii told *People Weekly*: ' "I was taking firefighters up in the elevator to the 24th floor to get in position to evacuate workers. On the last trip up a bomb went off. We think there were bombs set in the building." '

Other survivors remember explosions inside the Towers.

Kim White, 32, worked on the South Tower's 80th floor. She told *People*. ' "All of a sudden the building shook, then it started to sway. We didn't know what was going on. We got all our people on the floor into the stairwell . . . at that time we all thought it was a fire . . .We got down as far as the 74th floor . . . then there was another explosion." '

Survivors also remember that instructions to stay in the buildings were broadcast even AFTER each Tower was struck by an exploding airliner.

Nancy Cassidy, 42, was personnel manager for the Mizuho Capital Markets trading company on the South Tower's 80th floor. She fled her office just after American Airlines Flight 11 struck the North Tower and she saw fireballs roil in that building next to her window. She and about fifty others rushed down a stairwell.

Nancy Cassidy was quoted in New York's *Newsday* of 9/13/01. ' "All of a sudden you heard, 'Shhh,'" she said. "Everyone was quiet. That's when they made that announcement: 'Building One is in a state of emergency; Building Two is secure. You're fine, you can return to your work stations.' " '

Nancy Cassidy told *Newsday* : ' "It could be that because of that announcement, some people from my company went back upstairs and now may be gone," she said.'

In the North Tower employees were told to stay in their building even as the Boeing 767 burned above them.

Newsday related: 'Michael Cartier, 24, of Jackson Heights, said his sister Michelle, who worked in Tower One told him that after the first plane struck, "People began to evacuate, but an announcement over the intercom said everything was all right, no need to evacuate."

"If this is true," Michael Cartier said, "they told people to go back to their desks. There should be an investigation." '

Tower One was the North Tower.

Dan Baumbach, 24, a software engineer on the 80th floor of the North Tower when he Boeing 767 struck his building, took off downstairs with a group from his office.

Newsday related: 'But heading down the stairs, he and four other co-workers suddenly came upon 100 others, who were told by a building official, "We'll get you out; be calm, just stay here."

"There was no way we were going to stay there," said Baumbach, 24, who was then warned: "You can try it, but it's at your own risk."

Many stayed. Baumbach did not.

At 10-story intervals, he had to walk through burning corridors. Bizarrely, no sprinklers or alarms had been activated.'

H'mm!

The lack of activation or alarm inside the Twin Towers may remind you of the same lack of alarm or activation inside the Pentagon before workers died there.

About 7 hours later on that day of horrors, WTC Building 7, the 47-story former headquarters of sunken junk-bond colossus Drexel Burnham Lambert, the firm whose failure set off the $500-billion Savings & Loan losses of the latter 1980s, collapsed.

WTC 7 was home to the Emergency Command Center or "bunker" that Mayor Rudolph Giulani had installed after an FBI-assisted bomb exploded on February 20, 1993 in the parking-garage underneath Tower 2.

WTC 7 was also home to offices of the CIA, the U.S Department of Defense and the U.S. Secret Service.

Network coverage of the " '9/11' " morning shows an explosion smoking up from WTC 7 even BEFORE the South Tower fell. The explosion was later attributed to fires bursting out in the several huge tanks of diesel fuel in WTC 7 that were there to serve in case of emergency (10,000 gallons for Giuliani's Command Center, 12,000 for the Smith Barney investment-banking firm, and more: a total of 42,000 gallons.)

Coverage shows, however, no flames accompanying the first WTC 7 explosion: Only a cloud of white dust.

Within minutes of the first WTC 7 explosion, before either Tower fell, Mayor Rudolph Guilani and close associates fled the "headquarters" they'd set up at 75 Barkley Street. "We were operating out of there when we were told that the World Trade Center was gonna collapse," Rudolph Giuliani told Peter Jennings of ABC News that morning, "and it did collapse before we could get out of the building."

H'mm!

How could anyone have foreseen a collapse that was otherwise said to be unprecedented and unexpected? Who warned the Mayor whose pre-9/11/01" 'clean-up' " of New York City has often been compared to Mussolini's of Italy? Why weren't firefighters inside or around the World Trade Center's Twin Towers also warned?

You may remember that 343 New York City firefighters died on the " '9/11' " morning.

In August of 2002 the *New York Times* reported that two of those New York City firemen, Battalion Chief Orio J. Palmer and Fire Marshal Ronald P. Bucca, had reached the 78th floor, the Sky Lobby, of the South Tower within a few minutes of that building's collapse.

'Once they got there,' the *Times* piece recounted, 'they had a coherent plan for putting out the fires they could see and helping victims who survived.... At that point, the building would be standing for just a few more minutes, as the fire was weakening the structure on the floors above him. Even so, Chief Palmer could see only two pockets of fire, and called for a pair of engine companies to fight them.'

The occasion for the *Times* piece was release by the U. S. Justice Department of a ' "lost tape" ' of communication between New York Fire Department personnel that New York ort Authority Police recorded on the morning of 9/11/01. The existence of this tape was revealed to the NYFD last January, but the NYFD refused to pledge secrecy as to its content. It was played on August 2, 2002 to sixteen survivors of NYFD firefighters in a Manhattan hotel.

Orio J. Palmer's widow said: ' "I didn't hear fear, I didn't hear panic. When the tape is made public to the world, people will hear that they all went about their jobs without fear, and selflessly." '

We know that WTC 7 was another valuable holding of Silverstein Properties.

In February of 2002 Silverstein Properties won $861 million from Industrial Risk Insurers to rebuild on the site of WTC 7. Silverstein Properties' estimated investment in WTC 7 was $386 million. So: This building's collapse resulted in a profit of about $500 million.

'Broad Human Interests'

Other facts about the Twin Towers and " '9/11' " relate to that most material of concerns: Money.

On April 26 of 2001 the Board of Commissioners for the Port Authority of New York and New Jersey awarded Silverstein Properties and mall-owner Westfield America a 99-year-lease on the following assets: The Twin Towers, World Trade Center Buildings 4 and 5, two 9-story office-buildings, and 400,000 square feet of retail space.

The partners' winning bid was $3.2 billion for holdings estimated to be worth more than $8 billion. JP Morgan Chase, a prestigious investment-bank that's the flagship firm of its kind for Rockefeller family interests, advised the Port Authority, another body long influenced by banker and builder David Rockefeller, his age then 85, in the negotiations.

The lead partner and spokesperson for the winning bidders, Larry Silverstein, age 70, already controlled more than 8 million square feet of New York City real estate. WTC 7 and the nearby Equitable Building were prime among these prior holdings. Larry Silverstein also owned Runway 69, a nightclub in Queens that was alleged 9 years ago to be laundering money made through sales of Laotian heroin.

Let's pause to scan this last sidelight. On September 16, 2001 Ernesto Cienfuegos wrote in the Los Angeles newspaper *La Voz de Aztlan*: 'In July 1993, Harry P. Miller, a Vietnam veteran, filed a complaint in a federal district court of New York against Larry Silverstein, the owner of "Runway 69," a Queens dance club, that included as defendants President Clinton and Colin Powell. The allegations of Miller's complaint were that the named defendants committed or aided others in committing illegal acts, including assassinations, over a twenty-five year period, beginning amidst the

Vietnam War, in furtherance of a conspiracy to distribute Laotian heroin. He asserted that the defendants were engaged in heroin trafficking and that "Goldfingers International," a business that supplies nude dancers to nude dance clubs, was laundering the proceeds of the conspiracy through "Runway 69." '

Now, given what's been shown so far even within the confines of the short book you hold, is this association of Silverstein, Clinton and Powell fantastic or far-fetched to you?

We know from many sources--Alfred McCoy's The   Politics of Heroin in Southeast Asia and Peter Dale Scott's Deep Politics are rich in documentation--that United States' intelligence-services began to smuggle opium and heroin from Burma, Thailand and Laos in the 1950s. Their traffic especially expanded through Vietnam in the late 1960s/early 1970s. We know that tons of heroin flooded ghettos of Black and Brown people in the U. S., depressing threats of revolution, at the same time as 30,000 U.S. servicemen in Vietnam were addicted to heroin.

As to what's happening now, we'll soon see how important the laundering of illegal narcotics is to the most central of U.S. financial institutions, including Citibank, the Chase Bank, JP Morgan Chase, and the entire New York Stock Exchange.

For the 2001 Twin Towers' deal Larry Silverstein's main source of promised financing came from a group headed by another realtor, Lloyd Goldman, who also possessed enormous holdings in New York City.

His deal done, Larry Silverstein told the the *Real Estate Journal*, an offshoot of the *Wall Street Journal*: ' "This is a dream come true. When we first became associated with the Port Authority with 7 World Trade Center, we looked at the asset of the World Trade Center with tremendous interest. We will be in control of a prized asset. There is nothing like it in the world," he said.'

Mortgaging for the winning bid came from the General Motors Acceptance Corporation.

General Motors, you may know, is another giant engine of capital and oil that's for generations had the Rockefeller family among its controlling investors.

We should here take a preliminary moment to note the history of some the United States' ruling-class families.

We should note a representative few of the appalling schemes and partnerships--partnerships using Wars, Governments and fascists--by which these families have profited in the 20th century. This preliminary review of conspiracies will help us to understand, I believe, " '9/11.' "

We should then proceed to seeing how the World Trade Center got built.

Like their partners and/or relatives the Roosevelts, Duponts, Harrimans, Warburgs, ... , the Rockefeller and Bush families are long-time players for global power.

Let's start with one telling fact. Both John D. Rockefeller Jr. (father of David and Nelson), and Prescott Bush, (grandfather of our selected President and father of George Herbert Walker Bush), materially aided the National Socialist Party of Germany, Hitler's Nazis, in the 1920s and 1930s and into World War II through businesses such as the Chase Bank and Standard Oil of New Jersey (Rockefeller) and the Hamburg-Amerika Shipping Line and the Silesian American Corporation (Bush).

The Rockefellers' Chase Bank solicited accounts in Nazi France as late as 1944.

In 1941 Prescott ("Press") Bush, a nominal Republican, and his partner Averill Harriman, a Democrat, bought controlling interest in the Silesian-American Corporation from their partner, Fritz Thyssen, Thyssen the main financier of Nazis' seizure of power and author of a book titled I Paid Hitler. The Silesian-American Corporation continued to operate in Nazi-occupied Poland. Partly a mining company, the S-A Corp. availed itself of the increasing, mostly Jewish slave-labor at a nearby " 'Camp' " known as Auschwitz. Prescott Bush, a Republican, and his partner, W. Averill Harriman, a Democrat, thus profited from said slave-labor till the S- A. Corp.'s assets and those of other holdings of theirs (the Union Banking Corporation one) were seized under the United States' Trading with the Enemy Act in 1942.

These few facts may help ordinary, intelligent and compassionate people better understand what other facts about the construction and destruction of the World Trade Center Towers suggest or mean. Later--in 'Lords of the "New World Order" '--we'll scan a history of

U.S. ruling-class families over a span of more than a century, beginning with the Spanish-American War, focusing on members of the Bush and Rockefeller clans.

In 1952 Prescott Bush was elected to be a U. S. Senator from Connecticut. For the next 8 years "Press" (so he was addressed in 1937 by his and Harriman's attorney with Nazis, John Foster Dulles, the United States' Secretary of State between 1952-60) was a regular golf-partner of President Dwight D. Eisenhower, the General who commanded U.S. forces in Europe during World War II.

During the exact middle of this decade, the 1950s, David Rockefeller, the youngest son of John D. Rockefeller, Jr. and the grandson of the United States' first billionaire, became Chairman of his family's Chase Bank. David, born in 1915, already was known among his peers as wonderfully capable. He was working with great diligence and industry to make Manhattan south of Wall Street a new financial center of the world. In 1956 he formed the Downtown-Lower Manhattan Association, packing it with financiers from old wealth such as S. Sloan Colt of Banker's Trust, Henry S. Morgan of Morgan Stanley, and Robert Lehman of Lehman Brothers.

By 1961 David, the youngest son, the banker and builder, had erected a 60-story headquarters for his newly merged Chase and Manhattan Banks on a single block of Cedar Street. One Chase Plaza was the first skyscraper in lower Manhattan in a generaton. For it to flourish optimally--for the whole new Manhattan of global financing and projection that he envisioned to flourish optimally--David Rockefeller needed a nexus of similar institutions nearby. He needed ... a World Trade Center--something that would outsize and outdo other Centers that Rockefellers had previously built.

David's brother Nelson, born in 1908, the second-eldest of five brothers, had kindred ambitions. In 1958 Nelson was elected Governor of New York over W. Averill Harriman, the former partner, we know, of Prescott Bush, George Herbert Walker, Adolf Hitler and Benito Mussolini.

This same year, David announced and the *New York Times* endorsed a Lower Manhattan Plan that would put a World Trade Center on 20 square blocks of the East Side, displacing the Fulton Fish Market and the Washington Produce Market.

In 1961 the WTC's prospective site shifted westward, as the State of New York's Port Authority assumed control of the project and the Port Authority acquired the Hudson Tubes that would subsequently transport PATH trains to and from New Jersey. 16 square blocks that then featured a bustling community of electronics' retailers ("Radio Row"), restaurants, markets, and clothing-stores, were to be razed for " 'redevelopment.' "

Other " 'urban renewal' " would remove the Fulton Fish Market and the Washington Produce Market from lower Manhattan. Shipping that employed thousands of skilled laborers would also be taken away. Instead, New York City would have a project of ' "catalytic bigness" ' (David Rockefeller), the World Trade Center, in the district that was ' "the heart pump of the capital blood that sustains the free world" ' (Warren Linquist, David Rockefeller's lead aide).

Eric Darton's <u>Divided</u> <u>We</u> <u>Stand</u>, a book that's subtitled <u>A</u> <u>Biography</u> <u>of</u> <u>New</u> <u>York's</u> <u>World</u> <u>Trade</u> <u>Center</u>, summarizes the final development: 'The project took seven years and a billion dollars to build. It needed immense political muscle, supplied by David Rockefeller at the Chase Manhattan Bank and his brother Nelson, then governor of New York, who stocked one tower with state office workers when the building failed to attract clients.'

Most vitally, risk-free subsidization from the State of New York (Nelson was re-elected Governor in 1962 and 1966, outspending his opponents at least 2 to 1) let the WTC-project push through economic ups and downs, lawsuits and protests. State Supreme Court and City Planning Commission decisions also furthered it.

The one billion dollars was taken from public funds without the public's authorization. As Mario Cuomo told a radio-interviewer in 1996 (when he was no longer Governor of New York), a Public Authority is ' "something above democracy, absolutely, that's why it was invented by politicians, to keep the people away from the operation, and to insulate the politicians." '

Sixty-two workers died in accidents during the Twin Towers' construction.

In 1973 Governor Nelson Rockefeller dedicated the new World Trade Center and moved 20,000 New York State workers into the vacancy of Tower Two.

In 1973, too, with the United States losing its war on the ground in Vietnam, David Rockefeller, advised by future or then National Security Advisors Zbignew Brzezinski and Henry Kissinger, founded the Trilateral Commission.

The Trilateral Commission was like an international version of the Downtown-Lower Manhattan Association.

It was also like a supranational version of the Council on Foreign Relations that has shaped U. S. since its founding by bankers and industrialists in 1921.

Executives from Corporations, Government and academia made up the Trilateral Commission along with European nobility. Men from nations in the industrialized North (the U.S., Britain, Germany, France, Italy, Japan, Canada) dominated the Commission's membership. The Trilateral Commission divided the " 'free world' " into three regions for " 'development.' "

David Rockefeller wrote then: 'Broad human interests are being served best in economic terms where free market forces are able to transcend national boundaries.'

The Trilateral Commission's premise was, however, a lie.

The basic concept of 'free market forces' is a lie--another form of 'Big Lie', whether it's voiced consciously or not.

'Free market forces' have nothing to do with the ability of Western economies to take more each year in interest from Southern nations' debts than the principal of said debt.

As capitalism depends on exploitation, money-lending and speculation to sustain itself (through Banks, Exchanges of commodities and stocks), it depends on brutal and material power (through legislative bodies, Police, Sheriffs and international Armed Forces) to carry on its inequities.

The forced, worsening imbalance between Northern and Southern nations' economies means that Southern nations' revenue from resources (oil, bananas, bauxite, coffee, copper, diamonds, gas, gold ... manganese, nickel, titanium, zinc, ...) and their people's 12-hours-a-day labor are ultimately cost-free to their exploiters. It means that these nations and their peoples can never escape debt. That is, their people can never escape the crushing, grinding, distorting pressures of poverty.

The supranational exploiters' methods are thus to me worse than local mafias. The supranational exploiters and their means never let a farm or shop or workers and families gain a penny or peso against debt.

They have old and new Laws on their side. Their methods of loan-sharking, theft and degradation are sanctioned by international Agreements (the General Agreement on Tariffs and Trade or

G.A.T.T., the North American Free Trade Agreement or N.A.F.TA.) that are never put to a vote by the working people they affect.

Further, supranational groups (the World Trade Organization foremost) have sought more and more to 'transcend' any control by local or national Governments.

These groups want to be a law among themselves.

They want, in fact, return to a feudal order that will be extended across continents.

Their intentions are at best arrogant and mistaken, blinded by their removes from the poverty, suffering and rebellion that their further, depriving means--such as the International Monetary Fund's 'Structural Adjustment Programs' (SAPs)--engender in billions of working families worldwide.

Their markets are NOT 'free', their trade is NOT 'fair', and their 'neo-liberal' New World is really an old one. Their world is of neo-colonial imperialism: A New World for Corporate Empires.

David Rockefeller, for one, he who's now 86, he the "unelected if indisputable chairman of the American establishment", he who still sits "at the hub of a vast network of financiers, industrialists, and politicians whose reach encircles the globe", he one of the most capable, confident and powerful beings of his generation, used the same anti-democratic methods to get the World Trade Center built as he's used to direct the course of all humanity over the past 50 years.

And yet David Rockefeller's methods, his game, we'll see, isn't working for even his grandchildren and their grandchildren.

A Good Investment, ... A Powerful Proof Statement

' "We want to show in September 2002 just how far
we've come," Tatlock said. "We want to have a
powerful proof statement in September 2002. " '
Anne Tatlock, Chief Executive Officer, Fidiciuary
Trust, *San Francisco Business Times,* 2/1/02

Larry Silverstein made a sweet deal for himself prior to the fall of the Twin Towers and WTC 7.

Of the promised 3.2 billion for the 99-year lease that was estimated to be worth $8 billion, Larry Silverstein committed only $15 million of his Properties' money--that is, less than half of .01% of the total financiing.

He and his partners (mall-builder Westfield America and a group headed by Lloyd Goldman) immediately took out insurance polices worth more than $3.2 billion for their dream-come-true new holding.

On November 5, 2001 the *Real Esate Journal* reported on the progress that Larry Silverstein, Lloyd Goldman and their partners had made toward rebuilding on the Twin Towers' site. The *REJ* article stated that Silverstein had the support of New York Senators Charles Schumer and Hillary Clinton (Larry Silverstein had hosted parties for both politicians on his yacht the *Silver Shalis*) as well as Sen. Majority Leader Tom Daschle, Sen. Minority Leader Trent Lott and House Speaker Dennis Hastert. *REJ* reported that the mogul had hired Brad Card, brother of White House Chief of Staff Andrew Card, to 'work' politicians in New York. He was lobbying for caps on liability from the WTC carnage and pursuing lawsuits against insurers. He talked of building four 50-story buildings and a memorial on the site.

The 11/5/01 *REJ* article concluded: 'It also may end up being a good investment. In the end, Mr. Silverstein may wind up controlling 11 million square feet of attractive, lower-rise modern space instead of 11 million square feet of 30-year-old space in New York's tallest and most conspicuous buildings.

"It should prove to justify the time, energy and the psychic impact of what we've been through," Mr. Silverstein says.'

In Feburary 2002 Silverstein Properties won $861 million from Industrial Risk Insurers to rebuild on the site of WTC Building 7.

Regarding the Twin Towers, Larry Silverstein and his partners are locked in lawsuits with Swiss Reinsurance, the Towers' main insurer, over whether the 9/11 attacks were one 'occurrence' or two. The lease-holders would receive $3.55 billion as a settlement if the attacks are considered one occurence. They would receive $7.1 billion--that is, more than twice their investment, an investment that was itself only 20% paid for (and in the case of Silverstein Properties less than half of .01% paid for) if the attacks are determined to be two occurences.

Whatever the result of the dispute with Swiss Reinsurance, Silverstein Properties will receive billions in insurance moneys and possibly more in State and Federal Funds to rebuild on the WTC site.

At the time of their destruction the Twin Towers and WTC 7 needed extensive work to stay competitive as office-space in Manhattan. As early as 1993--the year of the basement-garage bombing by ' "Muslim terrorists" ' that the FBI had anticipated from at least 1985 onward--the WTC 'was already passing its prime as office space, overtaken by a generation of more recent, cybernetically "smart" buildings with higher ceilings and greater built-in electrical capacity,' according to Eric Darton's <u>Divided</u> <u>We</u> <u>Stand.</u>

Darton continues: 'To maintain the trade center as class-A office space commanding top rents, the PA '(the Port Authority, then the WTC's owner) 'would have had to spend $800 million rebuilding the electrical, electronic communications, and cooling systems.'

The new Lower Manhattan Development Corporation, created by Governor George Pataki and Mayor Rudolph Giuliani in November 2001, is to decide on uses of the Twin Towers' site. The Lower Manhattan Developement Corp.is chaired by John Whitehead, he the former Chief Executive Officer of the Goldman Sachs investment-banking firm and former Deputy Secretary of State in the George Herbert Walker Bush Administration, he another close associate of the Rockefeller family's.

Now I feel obliged to look at who died and who did not in the World Trade Center attacks last Sepember 11.

2,952 people is the current total of dead from there on that day (we'll never know how many undocumented workers remain uncounted beyond the official dead). 129 were passengers or crew aboard the airliners. 479 were public-service personnel such as firefighters and New York City Police. The remaining 2,344 were office-workers

We can be thankful that the current total is times less than the numbers that were broadcast on the day of " '9/11' " and in the several weeks afteward.

Only one Chief Executive Officer is among the total. David Alger of Fred Alger Management headed a firm with offices on the North Tower's 93rd floor, a firm that lost 34 others on 9/11.

The largest employer of workers in the Twin Towers was Morgan Stanley Dean Witter.

The *Wall Street Journal* of 9/12/01 quoted Phil Purcell, Chairman and CEO of MSDW, a brokerage and investment-banking firm:

' "Some 3.500 people working for Morgan Stanley's individual-investor businesses were based in the World Trade Center complex, and we are working diligently with local authorities to determine the facts regarding their safety." '

We can be thankful that only ten Morgan Stanley Dean Witter employees were killed last September 11.

We can also be thankful that only one Israeli died in the World Trade Center on that day.

Early reports led to fears that dozens or even hundreds of Israelis might have died on " '9/11.' "

On September 12, 2001 the *Jerusalem Post* wrote that according to Israel's Foreign Ministry and its Consular offices about 4000 Israelis had been employed in the World Trade Center Towers. Four days later, September 16, addressing Congress, President George W. Bush linked Israel's tragedy to the United States' by saying that 130 Israelis had died in the attacks on the WTC.

On September 22, 2001, however, the *New York Times* ran a piece that corrected President GWB. 'There were, in fact,' the *Times* wrote about fatalities from 9/11, 'only three Israelis who had been confirmed as dead: two on the planes and another who had been visiting the towers on business and who was identified and buried.'

That is, there was only one death out of one nationality's initial, supposed pool of 4000 in the Towers.

That's a statistical anomaly of huge proportions.

Two other facts help to explain this anomaly.

In August of 2001 Israel's intelligence-service, the Mossad, repeatedly warned the United States that attacks such as those of " '9/11' " were imminent. The Mossad sent agents to the CIA in Washington with this alarm.

Further, on the morning of 9/11 an Israel-based instant-messaging company, Odigo, e-mailed employees in its South Tower offices that they should not go to work because their building was likely to be attacked.

The investment-banking firm of Goldman Sachs may also have warned its WTC workers. The 9/14/01 edition of *CounterPunch* reported: '*CounterPunch* has also learned that an internal memo was sent around Goldman Sachs in Tokyo on September 10 advising all employees of a possible terrorist attack. It recommended all employees to avoid any American government buildings.'

Odigo's message and the reported Goldman Sachs' warning
somehow weren't conveyed to the tens of thousands who did come
to work at the World Trade Center last September 11. Nor were those
thousands warned by U.S. Government Agencies and officials.

Fidicuary Trust is yet another investment-banking firm.
Like J.P. Morgan and Lazard Freres before it, Fiduciary Trust wants
to serve big money or an exclusive elite. It's 'for institutions and
wealthy clients.' Five months prior to 9/11/01, Fiduciary Trust was
bought by Franklin Resources of San Mateo, California for $825
million .

Fidicuary Trust employed 645 people on five floors on or above
the 90th in the WTC's South Tower. 87 of those employees were
killed due to the " '9/11' " destruction.

Fiduciary Trust's Chairman and CEO, Anne Tatlock, 62, was gone
from her headquarters on " '9/11.' "

The February 1, 2002 *San Francisco Business Times* reported: 'On
the morning of Sept. 11, Tatlock herself had just arrived with a small
group of business leaders at Offutt Air Force Base in Omaha for a
charity event hosted by Warren Buffett. She then heard the news of
the first plane hitting the World Trade Center's north tower.'

H'mm! Or: H'mm? We should pause here to note other, curious
and coincidental facts.

Offutt Air Force Base in Nebraska is home to the United States'
Stragetic Air Command Center.

The SACC is a two-level, 14,000 square-foot underground
structure that links directly with the National Military Command
Center in the Pentagon.

The SAAC may be imagined as a vaster, 21s-century model of the
bunker in which Peter Seller's Dr. Strangelove wanted to wage
nuclear war in Stanley Kubrick's 1963 movie..

The press-release for the SAAC states: 'Within seconds, vital
operational data can be displayed on the large wall display screens or
individual computer monitors.... The Senior Controller also has a
direct line to the National Military Command Center in Washington,
DC, and to the other major command headquarters. This system,
called the Joint Chiefs of Staff Alerting Network, allows CINCSTRAT
(the Commander in Chief of the Stragetic Air Command) prompt
contact with the President, the Secretary of Defense, the Chairman of
the Joint Chiefs of Staff, and other unified commanders.... Through

satellites and radio networks (VLF, LF, UHF and HF), the Command Center can communicate with aircraft in flight over any part of the world. A principal purpose of these networks is to pass National Command Authority orders to the alert forces.... Although CINCSTRAT can launch aircraft for survival, only the President can order nuclear strikes.'

From the above paragraph, you may gather that the SAAC should have helped to track and intercept the four off-course airliners last September 11.

You may know, too, that Warren Buffet is one of the world's leading financiers. His fortune of more than $50 billion makes him widely listed as one of the five richest men in the U. S.

H'mm! Or: H'mm?

You also may now be exclaiming at certain coincidences.

How was it that 'a small group of business leaders' were flown to Nebraska and this particular Air Force Base--the AFB that's the 'nerve-center' of U.S. air-defenses--and flown there for a 'charity event' hosted by Warren Buffet--very early on the morning of 9/11/01?

Who other than Anne Tatlock were among the 'small group of business leaders' is yet another question.

And these questions are but a few among the deeper details of "9/11' "' that have yet to be answered.

President George W. Bush went to Offutt AFB later in the 9/11/01 day. President GWB left Barksdale AFB in Shreveport, Louisiana at 1:48 Central Daylight Time, arriving at Offutt AFB in the next hour.

From there he consulted by phone with his National Security Council.

In March of 2002 financial speculator Warren Buffett predicted that the use of nuclear weapons by terrorists was ' "inevitable." '

In August of 2002 we in the U.S. have become familiar with the charges by Strangelove-like Cabinet officers such as Dick Cheney and Donald Rumsfeld that Saddam Hussein's Iraq wants to wield nuclear weapons against us.

Fiduciary Trust appears to have also profited from the destruction on " '9/11." '

The 2/1/02 *San Francisco Business Times* reported: 'Through the first two weeks after the attacks, Franklin had paid out $16.46 million in benefits payments to victims' families', but that the firm could 'write off $19.8 million in lease, property and equipment leases', and that it could also 'recover an estimated $27.2 million from insurance.'

The difference between $47 million ($19.8 million plus $27.2 million) and $16.46 million is about $30 million. Fiduciary Trust's payments to victims' families' average about $200,000 per family.

Further, Fiduciary Trust's 'integration' with Franklin Resources has been enhanced after September 11, the 2/1/02 *San Francisco Business Times* reported.

'With most of Fiduciary's physical assets destroyed, the firm's back-office integration with Franklin--an ever-risky blending of culture and technology--also was bumped up.

"We are now a year or more ahead on integration plans," Tatlock said.

Plus, Franklin and Fiduciary launched FTI Institutional, its global sales effort aimed at institutional investors.

Given the overarching tragedy, however, Franklin and Fiduciary officials, as well as Wall Street analysts, resist calling the changes a silver lining.

"We want to show in September 2002 just how far we"ve come," Tatlock said. "We want to have a powerful proof statement in September 2002." '

First Looks, Last Looks

Let's look back at the WTC Buildings' collapse.

On September 14, 2001 a relatively obscure newspaper, the *Albuquerque Journal,* ran a story that was headed
' "Explosives Planted In Towers," New Mexico Tech Expert Says.'

Van Romero, Vice President for Research at the New Mexico Institute of Mining and Technology, told the *Albuquerque Journal* on 9/14/02: ' "My opinion is, based on the videotapes, that after the airplanes hit the World Trade Center there were some explosive devices inside the buildings that caused the towers to collapse." '

Van Romero is 'a former director of the Energetic Materials Research and Testing Center at Tech, which studies explosive materials and the effects of explosions on buildings, aircraft and other structures,' the newspaper in New Mexico wrote.

'Romero said the collapse of the structures resembled those of controlled implosions used to demolish old structures....

"It could have been a relatively small amount of explosives placed in strategic points," Romero said. The explosives likely would have been put in more than two points in each of the towers, he said.

The detonation of bombs within the towers is consistent with a common terrorist strategy, Romero said.

"One of the things terrorist events are noted for is a diversionary attack and secondary device," Romero said.

Romero said that if his scenario is correct, the diversionary attack would have been the collision of the planes into the towers.'

On the afternoon of September 11 another engineer, David Rostchek, reviewed TV coverage of that morning's catasrophe in lower Manhattan. He posted his observations on the Internet.

David Rostchek remarked on how smoke from the fires in the North and then the South Tower turned from white to black, a change that showed the fires were cooling due to lack of oxygen, a change we've also noted.

'Then, later,' Rostchek wrote, 'the second building suddenly crumbles into dust, in a smooth wave running from the top of the building (above the burned part) down through all the stories at an equal speed. The debris falls primarily inward. The tower does not break off intact and collapse into other buildings... The crumbling comes from the top (above the damage). It moves at a uniform rate. All of the structural members are destroyed in a smooth pattern, so there is no remaining skeleton. The damage is uniform, symmetric, and total.

In summary, it looks exactly like a demolition--because that's what it is.'

Last September, too, on the ABC News Website for 9/11 a bystander on the ground below the Towers described what she saw and heard: ' "Lots of smoke and then the next thing I heard was an explosion in the building from the top, the south building just crumbled, just completely went down, I saw it," said witness Joan Fleischer.'

In July of 2002 the Public Broadcasting Corporation--PBS sponsored by many of the financial institutions and oil-companies that had or have offices in the World Trade Center--presented a documentary titled 'Why the Towers Fell.'

Over the course of this documentary's hour several professors and engineers elaborated on the depiction/explanation that the 767s' impact and the subsequent fire had caused the Towers' beams to deform, snap loose and collapse.

Not once, however, was any substance in either Tower identified as able to burn hot enough to deform steel. One of the North Tower's two above-the-impact-zone survivors, in fact, Brian Clark, said that he'd seen nothing like "an inferno" as he passed downstairs through the impact-zone.

In August of 2002 the *New York Times* corroborated this eyewitness with the piece that I've already quoted--that about the two New York City firemen, Battalion Chief Orio J. Palmer and Fire Marshal Ronald P. Bucca, who reached the 78th floor, the Sky Lobby, of the South Tower, about 45 minutes after United Airlines 175's impact.

Here's more of what the *N Y Times* wrote: 'Once they got there, they had a coherent plan for putting out the fires they could see and helping victims who survived.... At that point, the building would be standing for just a few more minutes, as the fire was weakening the structure on the floors above him. Even so, Chief Palmer could see only two pockets of fire, and called for a pair of engine companies to fight them.'

Transcript of talk between FDNY Batallion Seven Chief Orio Palmer and other firefighters on 9/11/01. Triathlete Palmer and Fire Marshal Ronald Bucca had climbed to the South Tower's 78th floor Sky Lobby by 9:52 a.m., six minutes before that Tower suddenly began to explode. The New York Times *wrote: 'Nowhere on the tape is there any indication that firefighters had the slightest indication that the tower had become unstable or that it could fall.'*
For a more complete transcript see http://www.thememoryhole.org/ 911/firefighter-tape-excerpts.htm .

9:52 a.m.
Battalion Seven Chief (Orio Palmer): "Battalion Seven ... Ladder 15, we've got two isolated pockets of fire. We should be able to knock it down with two lines. Radio that, 78th floor numerous 10-45 Code Ones."
Ladder 15: "What stair are you in, Orio?"
Battalion Seven Aide: "Seven Alpha to lobby command post."
Ladder Fifteen: "Fifteen to Battalion Seven."
Battalion Seven Chief: "... Ladder 15."
Ladder 15: "Chief, what stair you in?"
Battalion Seven Chief: "South stairway Adam, South Tower."
Ladder 15: "Floor 78?"
Battalion Seven Chief: "Ten-four, numerous civilians, we gonna need two engines up here."
Ladder 15: "Alright ten-four, we're on our way."
...

9:57 a.m.
Battalion Seven Chief: "Operations Tower One to floor above Battalion Nine."
Battalion Nine Chief: "Battalion Nine to command post."
Battalion Seven Operations Tower One: "Battalion Seven Operations Tower One to Battalion Nine, need you on floor above 79. We have access stairs going up to 79, kay."
Battalion Nine: "Alright, I'm on my way up Orio."

9:58 a.m.
Battalion Seven Chief: "Battalion Seven to Ladder 15."
Communication from Orio Palmer ends.

'To put it in a terminology that harkens back to the more brutal age of ancient empires, the three grand imperatives of imperial geostrategy are to prevent collusion and maintain security dependence among the vassals, to keep tributaries pliant and protected, and to keep the barbarians from coming together.'
    Zbigniew Brzezinski, The Grand Chessboard, 1997

"The Morning News *is wet from the rain*
Letters are bleeding down the page
Morning News *fill my head It said business is fine*
War and business makes the man
He stole the sky in the Indian land"
    Laura Nyro, "The Morning News", 1977

'O God the whole host and foolish illusion and entire rigamarole and madness that we erect in the place of onelove, ...'
    Jack Kerouac, The Subterraneans, 1953

OIL, OPIUM, COCA,
BANKS, STOCKS & POWER

'According to the Department of Justice, the US
launders between $500 billion-$1 trillion annually.
I have little idea what percentage of that is narco
dollars, but it is probably safe to assume that at least
$100-200 billion relates to US drug import-exports
and retail trade....
Many of the members of our global leadership were
trained in wartime narcotics trafficking in Asia during
WWII. George H. W. Bush and his generation watched
our ally Chang Kai Shek finance his army and covert
operations with opium.'
Catherine Austin Fitts, 'Narcodollars for Dummies'

'When in doubt, it is always worthwhile to take a look
at a map, where are raw materials resources, and the
routes to them? Then lay a map of civil wars and
conflicts on top of that--they coincide. The same is the
case with the third map: nodal points of the drug
trade. Where this all comes together, the American
intelligence services are not far away. By the way, the
Bush family is linked to oil, gas, and weapons trade,
through the bin Laden family." '
Andreas von Buelow, former Minister of Technology
for Germany, *Tagesspeigel*, January 13, 2002

How the Money Works

" '9/11' " triggered the U.S-led invasion of Afghanistan.
It also set off the " 'global' and " 'endless " 'War on Terror' that
President George W. Bush, lesser Republican and Democrat officials,
and countless newspapers and TV outlets have proclaimed over the
past nine months.
In the columns from Fall of 2001that precede this study of
" '9/11' ", you can read about preparations and threats to invade
Afghanistan by U.S. officials' that occurred months before
September 11 in 2001.

The most graphic of these threats was delivered by Thomas Simons, former Ambassador to Pakistan, as one of three U.S. negotiators at a meeting in Berlin in July 2001 with representatives of the Taliban and six nations that border the oil-rich Caspian Sea. Naif Naik, former Pakistani Minister for Foreign Affairs, was among those present. Jean-Charles Brissard, the French investigative journalist who's co-author of the best-selling <u>Bin</u> <u>Laden:</u> <u>The</u> <u>Hidden</u> <u>Truth</u>, quoted Naik that Simons said: '' "Either you accept our offer of a carpet of gold, or we bury you under a carpet of bombs." '

The prime objective of the July 2001 negotiations was pipelines. Construction of secure pipelines for oil and gas from Turkmenistan, Kazakhistan, and Uzbekistan south through Afghanistan and then through Pakistan to the Arabian Sea would serve rapidly expanding markets in China and elsewhere in the Far East.

Such pipelines were and are thought to be more profitable and less vulnerable than routes through Russia or Iran or Kosovo. They'd been sought by Unocal (Union 76) and other major oil-and-gas Corporations for several years prior to the Taliban's refusal to surrender Usama bin Laden in 1998.

Naif Naik recalled that the discussions in Berlin turned around ' "formation of a government of national unity. If the Taliban had accepted this coaltion, they would have immediately received the internatinal economic aid... And the pipelines from Kazakhistan and Uzbekistan would have come." '

The Taliban evidently refused both inducements and threats. They kept open the prospects for a regional pipeline that they could more control. On September 3 Afghanistan's neighbor, Pakistan, launched the Interstate Gas Company to pursue 'regional pipeline options' from Iran, Qata, Turkmenistan and the United Arab Emirates. Pakistan and the United Arab Emirates were then two of only three nations in the world that recognized the Taliban as Afghanistan's legitimate government.

Eight days later the attacks of 9/11/01--attacks that were at least anticipated and avoided by some in the U.S. Government and in the WTC, we know--struck.

Opium was the other major economic interest in Afghanistan. Prior to the Taliban's eradication of poppy fields in 2000-2001, Afghanistan was the world's main supplier of opium, the source of heroin. Profits from Afghanistan's opium were estimated by the

United Nations to make up $100-150 billion of the $400-500 billion annual take from illegal narcotics around the world.

Between 1979-89, profits from the opium trade sustained the CIA-funded war against the Soviet Union.

In the seven years after 1989 warlords continued to reap tens of millions of dollars in revenues from opium even as their power-struggles ravaged Afghanistan

By Spring of 2001, however, the Taliban had eliminated opium-growing from the territory under their control, turning fields of poppies into fields of wheat. The U.N. estimated Afghanistan's annual crop of opium to be reduced from more than 4000 metric tons to 185, all of the remaining production under the control of " 'Northern Alliance' " warlords who still held about 10% of Afghanistan.

We'll soon see how critical the "cash-flow" of profits from illegal narcotics is to Banks and Stock Exchanges and State economies throughout the industrialized world. We'll see why and how these institutions would founder without their regular fix of such "dirty money."

To be specific: Wall Street and subordinate financial nexuses of " 'globalization' ", all served by the CIA and similar agencies (seven of the eight CIA Directors since World War II have been attorneys or investment-bankers from Wall Street) rely on heroin and cocaine for a "black market" of super-profits that are laundered through their most essential institutions.

In short, Banks need Crack.

In June of 2002, nine months after " '9/11' ", it's boom-time for opium and oil-and-gas in Afghanistan.

Last November the U.S. and Britain consolidated their invasion of Afghanistan by setting up their first Bases nearby Kabul and Kandahar. At the same time, fields in the newly conquered territory were rapidly resown with poppies for heroin instead of wheat for bread.

On November 21, 2001 the British newspaper *The Independent* ran this headline: 'Opium Farmers Rejoice at the Defeat of the Taliban.'

Four days later another British paper, *The Observer*, ran this headline: 'Victorious Warlords Set To Open the Opium Floodgates.' *The Observer* told how reinstated warlords of the Northern Alliance were encouraging farmers to plant ' "as much opium as possible." '

On December 4, 2001 the online *Asia Times* credited the United
States with Ayub Afriti's release from prison in Karachi, Pakistan on
November 29. Ayub Afriti had by then served a few weeks of his
seven-year sentence for the export of 6.5 tons of hashish. Afriti's
reported mission was to gather the support of three warlords--Haji
Abdul Qadeer, Haji Mohammed Zaman and Hazrat Ali--for a new
government in Afghanistan. According to the *Asia Times*: 'These
commanders used to be the biggest heroin and opium mafia in
Afghanistan's Pashtun.'

On February 18 the *Financial Times* of London summed up the
industry of the reinstated warlords and of the farmers within their
domains: This year's crop of opium in Afghanistan was expected to
be 3500 to 4500 metric tons.

The bumper harvest would mean multiples more of heroin for
addiction, degradation, theft, murder and money-laundering around
the world.

Why Banks Need Crack

For the opium-related timeline that's immediately above
I'm again indebted to Michael Ruppert and his *From The
Wilderness* Website.

For education about 'how the money works' from the laundering
of profits in illegal narcotics for Banks, Brokerages, Corporations,
and Stock Exchanges--that is, how such laundering works for all of
the most essential and pillarlike institutions of global capitalism--I'm
especially indebted to Catherine Austin Fitts and her <u>Narcodollars</u> <u>for</u>
<u>Dummies</u> and to Al Giordano and other contributors to his *Narco
News Bulletin*.

Catherine Austin Fitts was an insider for more than 15 years among
major movers of capital. Her biography states that she's a former
Managing Director and Member of the Board of Directors of Dillon
Read & Co, Inc, a former Assistant Secretary of Housing and a
Federal Housing Commissioner in the first Bush Administration, and
the former President of The Hamilton Securities Group, Inc.

Dillon, Read is among the most old-line Wall Street investment-
banking firms. In 1926 Clarence Dillon of this firm was the agent
for partnering Prescott Bush, W. Averill Harriman and George

Herbert Walker with Nazi funders Fritz Thyseen and Friedrich Flick
in the German Steel Trust.

In the Department of Housing and Urban Development Catherine
Austin Fitts worked under Secretary Jack Kemp.

She writes that she then declined a position as one of the Governors
of the Federal Reserve Bank to start the Hamilton Securities Group in
1991. She writes that by the mid 1990s 'Hamilton was doing well
and poised for significant financial growth' due to its 'leadership in
digital technology, financial software and analytic tools.'

Catherine Austin Fitts then discovered patterns of waste and fraud
and probable crime that she felt obliged to point out to her
Government clients.

In her plain-speaking style she writes: 'One of my software tool
innovations, Community Wizard, helped communities access data
about how all the money works in their place. Accessible through the
World Wide Web, Community Wizard was illuminating an unusual
pattern of defaults on HUD mortgages and other government and
homeowner losses in areas in which the CIA had admitted to
facilitating cocaine trafficking by Iran/Contra supporters.'

That is, Fitts and Hamilton Securities pointed out that the same
Black and Brown people who were most afflicted by the 1980s'
invasion of Crack cocaine into their communities, an invasion that
Gary Webb's book Dark Alliance (first a *San Jose Mercury News*
series) showed to be assisted or ignored by the CIA and FBI, were
losing their homes to foreclosures administered by another arm of the
U.S. Government, HUD.

Fitts was harassed after her revelations. The Internal Revenue
Service audited Hamilton Securities 18 times. She spent more than $6
million in legal and administrative fees and had to abandon
Hamilton. Relief from Federal pressures came only after *Insight*
magazine published a profile/expose in 2001. Fitts writes: 'A follow-
up article by *Insight*'s Paul Rodriguez described the closed
investigation as something that "many inside both HUD and the
Department of Justice regarded as a political vendetta against Fitts." '

Fitts hasn't abandoned her fight to expose corruption
and empower communities. She's instead become more sweeping in
her disclosures and condemnation. She notes that trillions (yes,
trillions--one thousand times one billion) of dollars are unaccounted
for in the Departments of Defense and HUD over the past three years.

She perceives that people in general are much less safe and at ease now than when she was a girl in West Philadelphia in the 1950s despite the New York Stock Exchange's rise of more than 9500 points (or more than 2000%) during the past five decades. She wants to restore what she terms the Solari Index--an an Index that registers the security, ease and cohesion within a community --to a state of both prosperity and safety for people in general.

Fitts blames the use of profits from illegal drugs ('our addiction ot narco-dollars') for the transformation of the U.S. Government into a 'criminal syndicate' that's grown rotten in all of its Branches.

She shows that illegal drugs' profits themselves multiply 20 times through the power of "the pop" on Wall Street.

She writes: 'The power of narco dollars comes when you combine drug trafficking with the stock market.'

She continues: 'The "pop" is a word I learned on Wall Street to describe the multiple of income at which a stock trades. So if a stock like PepsiCo trades at 20 times it's income, that means for every $100,000 of income it makes, it's stock goes up $2 million. The company may make $100,000, but its "pop" is $2 million. Folks make money in the stock market from the stock going up. On Wall Street, it's all about "pop." '

This 20-times-more-from-Pop formula invites infusion of capital from illegal and untraceable sources. 'So if I have a company that has a $100,000 of income and a stock trading at 20 times earnings,' Fitts write, 'if I can find a way to run $100,000 of narcotics sales by a few teenagers in West Philadelphia through my financial statements, I can get my stock market value to go up from $2 million to $4 million. I can double my "pop." '

That is, Banks and indeed any entity that trades on or through a Stock Market can make 20 times a dollar for every dollar sold of Crack, cocaine or heroin.

Fitts writes: 'According to the Department of Justice, the US launders between $500 billion-$1 trillion annually. I have little idea what percentage of that is narco dollars, but it is probably safe to assume that at least $100-200 billion relates to US drug import-exports and retail trade.'

So: The simplest way to figure the value of illegal narcotics' profits to the central institutions of U..S finance is to multiply Fitts' estimate for laundering of narco dollars by 20. If we multiply the estimate of

'$100-200 billion' by 20, the result is two to four trillion dollars.
Two to four trillion dollars per year make an amount that's 100% to
200% of the United States' annual Federal budget.

Let me repeat and emphasize: TWO TO FOUR TRILLION
DOLLARS PER YEAR MAKE AN AMOUNT THAT'S 100% TO
200% OF THE UNITED STATES ANNUAL FEDERAL BUDGET

H'mm! H'mm!--H'mm!--H'mm!

The annual amount of "pop" lets us see now how much Banks need
Crack.

We can appreciate more fully how large and cruel is capitalism's
own addiction.

Fitts goes on to make further connections. She writes: 'Many of the
members of our global leadership were trained in wartime narcotics
trafficking in Asia during WW II. George H. W. Bush and his
generation watched our ally Chang Kai Shek finance his army and
covert operations with opium. I am told that the Flying Tigers were
the model that taught Air America how to fly dope.'

She adds: 'If you trace back the history of the family and family
networks of America's leaders and numerous other leaders around the
world, what you will find is that narcotics and arms trafficking are a
multigenerational theme that has criss-crossed through Asia, North
America, Europe, Latin America and Eurasia and back through the
City of London and Wall Street to the great pools of financial capital.
Many a great American and British fortune got going in the Chinese
opium trade.'

Fitts and Ruppert and other investigators mentioned in this book
are admirable in their courage and acuity.

Fitts' prime example of the value of narco-dollars to global finance
is ' "the cold call" ' that Richard Grasso, President of the New York
Stock Exchange, paid to Raul Reyes, one chief of Colombia's largest
guerrilla army, the F. A. R. C., in late June of 1999.

At that time the FARC was reputed to be taxing the traffic of
billions of dollars of Andean coca each year. Richard Grasso, the
President of the New York Stock Exchange flew over 2000 miles to
Colombia and then to the FARC's Switzerland-sized enclave to meet
the Marxist guerrilla.

Richard Grasso then told the Associated Press: 'The purpose of the
trip was ' "to bring a message of cooperation from U.S. financial
services." '

The FARC, however, held to their position that a more comprehensive and cooperative solution to the problem of illegal narcotics and the far more profitable crimes (up to 20 times more profitable) that flourished from said criminality would be the decriminalization of coca and cocaine. Grasso made no sale.

The next year, 2000, the Clinton Administration and Congress approved 'Plan Colombia', throwing $1.3 billion U.S. dollars into Colombia for the stated purpose of wiping out the harvests of coca and opium there. The Bush Administration has since enlarged this Plan's funding and given Colombia's military freer rein to attack the FARC and Colombia's second, Marxist/Gueveraist guerilla group, the E.L.N.

One result of Plan Colombia so far is a net gain in the output of cocaine and opium from South America, a gain partly due to increased output through the paramilitary group, the Autodefensas Unidades de Colombia (AUC) , that's allied with Colombia's military. Another result is more widespread and deadly mass-murder of noncombatants in Colombia's civil war.

War provides much business in itself to leading Corporations..

War means sales of weapons. War makes huge profits for U.S.-based Corporations such as General Electric (NBC), Halliburton, Boeing, JP Morgan Chase, and many more. War is another staple of Corporations' 'supranational' economy.

Catherine Austin Fitts points out how the wars in Colombia and elsewhere share elements of profitability.

'You also see the arms-drugs relationship as you estimate how the money works on the private profits from various taxpayer funded wars,' she writes. 'Vietnam, Kosovo, Plan Colombia, Afghanistan, what do they all have in common? Drugs, oil and gas, arms. Add gold, currency and bank market share and you have the top of my checklist for understanding how the money works on any war or "low intensity conflict" around the globe.'

Andreas von Buelow, the former German Minister of Technology, has noted similar connections. His words bear one more repetiton. Von Buelow replied to his *Tagesspeigel* interviewer in January 2002: ' "In the analysis of political processes, I am allowed to look and see who has advantages and disadvantages, and what is coincidental. When in doubt, it is always worthwhile to take a look at a map, where are raw materials resources, and the routes to them? Then lay a map of civil wars and conflicts on top of that--they coincide. The same is the case with the third map: nodal points of the drug trade. Where this all comes together, the American intelligence services are not far away. By the way, the Bush family is linked to oil, gas, and weapons trade, through the bin Laden family." '

Of Oil and Gas and Central Asia

' ... an enormous concentration of natural gas and oil
reserves is located in the region, in addition to
important minerals, including gold....'
Zbignew Brzezinski on Central Asia in his 1997
book The Grand Chessboard

You may now be quite disturbed and perhaps amazed by the criminal networks that prosper from opium and coca. How the world and money work--from Afghanistan to Colombia to children shot down and shot up in U.S. neighborhoods--can cause any parent's gut to clench.

Let's now go back to oil-and-gas, profits from which make up another of the world's most major and essentially destructive enterprises.

Since last December international media has revealed that both the newly appointed Prime Minister of Afghanistan, Hamid Karzai, and the United States' special envoy to Afghanistan, Zalamy Khalizad, were paid by Unocal (Union 76) in the 1990s.

On February 9, 2002 Prime Minister Karzai, the former Unocal consultant, and Pakistan's President-via-military-coup, General Peshawar Musharraf, announced a pact to "cooperate in all spheres of activity."

Prime among these activites are the Turkmenistan-Afghanistan-Pakistan pipelines of oil and gas to the Arabian Sea that U. S. Ambassador to Pakistan Wendy Chamberlain declared to be "back on the table" after a meeting with Pakistan's Minister of Oil on October 9, 2001, two days after U.S. bombers began to devastate Afghanistan.

Pakistan is to provide $10 million to pay Afghan workers on the pipeline or pipelines.

How much are the prospective trans-Afghanistan pipelines worth to U.S. and other Western oil Corporations? Again: Billions unto trillions of dollars.

Two of Larry Chin's typically excellent pieces for *Online Journal*, dating from February and March of 2002, titled 'Enron: Ultimate Agent of American Empire' and 'Players on a Rigged Grand Chessboard', detail the Corporate and Government players involved in U.S.-led moves to control the flow of oil from Central Asia in and around the Caspian Sea.

Central Asia contains an estimated 6 trillion cubic meters of natural gas and 10 billion barrels of oil.

Along with Unocal, every major U.S. seller of oil and gas has a stake in Central Asia. Their total capital- commitment there before " '9/11' " is more than $10 billion. Their potential take from this investment over the next three decades is more than $5 trillion.

Larry Chin writes: 'American companies with unrequited heavy investments in the region's oil fields included ExxonMobil, Chevron Texaco, BP-Amoco, Phillips, Total/Fina/ELFm Unocal, Halliburton and Enron.

Enron's investment alone, as reported by the *Albion Monitor*, exceeded $3 billion in a power-generating station in Dhabol, India that was floundering in red ink because Enron could not access inexpensive natural gas via a proposed trans-Afghani pipeline fromTurkmenistan.'

The now-bankrupt Enron Corporation also was invested in 11 oil-fields in Uzbekistan and in a proposed Trans-Caspian pipeline that it, General Electric and Bechtel were to build. These three partners' project was to connect with pipelines westward to Baku and onward to Kosovo and the Mediterrean. Their project was also to connect with the afore-mentioned pipelines southward through Afghanistan and Pakistan to the Arabian Sea and onward to exponentially lucrative markets in the Far East.

The Far East's markets are a gigantic prize for Corporations that sell fossil-fuels. Consumption of oil and gas in the Far East is expected to rise 10-fold in the next 20 years against a 10% rise in Europe.

Enron, Exxon, Chevron, Unocal, Halliburton, et cetera (all campaign-funders with major investments in the Bush Administration and all with former executives high-up in the Bush

Administration) were thus frustrated by the Taliban's evident refusal to give up control of the pipeline--projects that could yield the greatest profits from Central Asia's oil and gas.

To oust the Taliban, they needed what the U.S. military terms 'a pretext.' They also needed to call in the print and broadcast media they own or control.

'The public supported America's engagement in World War II largely because of the shock effect of the Japanese attack on Pearl Harbor.'
Zbignew Brzeniski, The Grand Chessboard, 1997

' ... the government should be charged with a systematic response that, one hopes, will end the way that the attack on Pearl Harbor ended--with the destruction of the system that is responsible for it. That system is a network of terrorist organizations sheltered in capitals of certain countries.'
Henry Kissinger in a dispatch to *Newsweek* online, 21:04 Eastern Daylight Time on 9/11/01

Four years prior to " '9/11' " Zbigniew Brzezinski--a strategist for David Rockefeller on the Trilateral Commission and the Council on Foreign Relations, we know, before and after he was the architect of entrapping the Soviet Union in Afghanistan while National Security Advisor to President Jimmy Carter--published a book that's titled The Grand Chessboard.

Brzezinski's ... Chessboad sets forth urgent reasons for the United States' military to enter Central Asia and establish dominance. His reasons are the riches there in oil and gas (opium is not mentioned) and the proximity there of the U.S.'s only possible rivals for hegemony among nation-states, Russia and China.

Brzezinski's world-view is as mad as his major backers'--as arrogant, abstract, and removed from people's suffering.

He argues that the United States should subjugate both Europe and Asia so that the U.S may maintain these whole continents (and by extension the nations and peoples of the Earth's other, implicitly less consequential continents) as 'vassals' to the U.S.'s sole superpower-dom.

Here's what and how Zbignew writes: 'In that context, how America 'manages' Eurasia is critical. Eurasia is the globe's largest continent and is geopolitically axial. A power that dominates Eurasia would control two of the world's three most advanced and economically productive regions. A mere glance at the map also suggests that control over Eurasia would almost automatically entail Africa's subordination, rendering the Western Hemisphere and Oceania geopolitically peripheral to the world's central continent. About 75 per cent of the world's people live in Eurasia, and most of the world's physical wealth is there as well, both in its enterprises and underneath its soil. Eurasia accounts for 60 per cent of the world's GNP and about three-fourths of the world's known energy resources.'

You see how simple the whole Earth can be--when you want to 'control' it!

Central Asia offers even more 'underneath its soil' than it does as an eminence for 'geopolitical' oversight.

Zbignew (who begs for Dostoyevskyan satire and Strangelove-like impersonation) writes: 'But the Central Balkans are infinitely more important as a potential economic prize: an enormous concentration of natural gas and oil reserves is located in the region, in addition to important minerals, including gold.'

But, this adviser to Rockefellers and Presidents notes, the U. S. public is not much inclined to war for power's sake. 'It is also a fact that America is too democratic at home to be autocratic abroad.... the pursuit of power is not a goal that commands popular passion, except in conditions of a sudden threat or challenge to the public's sense of domestic well-being.... Democracy is inimical to imperial mobilization.'

And Zbignew observes that the United States is not so homogenous as it once was--it has more a mix of races. His brittle, ponderous, Establishment-English-as-a-second-language style writes: 'Moreover, as America becomes an increasingly multi-cultural society, it may find it more difficult to fashion a consensus on foreign policy issues, except in the circumstance of a truly massive and widely perceived direct external threat.'

So, then, needing '... a truly massive and widely perceived external threat' to throw Americans into a 'supportive mood' for international war, what are the world's would-be managers to do?

Zbignew remembers: 'The public supported America's engagement
in World War II largely because of the shock effect of the Japanese
attack on Pearl Harbor.'

At 9:04 E.D.T. on the night of " '9/11' " the *Washington Post*
printed a commentary by Henry Kissinger, another former National
Security Advisor, one even more self-important, fatuous and
deserving of savage satire than his successor Zbignew.

Henry, the Secretary of State to Richard Nixon and Gerald Ford
and Zbignew's colleague on the Council of Foreign Relations and the
Trilateral Commission, wrote: ' ... the government should be charged
with a systematic response that, one hopes, will end the way that the
attack on Pearl Harbor ended--with the destruction of the system that
is responsible for it. That system is a network of terrorist
organizations sheltered in capitals of certain countries.'

To be sure--down with the system of a network of terrorist
organizations (the statesman clears his throat and dips his nose as his
wattle quivers) sheltered in capitals of certain countries.

Henry Kissinger then elaborated on 'the process' that should go
forward and on its likely targets. 'The principal part has to be to get
the terrorist system on the run,' he wrote. '... We do not yet know
whether Osama bin Laden did this, although it appears to have the
earmarks of a bin Laden-type operation. But any government that
shelters groups capable of this kind of attack, whether or not they can
be shown to have been involved in this attack, must pay an
exorbitant price.'

So, only 12 hours after the airliners struck, presenting the U. S.
public with that wished-for 'massive external threat' to 'domestic
well-being', Henry echoed Zbignew about 'Pearl Harbor' and then
set forth 'the process' that the G.W. Bush Administration should
follow.

H'mm!

Quick work, Henry!

What another set of coincidences! And how coincidental
that all the 'governments' and 'capitals' that Henry's *Post* piece
targets are connected to billions and trillions of potential U. S. dollar-
profits from oil, gas, and/or opium or coca!

How full of wondrous coincidences is the 'geopolitical' world!

On May 30, 2002, President Karzai of Afghanistan, President
Niyazov of Turkmenistan, and President Musharraf of Pakistan met
in Islamabad, Pakistan and signed a memorandum of understanding
to proceed with a trans-Afghanistan gas pipeline.

In the 60 days prior to these three Presidents' meeting, media in Britain and France reported that Unocal and the World Bank are certain or likely funders for gas and/or oil pipelines across Afghanistan.

'We have about 60% of the world's wealth but only 6.3% of it's
population. In this situation we cannot fail to be the object of envy
and resentment. Our real task in the coming period is to devise a
pattern of relationships which will permit us to maintain this position
of disparity. We need not deceive ourselves that we can afford today
the luxury of altruism and world benefaction. We should cease to talk
about such vague and unreal objectives as human rights, the raising
of living standards and democratisation. The day is not far off when
we are going to have to deal in straight power concepts.'
    George F. Kennan, chief of Policy Planning for the
    United States' State Department, on February 24, 1948.

'I say, when your heart turns cold
It cause your soul to freeze
It spreads throughout your spirit
Like a ruthless, feeling disease
The walls, the walls that once were down
Now stand firm and tall
Safe from hate, love, pain, joy,
Until you feel nothing ...
You forget ideals
And turn off the reason
To make sure the product gets sold"
    Tupac Amaru Shakur, "When Ure Heart Turns Cold"

LORDS OF A FEUDAL 'NEW WORLD ORDER'

'We are witnessing the creation of a supranational
control of the world's necessities. The old notions of
sovereignty no longer govern the facts.'
Walter Lippmann, N Y Times columnist, 1917

'Earth's population will be forced to colonize two
planets within 50 years if natural resources continue
to be exploited at the current rate, according to a
report out this week.'
Mark Townsend and *Jason Burke* on a World
Wildlife Fund report, the *Observer*, Britain, 7/7/02

Still Coming Down On Sunny Days

Who are these people who use terror--or "tear'r" in President G. W.
Bush's faux tough-Texan pronunciation--so coldly for 'geopolitical'
ends--ends that we must now perceive are as crazy as they are
greedy, arrogant, and both murderous and suicidal?

During the 2000 U.S. Presidential campaign, media in Europe
reported that George W. Bush and Al Gore descend from Kings of
England.

On October 17, 2000 Reuters News Service wrote: ' "It is now clear
that Mr Gore and Mr Bush have an unusually large number of royal
and noble descents," said Harold Brooks-Baker, publishing director
of Burke's Peerage.

"In point of fact, never in the history of the United States have two
presidential candidates been as well endowed with royal alliances." '

By being a descendant of Edward I, the first King of England, the
Reuters agency wrote, 'George W. Bush is also a cousin of former US
president Richard Nixon, who resigned from the White House in
1974 for his part in the Watergate scandal.

Al Gore, however, Reuters wrote, 'does have direct links to the
holy Roman Empire.'

Reuters explained about the Democrats' candidate: 'He is a
descendant of Roman Emperors Louis II, Charles II and Louis I
and is therefore also a direct descendant of Charlemagne--the
eighth-century Emperor.

The problem is, Gore's Charlemagne links also make him a cousin of George W Bush.'

So the Bush and Gore families--like the Dupont, Hearst, Rockefeller, Roosevelt, Warburg, ... families--have generations of practice with privilege. Terms and concepts such as 'vassals' and 'tributaries' appear to them parts of a natural order, whether 'New World' or old, and "just another day's work."

Let's now have a closer look at the history of the United States' ruling elitists since the turn into the 20th century. We'll see how often people's natural compassion for one another and love of homeland have been duped into Wars that serve the interests of a few. Much of this history is told in Joel Andreas' excellent, comicbook-like Addicted to War, co-published by AK Press and Frank Dorrel.

The United States' reach for global power effectively began in 1898 with the so-called Spanish-American War.

Four years earlier, in 1894, Senator Orville Platt of Connecticut stated forthrightly: "I firmly believe that when any territory outside the present territorial limits of the United States becomes necessary for our defense or essential for our commercial development, we ought to lose no time in acquiring it."

In 1897 Secretary of the Navy Theodore Roosevelt was both more specific and more general. "Teddy" said: "I would welcome any war, for I think this country needs one."

By 1898 Spanish troops were losing to natives' armed struggle in Cuba and the Phillipines. Claiming to support said natives' desire for independence, the United States declared war on Spain.

Spain gave up both territories after little fighting by U.S. forces. The United States then declared the Phillipines, Puerto Rico and Guam to be its colonies.

Filipinos resisted their new boss. In 1900 Mark Twain, Vice-President of the Anti-Imperialist League, wrote: 'I have seen that we do not intend to free but subjugate the Philippines. And so I am an anti-imperialist.' At least 600,000 Filipino people were killed by U.S. forces between 1898-1914.

As for Cuba, the Platt Amendment, authored by the Senator from Connecticut, declared that the U.S. was to decide Cuba's foreign and financial policies; was to have a military Base in Cuba forever; and was to have the option of invading Cuba with its Marines whenever it chose.

The United States invaded Cuba four times in the next 35 years.

Tambien, it invaded Haiti and Panama twice, Mexico three times, Colombia and the Dominican Republic four times, Nicaragua five times and Honduras seven times.

Every one of these invasions served U.S. Corporations. United Fruit wanted bananas, Anaconda wanted copper, Standard Oil wanted oil, and they all wanted "no problem" from the native workers whose labor brought forth these fortunes-building resources.

General Smedley Butler led many United States Marines' invasions from the turn-of-the-century forward.

In 1934 the retired Marine General wrote: 'I spent 33 years and 4 months in active miltiary service. I spent most of my time as a high-class muscle man for Big Business, for Wall Street and the bankers. In short, I was a racketeer, a gangster for capitalism... I helped purify Nicaragua for the international banking house of Brown Brothers in 1902-1912. I brought light to the Domincan Republic for American sugar interests in 1916. I helped make Honduras right for American fruit companies in 1903. In China in 1927 I helped see to it that Standard Oil went on its way unmolested.'

Brown Brothers Harriman, a merger of British and U.S. investment-banking firms, you'll remember, was the firm for which Prescott Bush, great-grandfather of GWB, was Managing Director during its service to Nazi Germany, Standard Oil and General Motors during World War II.

Standard Oil, we know, was the main fount of the Rockefeller family fortunes.

Both World Wars also profited the U.S. ruling-class.

As the sinking of the *Maine* in Havana's harbor prompted mass outrage in the United States and this nation's entry into the Spanish-American War, the forewarned sinking of the *Lusitania* by Germany, causing 128 U.S. civilian deaths, prompted mass outrage in 1915.

Financier J.P. Morgan especially needed the U.S. to enter World War I. Billions of dollars of U.S. capitalists' debt were at stake along with whatever might be their share of the colonial world. The then U.S. Ambassador to England, W.H. Page, said that entering this war was "the only way of maintaining our present pre-eminent trade status."

130,274 U.S. soldiers died in World War I. More than 20 million people were killed by this World War altogether.

(Let's glance now at a revealing sidelight. In 1924 the aforementioned W. H.--Walter Hines--Page, co-founder of the Doubleday & Page publishing firm, had a School of International Relations at Johns Hopkins University funded in his name by then U.S. Vice-President Charles Gates Dawes. Charles Gates Dawes endowed this School with money that he won as recipient of a Nobel Peace Prize. Charles Gates Dawes won his Peace Prize for his role in extracting capital from Germany after World War I. And the crippling of German society from this extraction of capital set the stage for Nazis' rise in the latter 1920s.)

Much of U.S. business and media celebrated Fascism in the 1930s. *TIME* and Charles Lindbergh praised Mussolini's " 'Corporate State.' ". Henry Ford and the Rockefeller family funded Hitler from the 1920s forward. Many of the United States' key corporate institutions (General Motors, the Chase Bank, the Union Bank, General Electric, ...) trafficked profitably with Nazi Germany as World War II and the Holocaust proceeded.

We know that the Rockefeller-run Chase Bank solicited Nazi accounts in France as late as 1944.

Prescott ("Press") Bush, father of GHWB and grandfather of GWB, came into collaboration with Nazis through his father-in-law, George Herbert ("Bert") Walker, an early fan of the message and potentials of Adolf Hitler.

Ex-boxer Bert Walker had previously taken his banking business from St. Louis, Missouri to the address of 1 Wall Street and partnership with the richer blue-blood Averill W. Harriman. Averill Harriman's father, the railroad magnate William, was a protege and ally of John D. Rockefeller's.

From 1926 onward Bert Walker, Prescott Bush and Averill Harriman joined with German industrialist/banker Fritz Thyssen in funding Adolf Hitler's small but growing National Socialist Party. Their funding--much of it funneled or laundered through the Hamburg Amerika (HAPAG) shipping line--let Hitler increase his private armies of "brown shirts."

Prescott Bush was himself the son of an industrialist who had partnered with a Rockefeller scion. As head of small arms and ammunition on the War Industries Board under President Woodrow Wilson during World War I, Samuel Prescott Bush had helped Percy Rockefeller, son of William Rockefeller (William the brother of Standard Oil's founder John D.), take over Remington Arms and thereby corner small-arms manufacturing in the U. S.

Samuel P. Bush owned the Buckeye Steel Castings Company, which supplied parts to Railroads owned by E. H. Harriman, the father of Averill W. Harriman and another beneficiary of financing by the Rockefeller family.

"Press" Bush, a 1919 graduate of Yale and an initiate of the Skull & Bones secret-society there, married Bert Walker's daughter, further binding families and alliances.

Now let's pause to focus on a hidden piece of history.

The aid of Bush, Harriman and Walker to Nazis' rise during the 1920s. '30s and '40s--their well-paid aid along with the well-paid aid of intimately related U. S. capitalists--is one of the great, little-known stories of the past century.

I can't begin to detail it here. I can, however, recommend Webster G. Tarpley's and Anton Chaitkin's <u>George Bush: The Unauthorized Biography</u> and summarize some of the financiers' broad strokes over two decades (1922 to 1942).

As mentioned earlier in relation to Wall Street's Dillon, Read investment-banking firm, W. Averill Harriman, George Herbert Walker and Prescott Bush partnered with German magnates Fritz Thyssen and Friedrich Flick to assist the Nazi Party during the 1920s and early 1930s. They helped the Nazis with guns and propaganda (delivered via Remington Arms and via their co-owned Hamburg-Amerika Shipping). Thyssen and Flick, partners with the three U. S. principals in the German Steel Trust that Clarence Dillon had organized in 1926, also lent funds to Hitler.

At the same time Harriman, Walker and Bush profited from deals with the Soviet Union as it came under Joseph Stalin's control.

1932 and 1933 were crucial years for Germany.

Tarpley and Chaitkin write about Germany in 1932: 'The constitutional government of the German republic moved to defend national freedom by ordering the Nazi Party private armies disbanded. The U.S. embassy reported that the Hamburg-Amerika Line was purchasing and distributing propaganda attacks against the German government, for attempting this last-minute crackdown on Hitler's forces.'

In the ensuing street-fighting the Nazis' Brown Shirts and Black Shirts killed hundreds with Thompson submachine-guns that had been smuggled aboard Hamburg Amerika (HAPAG) ships.

Hitler became German Chancellor on January 30, 1933, anointed by industrialists, landholders and military.

Still, the Communist and Social Democrats held a plurality in Germany's legislature, the Reichstag, and the U.S. public's concerns about Nazis' methods had to be allayed.

Control of Germany remained uncertain.

On the night of February 27, 1933, Germany's legislative building, the Reichstag, burned to the ground. Communists were blamed for the arson. More of them were murdered and Nazis' power mounted.

Nazis' ascension immediately benefited Bush, Harriman and Walker. The partners made Jewish financier Max Warburg (the chief of Germany's intelligence-agency during World War I) their representative on the Board of the Hamburg Amerika Line. On March 27 Max Warburg reassured Averill Harriman about the nascent fascism: 'The Government is firmly resolved to maintain public peace and order in Germany, and I feel perfectly convinced in this respect that there is no cause for any alarm whatsoever.'

The Warburgs themselves threw worldwide weight.

On March 31, 1933, according to Tarpley and Chaitkin, 'the American-Jewish Committee, controlled by the Warburgs, and the B'nai B'rith, heavily influenced by the Sulzbergers (*New York Times*), issued a formal, official joint statement of the two organizations, counseling "that no American boycott against Germany be encouraged, " and advising "that no further mass meetings be held or similar forms of agitation be employed. "

The American Jewish Committee and the B'nai B'rith (mother of the "Anti-Defamation League ") continued with this hardline, no-attack-on-Hitler stance all through the 1930s, blunting the fight mounted by many Jews and other anti-fascists.'

Bush, Harriman and Walker benfited from a monopoly of trade with Nazi Germany. 'In May 1933,' Tarpley and Chaitkin wrote, 'an agreement was reached in Berlin for the coordination of all Nazi commerce with the U.S.A. The Harriman International Co., led by Averell Harriman's first cousin Oliver, was to head a syndicate of 150 firms and individuals, to conduct all exports from Hitler's Germany to the United States.'

This pact was 'negotiated between Hitler's economics minister, Hjalmar Schacht, and John Foster Dulles, international attorney for dozens of Nazi enterprises, with the counsel of Max Warburg and Kurt von Schroeder.'

Tarpley and Chaitkin added: 'John Foster Dulles would later be
U.S. Secretary of State, and the great power in the Republican Party
of the 1950s. Foster's friendship and that of his brother Allen (head
of the Central Intelligence Agency), greatly aided Prescott Bush to
become the Republican U.S. Senator from Connecticut. And it was to
be of inestimable value to George Bush, in his ascent to the heights
of "covert action government, " that both of these Dulles brothers
were the lawyers for the Bush family's far-flung enterprise.'

The Hamburg Amerika Line merged with the North German Lloyd
Line in September 1933, becoming HAPAG/LLOYD. The new Line
continued to carry Nazi agents, finances and propagranda between
Germany and other nations.

By 1940, however, a majority of the U.S. ruling elite sided with
England and agreed that war against Germany was again in its
' "pre-eminent" ' interest.

In October of 1940 the U.S. State Department and the nominally
non-Governmental Council on Foreign Relations, a body of
executives and academics founded and funded by the Rockefeller
family above all, met as partner bodies. Their sit-down decided that
this nation must prepare for war with Germany and at the same time
devise 'an integrated policy to achieve military and economic
supremacy for the United States' after the war.

A memorandum from the Council on Foreign Relations to the State
Department in 1941 may remind you of Zbigniew Brzezinski's
memorable phrasing of perspective in his 1997
The Grand Chessboard: 'Democracy is inimical to imperial
mobilization.'

The 1941 CFR memo advised: 'If war aims are stated which seem
to be concerned solely with Anglo-American imperialism, they will
offer little to people in the world.... The interests of other peoples
should be stressed ... This would have a better propaganda effect.'

Then, as in 2001, we may infer that 'a sudden threat or challenge to
the public's sense of domestic well-being.... a truly massive and
widely perceived direct external threat' might be thought useful to
'imperial mobilization.'

The 1941 CFR memo closely preceded the mass murder of more
than 2000 people at Pearl Harbor.

Let's look more closely at " 'Pearl Harbor.' " On December 7, 1941
Japanese forces attacked U.S. ships, planes and personnel at this base
and port in Hawaii. Documents in best-selling author John Toland's

Infamy and in Robert B. Stinnett's <u>Day</u> of <u>Deceit: The Truth about</u>
<u>FDR and Pearl Harbor</u> show that President Franklin Delano Roosevelt
and his closest advisors knew for days, if not weeks, that the Japanese
fleet, the *Kido Butai,* was advancing on Hawaii. Franklin Delano
Roosevelt, however, did not inform Pearl Harbor's commanding
officers, General Short and Admiral Kimmel, about the advancing
fleet.

In the Fall of 1941 Harold Ickes, FDR's Secretary of the Interior
and an advocate for Jews against Nazis' carnage, wrote in his diary:
'For a long time I have believed that our best entrance into the war
would be by way of Japan.'

John Toland explains reasons further in <u>Infamy</u>: 'The first bomb
dropped on Oahu would have finally solved the problem of getting
an America--half of whose people wanted peace--into the crusade
against Hitler.'

So this Roosevelt, too, got the war he wanted, one that his peers
advised was necessary. The Roosevelt Administration's withholding
of warning to commanders at Pearl Harbor was another of history's
conspiracies by a few to dupe masses into war.

Earlier in 1941 Prescott Bush and Averill Harriman took advantage
of the Nazis' war in Europe. They used their Union Banking
Corporation to buy out their partner Fritz Thyseen's interest in the
Silesian American Corporation.

The Silesian American Corporation in Poland was then mining
nearby a new concentration-camp called Auschwitz. Into the
following year, 1942, Bush's and Harriman's UBC subsidiary
employed inmates at Auschwitz as slave-labor in their mining.

Now, your stomach may have sunk while reading the few
paragraphs above. At the same time, a slow burn of disbelief and
outrage may be rising in you.

I relate the immediate history above so that we may better know
the character of the U. S. elitists whom we still face.

Ruthless conspiracies are their way of life.

By August of 1942 the U. S. was fully entered into World War II,
its troops fighting on both the European and Asian fronts. Invoking
the new Trading with the Enemy Act, our Government in that month
ordered seizure of all property of the Hamburg-Amerika and North
German Lloyd shipping lines.

Two months later it seized assets of the Union Banking
Corporation. The UBC's Managing Director then was Prescott Bush.

"Press" Bush, however, escaped fines or incarceration, as his son George Herbert Walker Bush would escape punishment from scrutiny of the Iran/Contra and Iraqgate scandals.

Instead, Prescott Bush (who resigned from the Union Banking Corporation in 1943) became Chairman of the United States' National War Fund!

And World War II went on killing with its killing of about 60 million civilians and soldiers.

According to the Internet's 'World War II Pages' by Phil Stokes, these are the numbers of that War's dead: 8,668,000 military and 16,900,000 civilians of the Soviet Union, 1,324,000 military and 10,000,000 civilians of China, 3.250,000 military and 3,810,000 civilians of Germany, 850,000 military and 6,000,000 civilians of Poland, 1,506,000 military and 300,000 civilians of Japan, 300,000 military and 1,400,000 civilians of Yugoslavia, 520,000 military and 465,000 civilians of Roumania, 340,000 military and 470,000 civilians of France, ... , 326,000 military and 62,000 civilians of Great Britain, ..., and 295,000 military of the United States.

Also, we can never forget the estimated 6 million dead due to the Holocaust that coincided with overt fascism's rise and that lasted throughout World War II in Europe.

World War II, however, did rescue capitalists in the West from economic Depression. And those who supplied both the Axis and the Allies with arms, oil and financing--these few profited all-around-- just as they had in World War I.

> *'After bombs' rain/ the War was done/ With the Bomb's reign/ the War was done/ Treaties were complete/ Plains greened with wheat/ Steel pressed into fins/ Northern empires still king* '--"Let The Children Come". 1990

Following World War II, capitalists in the United States did in fact achieve apparent 'supremacy' among colonial powers .

Britain and France were too depleted to keep their outright hold on territories in Asia, Africa and the Middle East. U.S.-based power moved in. The Truman Doctrine of 1947 coincided with the transformation of the United States' wartime Office of Secret Services into the Central Intelligence Agency.

This new Agency, the CIA, continued with the absorption of hundreds of Nazi agents into anti-Communist operations.

On February 24, 1948 the academic, diplomat and " 'liberal' " George F. Kennan--then chief of Policy Planning for the State Department--later adviser to Presidents Eisenhower, Kennedy and Johnson--stated what should be the new superpower's attitude.

Princeton graduate Kennan wrote: 'We have about 60% of the world's wealth but only 6.3% of it's population. In this situation we cannot fail to be the object of envy and resentment. Our real task in the coming period is to devise a pattern of relationships which will permit us to maintain this position of disparity. We need not deceive ourselves that we can afford today the luxury of altruism and world benefaction. We should cease to talk about such vague and unreal objectives as human rights, the raising of living standards and democratisation. The day is not far off when we are going to have to deal in straight power concepts. The less we are then hampered by idealistic slogans, the better.'

Between 1948 and 1961--using embargoes, narcotics, coups, proxy armies and death-squads--maintaining 'vassals' and 'tributaries'--and unhampered by any 'disparity' or idealism--the U.S. ruling-class subverted anti-imperialist movements or governments in Colombia, the Congo, Greece, Guatamala, Iran and Vietnam through its "old-boy" arm of the CIA.

In 1952 Prescott Bush became a Senator from Connecticut two generations after Orville Platt. "Press" then was a regular golfing partner of President Dwight Eisenhower, we know, while John Foster and Allen Dulles orchestrated U.S. " 'foreign policy.' "

Still, by end of the 1950s, the Soviet Union, the Chinese and Cuban Revolutions, and armed struggles for national liberation in Africa, Southeast Asia, and Central and South America blocked or worried Western imperialists.

Leading " 'the arms race,' ", the Lords of the U.S. still were far short of uncontested 'supremacy' on Earth.

Struggle and reaction heightened during the 1960s. Within the U.S., Blacks led the fights for genuine rights and equality. Their eventual militance arrived at 'Black Power.'

Worldwide, Vietnam represented many conflicts. Despite the United States' intrusion of more than a half-a-million troops at one time and a bombardment that exceeded all of World War II's, communists and nationalists in Vietnam won another protracted guerrilla war.

At the same time the "French connection" of opium/heroin from "the Golden Triangle" of Burma, Thailand and Laos to Europe and the United States--a CIA-directed flow that was strong-armed on the ground by the Taiwanese Kuomintang and Sicilian and Corsican mafias--and a flow that had funded anti-Communist movements and paramiltiaries in France, Italy and Greece shortly after World War II--addicted at least 30,000 U.S. service-men in Vietnam by 1970, according to an Insititue for Policy Studies history that was read into the *Congressional Record* by John Conyers of Michigan on May 7, 1998.

In May of 1970 the *Christian Science Monitor* reported on CIA ties to 'the extensive movement of opium out of Laos.' One charter pilot told the *Christian Science Monitor* then that 'opium shipments get special CIA clearance and monitoring on their flights southward out of the country.'

In the middle of the 1960s and in the middle of the Vietnam War, Martin Luther King Jr. was among the most eloquent, far-seeing, compassionate voices for justice.

On April 4, 1967 MLK Jr. talked about the empire around him in his 'A Time to Break the Silence' speech at Riverside Church in New York City. MLK Jr. said then: "We have no honorable intentions in Vietnam. Our minimal expectation is to occupy it as an American colony and maintain social stability for our investments. This tells us why American helicopters are being used against guerrillas in Colombia and Peru. Increasingly the role our nation has taken is the role of those who refuse to give up the privileges and pleasures that come from the immense profits of overseas investment."

In other words, the United States' military and other material power was directed at maintaining a great 'disparity' over the world's poor to serve 'those who refuse to give up the privileges and pleasures that come with the immense profits over overseas investment.'

MLK Jr. was among those assassinated or otherwise killed between 1963 and 1976. Other lights of revolutionary internationalism--such as Malcolm X, Fred Hampton, George Jackson and untold other Blacks in the U.S: Che Guevara, Carlos Fonseca, Father Camilo Torres in Latin America: and Anna Mae Aquash of the American Indian Movement (AIM) on the Pine Ridge Reservation of South

Dakota--were suspiciously or brutally killed during this span. So too were those of the ruling elite--John Fitzgerald Kennedy and Robert Fitzgerald Kennedy and perhaps Phillip Graham of the *Washington Post*--who appeared to threaten the 'privileges' of those who profited hugely from 'overseas investments'.

Still: '*Many stood and fought for lands they lived on.*'
During the 1970s liberation-movements with socialist plaforms persevered in armed struggle and won state-power in Angola, Guinea-Bissau, Mozambique, Nicaragua, and Zimbabwe. U.S. troops and other personnel left Vietnam. Oil-producing nations combined to set prices that rocked Western economies and consumers in 1973 and 1978.

In 1973 the Trilateral Commission was formed, we know, David Rockefeller its central founder and Zbigniew Brzezinski and Henry Kissinger among its leading members.

Democrat Jimmy Carter was a member of the Trilateral Commission and the Council on Foreign Relations before he became U. S. President in 1977. The inauguration of Republican Ronald Reagan and George H. W. Bush in 1981 was then needed to push the Trilateralist agenda of revived U. S. 'supremacy' forward.

In the 1980s Northern imperialists of the West devised complex, amazing and often criminal solutions to areas of difficulty for them around the planet.

The Soviet Union they entrapped in Afghanistan and sapped through an arms-race that cost trillions of dollars.

At the same time, Afghanistan's rising share of the world's opium-production, corresponding with the CIA's supply of billions of dollars of weapons to *Muhjadeen* warlords, increased to 800 tons per year. This rise made it, according to a statement by the U.S. State Department in 1986, 'probably the world's largest producer of opium for export' and 'the poppy source for a majority of the Southwest Asian heroin found in the United States.'

Elsewhere in Central Asia/the Middle East, Iran was entangled in a war with Iraq that killed more than one million people between 1980 and 1988. This war depleted and distracted both oil-rich nations at a time when either might have resisted Western Corporations' extractions from the Middle East. This war also brought billions of dollars to arms-sellers in the West.

At the same time, Northern imperialists mired Nicaragua, Angola and Mozambique in post-revoltionary wars through their funding of proxy armies.

Nicaragua was especially the United States' target. During the middle 1980s President Ronald Reagan warned that Sandinista-Cuban-Russian soldiers might invade Texas any day or night, now, unless Congress gave the anti-revolutionary *contras* a blank check.

Congress' subsequent reluctance or refusal to fund the *contras* prompted a strange, secret triangle--or a set of complementary channels--that was partially exposed as the Iran/Contra scandal in 1986-87.

Here's how this triangle--yet another conspiracy-- worked.

Reagan Administration officials (Oliver North, Admiral John Poindexter, CIA Director and the Rockefellers' Manhattan Institute founder William Casey among them) used the sale of weapons to Iran--the United States' nominal enemy--to fund *contras* based along the Honduran/Nicaraguan border.

At the same time, completing a third side of the triangle, U.S. agents or assets used money from said arms-sales to buy Colombian cocaine and transport it to Flordia, Calfornia, Texas, Louisiana and Mena, Arkansas. They thus augmented profits that then were partly passed on to *contra* commanders.

The imported cocaine, we know, was then made into the Crack that wracked Black and Brown inner-city neighborhoods in the middle 1980s. In 1986 *Newsweek* and other Corporate media presented lurid coverage of this " 'epidemic' ". Congress then passed the laws for mandatory sentencing for possession of Crack that would imprison hundreds of thousands of poor people in the next decade.

Soon afterward, we know, a Deputy Secretary of the Department of Housing and Urban Development, Catherine Austin Fitts, identified a similar " 'epidemic' " of HUD-ordered foreclosures in Crack-wracked neighorhoods.

Vice-President and former CIA Director George H. W. Bush was evidently at the center of the Iran/Contra conspiracy. GHWB's aide Donald Gregg talked daily with Oliver North's *contra*-supply manager, Felix Rodriquez, the Cuban exile who saw fit to steal the executed Che Guevara's Rolex watch off his wrist in 1967.

Nevertheless, George Herbert Walker Bush, like his father before him, escaped anything near incarceration. Instead, we know, in 1988 GHWB succeeded Ronald Reagan as President of the United States.

The first Bush Administration was rich in warfare and bloodshed

In December of 1989 George H. W. Bush invaded Panama to remove Manuel Noriega, his former partner as a CIA asset, after Noriega refused to let the U.S. stage *contra* attacks on Nicaragua from Panama.

In February of 1991 George H. W. Bush launched " 'the Gulf War' " against Iraq and Saddam Hussein, his favored Head-of-State and partner during the Iran/Iraq war. The previous July U.S. Ambassador April Glaspie had told Hussein that the U.S. had ' "no opinion on the Arab/Arab conflicts, like your border dispute with Kuwait." ' Thus Hussein was led to invade Kuwait, giving Great Britain and the U. S. their 'pretext' for war. The tricking of Hussein was again a conspiracy, hidden from the U.S.
public, and the invasion of Kuwait killed thousands of people. The war against Iraq killed hundreds of thousands.

The 1990-91 slaughters in both Kuwait and Iraq had several economic and 'geopolitical' results. The bloodshed there let the U.S. build a permanent military Base in Saudi Arabia; let the price of a barrel of oil rise by $7; let U.S. and Saudi contractors (including companies owned by the Bechtel and bin Laden families) make tens of millions of dollars; and postponed a severe economic downturn in the U.S. for one year.

Under Democrat Bill Clinton's Presidency, the 1990s continued to inflate speculative bubbles in Stock Markets at the same time as the U.S. military bombed and invaded whenever and wherever its directors chose.

After the Gulf War, the U.S. and Great Britain imposed no-fly zones over northern and southern Iraq. They kept Iraqi oil out of the world's open market. They thereby made tens of billions of dollars for Western oil-companies.

They also insisted on U. N. sanctions that have kept food and medicines from Iraq. These sanctions have killed at least 500,000 Iraqi children. In 1999 Clinton's Secretary of State Madeline Albright called these half-a-million dead children an ' "acceptable" ' price to pay for destablizing the regime of Saddam Hussein. Reports on the ground say that the sanctions have in fact strengthened the Iraqi people's loyalty to Hussein.

The U.S. bombed Iraq intensively in in 1993, 1994, and 1998-99. In the first 8 months of 1999 Anglo/American forces flew 10,000 sorties against Iraq.

On August 30, 1999 U.S. Brigadier General William Looney was especially triumphant and frank in the *Washington Post.*

Brigadier General Looney minced no words about the United States' dominance and ends in Iraq: ' "If they turn on the radars we're going to blow up their goddamn SAMs (surface-to-air missiles). They know we own their country. We own their airspace.... We dictate the way they live and talk. And that's what's great about America right now. It's a good thing, especially when there's a lot of oil out there we need." '

In 1993 the U.S invaded Somalia to protect interests of the Conoco Oil-Corporation there and to establish another miltiary Base beside the Red Sea and Middle East.

From 1993 onward the U.S. was also busy in Yugoslavia. It led the break-up or " 'Balkanization' " of Yugoslavia into small, ethnically divided nation-states (Bosnia, Croatia, Kosovo, ...). These lesser states abandoned nationalized industries and socialist protections for their people in return for International Monetary Fund and World Bank financing--that is, for the loan-sharking, imposed exports and ultimate deprivations that we've previously seen in Argentina, Brasil and elsewhere.

The break-up of Yugoslavia was promoted in Western media through horror-stories of Serbian massacares that later proved to be fraudulent. This break-up cost tens of thousands of people their homes or lives.

Oh, those boom-time '90s!

At the same time as the world's " 'lone superpower' " was firing its missiles and planting its feet wherever its leading Corporations chose--and opium and heroin were flowing through Pakistan and Kosovo--and cocaine and heroin were flowing through Colombia and Mexico--the speculative bubbles of industrialized economies and their Stock Markets grew more and more gigantic.

Up and up these bubbles blew, unbounded by facts and reason.

Biggest of them was the cybernetic " 'New Economy' " that was supposed to rocket along the Internet's "Superbahn" (Vice-President Al Gore, Democrat, circa mid-1990s).

Never before, Bill Clinton crowed in 1996 to the G-7 nations (the U.S., Britain, France, Germany, Italy, Canada and Japan--a group of Northern imperialists whose membership mirrors the Trilateral

Commission's supermajority) had capitalism and its prime nation-state, the U.S., been so prosperous.

Affluence was booming in an abstract bubble of greed,
seeing solidity in sand, deluded by wishes and speed.

By 1999 companies trading on NASDAQ, the Stock Market that most serves the Internet economy and the telecommunications industry, were valued at an average ratio that exceeded 50 to 1 of price versus earnings.

The New York Stock Exchange's average ratio was less inflated in that year--35 to 1--but still wildly above the 20-to-1 ratio of "pop" that's considerd the upper limit of rationality.

Now, by middle of the year 2002, scandals and/or bankruptcies and/or colossal losses are rocking giant Corporations of the oil-and-gas (Enron, Reliant, Pacific Gas & Electric), telecommunications (WorldCom), accounting (Arthur Anderson), and Internet (AOL/ Time Warner) realms.

Here's a quick survey of desperate principals and the ravaged, blasted landscape.

Reliant Resources now admits to overstating its 1999-2001 earnings by $7.8 billion, more than double the amount previosly admitted by WorldCom.

The commercial drug-company Merck tops Reliant with $14 billion in probably false earnings.

General Electric has joined General Motors among blue-chip Corporations that are widely supposed to have cooked their accounting books.

Fox News, that bastion of Corporate ideology, estimated on July 6, 2002, that $600 billion would be the total loss to the U.S economy this year due to accounting scandals.

Foreign capital is in full flight. ' "The international financial system is coming apart at the seams," ' says billionaire U.S. speculator George Soros. ' "Everybody's going home. The Swiss banks are going home...." '

The infusions of Federal capital into oil-based and Defense-contractor Corporations that followed " '9/11' "--and the rapacious theft of tens of billions from programs such as Social Security under the G. W. Bush Administration--are short-term fixes, helpng only a rich few of Executives while they ultimately weaken an already tottering system.

According to the *Washington Post* and *USA TODAY*, $34 billion was drawn from Social Security in 2001, while the House

Budget estimates that $160 billion will be drawn from Social
Security in 2002.

As a whole, the total loss of taxpapers' moneys from takes to
Federal Departments and programs over the last three years will
be $4.2 trillion dollars, Michael Ruppert estimates in a July 6,
2002 article on his From the Wilderness Website.

Please bear in mind again what I must remind myself: One
trillion is one thousand times one billion.

No wonder that New York City' employees' pension-fund has
lately lost $9 billion.

New York City employees'include those of the Fire and Police
Departments.

The hugest pillars of the world's financial Establishment--
names that this book's scans of conspiracy and plunder have
cited often--now are most overloaded with high-risk debts.

The Chase Bank acquired JP Morgan Company on the last day
of the year 2000. We know the Chase Bank's and JP Morgan's
connections to Rockefellers, Nazis, and to World War I and/or
World War II.

JP Morgan Chase is now at risk for an amount 571 times
greater than its assets. That is, JP Morgan Chase is at risk for
$23.5 trillion--there's that trillion again--in the "derivatives" it
holds.

What are "derivatives" in the banking world? Simply stated,
"derivatives" is the term for the means by which one institution
derives or assumes responsibility for the debts of another entity in
return for a substantial fee.

JP Morgan Chase has far outraced its peers in grabbing
"derivatives." and the fees attendant to "derivatives"--JP Morgan
Chase has 51% of this game among U. S. banks.

How can we relate such an unfathomable amount as $23.5
trillion to the everyday, working world? Adam Hamilton's Zeal
Intelligence newsletter writes that 'every man, woman, and child
in America all working together can "only" manage to produce
$10.4 trillion worth of goods and services every year. JPM's
derivatives book is almost two and a half times as large as the
entire US economy!'

Other U. S.-based giants have put themselves in similar peril.

The largest U. S. bank, Citigroup, taken over by Traveler's
Insurance in 1998, shows $1 trillion in assets, against JP Morgan

Chase's $799 billion, but Citigroup holds $9 trillion at risk in
derivatives.

Bank of America ranks third in assets, with $620 million,
against its many-times-greater risk of $10 trillion in derivatives.

So: Even a modest, 10%-of-total "run" of demands for payment on
the derivatives contracts that JP Morgan Chase, the Bank of America,
and Citigroup now hold would wipe out all three. Their fall would
take down other pillars of global capitalism in a Crash much more
severe than that which precipitated the Great Depression.

H'mm! H'mm and double-H'mm!

How have working-class and middle-class people been so deprived
and endangered?

Early in 2002 Waldon Bello, a Filipino sociologist, wrote on
'Capitalist Crisis and Corporate Crime' in the first issue of *Global
Outlook*. (You can also find this piece on the globalresearch.ca site.)

Waldon Bello wrote about capitalist overproduction. He wrote that
by 1997: 'The world auto industry was selling just 74 per cent of the
70.1 million cars it built each year. So much investment took place in
global telecommunications infrastructure that traffic carried over
fiber-optic networks was reported to be only 2.5 per cent of
capacity.... There was, as economist Gary Shilling put it, an
"oversupply of nearly everything." '

Because businesses were actually losing money, Corporations and
the Banks that served them had to engage in practices and devices
that were ever more removed from real earnings and losses.

That is, some appear to have engaged in conspiracies.

Bello wrote: 'With profit margins slim or nonexistent, survival
increasingly meant greater and greater dependence on Wall Street
financing, which increasingly came under the sway of hybrid
investment-commercial bankers like JP Morgan Chase, Salomon
Smith Barney, and Merrill Lynch, ... With little to show in terms of
an attractive bottom line, some firms took the route of trading future
promise for hard cash in the present, ... It was this seemingly
innovative technique of trading on illusion that resulted in the
stratospheric rise of share values in the high technology sector, ... '

The dot.com crash of 2000-2001, the resounding bust of that
" 'Boom' ", wiped out $4.6 trillion--trillion!--of mostly innocent
investors' wealth on Wall Street.

Amid such ruin, surviving businesses further extended their illusions in order to seem viable.

Still, Bello wrote: 'In the end, there was no getting around the fact that your balance sheet had to show an excess of revenue over costs to continue to attract investors. This was the simple but harsh reality that led to the proliferation of fancy accounting techniques such as that of Enron finance officer Andrew Fastow's "partnerships," which were mechanisms to keep major costs and liabilities off the balance sheet, as well as cruder methods like Worldcom's masking of current costs as capital expenditures.'

JP Morgan Chase was a consulting partner to both Enron and Worldcom.

On a single, recent day of trading, July 23, 2002, JP Morgan Chase lost 18.1% of its value.

Working-people both inside and outside the U.S. have suffered most under the systems of supranational Corporate Government over the past 30 years.

Imperial Capital!

Where and when capitalists have the powers of dictators or kings, they must naturally treat the masses under them as peasants to be worked, duped and robbed.

Since 1973 real wages as a whole for U. S. manufacturing workers have declined by increasing percentages. Their drop fell more in the 1990s with the stepped-up relocation of manufacturing by U.S.-based Corporations to "off-shore" plants. At least 800,000 such U.S. jobs were lost to this or that Free Trade Agreement in the past decade.

Workers elsewhere have been even more misled and abused.

Millions have joined assembly-lines in off-shore factories, earning as little as $2 per 12-hour shift, their ages as young as 8, but they've gained nothing in economic standing at the same time as they've lost a great deal of environmental well-being and indigenous cohesion within their societies.

On every continent and in every nation, workers' earnings against their cost-of-living has stagnated or receded.

Economic growth has especially fallen in nations of the Southern Hemisphere, making them even more needful of cash from the IMF and World Bank and private institutions of the North. Thus they're more vulnerable to austerity-measures and demands-for-exports. Such 'disparity' of exchange means less bread, health-care,

education, and even water for most of the world's people. Such are
the fruits of the methods of 'transcendant' exploitation and
speculation, theft and degradation, that we reviewed earlier.

And yet: Capitalism is not working even for its most essential and
pillarlike institutions.

Capitalists based in the U.S. now enjoy unprecedented dominance.
They <u>have</u> the 'military and economic supremacy' that was sought
just before the start of World War II. David Rockefeller <u>has</u> his 'free
market forces able to transcend national boundaries' as never before.
The United States <u>has</u> the 'control' that the faithful Zbignew
Brzezinski desired in his <u>The</u> <u>Grand</u> <u>Chessboard</u>.

And yet: Their present and the present of the whole of humanity is
an unprecedented, perilous mess.

On July 7, 2002 the *Observer* newspaper in London, England
wrote that a World Wildlife Fund study 'warns that the human race is
plundering the planet at a pace that outstrips its capacity to support
life.'

Mark Townsend and Jason Burke wrote about the WWF report:
'Earth's population will be forced to colonize two planets within 50
years if natural resources continue to be exploited at the current
rate, ... '

The *Observer* continued: 'The report, based on scientific data from
across the world, reveals that more than a third of the natural world
has been destroyed by humans over the past three decades.'

Between 1970 and 2002 the Earth's forest cover has shrunk by
about 12 per cent, biodiversity in the world's Oceans by 1/3, and
freshwater ecosystems by more than 55 per cent.

The United States leads in consumption and damage. 'The WWF
report shames the US for placing the greatest pressure on the
environment. It found the average US resident consumes almost
double the resources as that of a UK citizen and more than 24 times
that of some Africans.'

The realization penned by one of the comic-strip artists with whom
I laughed most as a boy in the 1950s, Walt Kelly in his Eisenhower-
era 'Pogo', is widely quoted now: 'We have met the enemy, and he is
us.'

And yet: We can choose our fates even under Snopesian criminals
(' "Idjits" ', William Faulkner called these characters of his) such as
some Rockefellers and Bushes.

' "We were in Trinidad and the next stop was Caracas. I'd just been informed by the Venezulean government that they could not guarantee his safety. They were uninviting him. He was having lunch at the time. He looked up at me as though I'd struck him. Then he said, 'After all that country has meant to me. And all I've done for them?' He shook his head." '

Nelson Rockefeller is disinvited from visiting Venezuala for the United States in May 1969, as recounted by his special assistant James Cannon, in Joseph Persico's The Imperial Rockefeller

"What I got--I got soul
What I got--I got pride
What I got--I got love
What I want--to be free
        Raise your hands in the air
        If you feel like me"
Tupac Amaru Shakur, "Can U C The Pride In The Panther"

"Lord, the smokestack is black
And the buildings shine like--buildings shine like--
        buildings shine like--gold"
Charley Patton, "Moon Going Down"

THE NEXT REVOLUTION

'Mankind's history has proved from one era to
another that the true criterion of leadership is
spiritual. Men are attracted by spirit. By power,
men are *forced*. Love is engendered by spirit.
By power, anxieties are created.'
Malcolm X, The Autobiography of Malcolm X

'We are all related. We are all one.'
Leonard Peltier, Native American activist and
artist, imprisoned since 1976 under false charges,
in his Prison Writings.

' "Consumer-power!" '
Aung San Suu Kyi, leader of resistance to
the fascist regime in Burma

Reviewing the Case

We began with " '9/11' ".

We supposed that investigating the terrible crimes against humanity
of 9/11/01 might expose the greater realities and greater forces which
ordinary, intelligent and compassionate people now have to face.

We've seen, I believe, that the stories told about " '9/11' " by
Government officials and Corporate media--together, our effectual
Corporate Government--can't be true.

We've established, I hope, the undeniable proofs for the three
defining facts that I put forth at the outset of this short book.

FACT #1) The airliners COULD NOT have struck their targets
last September 11 unless multiple arms of the U.S. Government
engaged in an unprecedented failure to carry out their mission to
intercept off-course airliners.

FACT #2) American Airlines Flight 77, a Boeing 757-200, COULD
NOT have been flown by the Arab who is supposed to have piloted
it.

FACT #3) And the World Trade Center's 110-story Twin Towers
and 47-story Building 7 COULD NOT have fallen as they did unless
they were demolished by explosives set off within their structures.

Evidence continues to mount that disproves the " '9/11' " story that's told by Government officals and Corporate media.

We know now from the *New York Times* early in the month of August 2002--a month of much sounding about the " 'need' " to invade Iraq and/or Saudi Arabia--that at least two firefighters reached the 78th floor of the South Tower and prepared to evacuate survivors, they reporting nothing like " 'a raging inferno' " there, a few minutes before that building collapsed.

We see more and more.

We've seen more than enough, I believe, to know that fascism from our Government is rushing toward even greater horrors and repression.

COULD the ruling elititsts of the United States allow or commit a crime so awful as the mass murder of thousands last September 11?

To me the answer to that question is a sure yes.

Remember the *Maine*. Remember the *Lusitania*.

Remember Pearl Harbor Remember how the ' "Day of Infamy" ' launched the U. S. into World War II by posing a 'massive external threat' to the 'domestic well-being' of normal, intelligent and compassionate citizens.

For an exact precedent of a plan by the United States Joint Chiefs of Staff to stage an 'incident' that would kill U.S. citizens and send this nation into war, we can look back to March of 1962.

Last Fall--on November 7, 2002--ABC News reported on the release of formerly 'Top Secret' documents from the National Security Archive that were obtained by James Bamford through the Freedom of Information Act.

Bamford revealed these documents in his book <u>Body</u> <u>of</u> <u>Secrets</u>.

They show a plot approved by all five Chiefs of Staff to stage what Bamford terms an accustomed "pretext" that would allow the United States to invade Cuba.

Here's how the account by ABC's David Ruppe began: "Code named Operation Northwoods, the plans reportedly included the possible assassination of Cuban émigrés, sinking boats of Cuban refugees on the high seas, hijacking planes, blowing up a U.S. ship, and even orchestrating violent terrorism in U.S. cities."

David Ruppe of ABC continued: "The plans were developed as ways to trick the American public and the international community into supporting a war to oust Cuba's then new leader, communist Fidel Castro.

America's top military brass even contemplated that they would cause U.S. military casualties as part of their "trick", just as the sinking of the *Maine* in 1898 caused such casualties. They wrote in their 'Operation Northwoods' "plans" of 1962: 'We could blow up a U.S. ship in Guantanamo Bay and blame Cuba,' then 'casualty lists in U.S. newspapers would cause a helpful wave of national indignation.' "

We may all recall the 'wave of national indignation' that arose after " '9/11.' "

The 1962 plans contain an exact precursor to " '9/11' ".

39 years before last September 11 and the evident probability that aircraft were flown by remote control into the World Trade Center and Pentagon targets, Operation Northwoods imagined--as quoted by Canadian TV journalist Barrie Zwicker in a piece for *Global Outlook*--that 'an exact duplicate for a civil registered aircraft' could be created.

Then: 'At a designated time the duplicate would ... be loaded with ... selected passengers, ...'

Then: 'The actual registered aircraft would be converted to a drone (a remove controlled unmanned aircraft).'

Then: 'The destruction of that aircraft will be triggered by radio signal.'

Then: The Cuban Government would be blamed for an infamous and ' "cowardly' " act of terror.

The March 13, 1962 'Operation Northwoods' memorandum from Admiral Lyman Lemnitzer, head of the Joint Chiefs of Staff, to Secretary of Defense Robert McNamara, states that the Joint Chiefs were responding to a request for 'brief but precise description of pretexts that would provide justification of U. S. military intervention in Cuba.'

Lemnitzer's revealing and damning memo is reprinted on page 39 of this edition of ... Facing Our Fascist State.

As a summary of the suspiciously faulty responses (absent or misdirected or late) by commanders of U.S. fighter-jets on the " '9/11' " morning, President G. W. Bush uppermost among them, let me quote the young researcher and writer Nafeez Mossaddeq Ahmed, Executive Director of the Institute for Policy Research and

Development in Brighton, England and author of a remarkably comprehensive study and source-book, <u>The</u> <u>War</u> <u>on</u> <u>Freedom:</u> <u>How</u> <u>and</u> <u>Why</u> <u>America</u> <u>Was</u> <u>Attacked,</u> <u>September</u> <u>11,</u> <u>2001</u>.

The 23-year-old's book was published in June of 2002. It's gotten almost no reviews in the U.S since then.

Nafeez Mossaddeq Ahmed wrote: 'In this opinion of this author, this' [the faults-ridden response] 'strongly suggests that significant, high-level elements of the U.S. military and Bush administration bear direct responsibility for the terrorist acts that occurred on the 11th of September on U.S soil, through what appears to be a combination of deliberate action and inaction.'

He continued: 'The facts on record weigh strongly in favour of this conclusion, providing reasonable grounds to believe that these officials were complicit in the 11th September attacks, through the active obstruction of routine protective systems, which are designed to automatically deflect the type of emergences that occurred on 11th September. This appears to have been maintained through the orchestrated prolongation (for up to one and a half hours) of systematic negligence as the attacks occurred, on the part of elements of the FAA, NORAD, the Pentagon, the Secret Service, the White House and the President--despite the clear danger they presented.'

We must know by know that the most appalling acts of cruelty--'pretexts' and mass murders from documented conspiracies--ARE possible for arms of our Corporate Government, a hidden government that's both fascist and feudal at its roots.

What Can Be Done, What Can Be Won

At a book-release party last April, as conversations and bottles of wine circulated through the two rooms of San Francisco Supervisor Matt Gonzalez's office, a well-known, local/international activist told me that she could not let herself believe that parts of the U. S. Government were responsible for the attacks of " '9/11.' "

"If I believed that, I'd just want to hide," she said. "It would mean that what we have to fight is just too big. Too evil. It would be too much for me."

I disagreed with her. We <u>have</u> to face these fascists, I insisted.

They're not going to stop, I said. We have to identify the enemy that we need to fight. We have to face what's in front of us, I said, if we're to have a chance at winning a future for our children.

Why has the present become so extreme?

Why have the old, lording families who rule working-people made such blatant and heinous plays for power and repression in the past year?.

The Earth is nearly exhausted of resources that are immediately profitable to Imperial Capital. Oil is the most vital and valuable of these resources, we know, and oil appears to be running short. For Britain oil-production and foreseeable imports of oil are expected to fall below national consumption around 2005. The same predicament is expected to begin a crippling of North American economies not later than 2012.

Therefore oil-plutocrats of the West are grabbing for fields of fossil-fuels wherever they suppose such grabs can be carried out-- Central Asia, Iraq, Saudi Arabia, ...

Their grabs, however, must fail--even if their grabs temporarily ravage lands, peoples and resources.

Their " 'wars' " in their " 'Endless War' " must fail--even if such " 'wars' " continue to be one-sided and shameful massacares that mostly kill civilians.

The Earth will win.

The Earth will rebel in concert with rebellion by the great mass of this planet's people.

And we'll win.

The Earth as a living body is already in revolt at those who stick her with shafts and foul her waters and poison her air.

Now, in the middle of 2002, unprecedented wild-fires jump across States' lines. Unprecedented Summer floods submerge Centrums of European municipalities. Swaths of Antarctica break off and float toward the shorelines of Chile and Australia and Atlantic City as the other Pole also melts.

Natives' prophecies are coming home to their colonizers.

These prophecies are coming home with a weight and multitude of causal consequence that feels mythic and moral.

The "end times", the "end days", people who still work the
earth around the world say in regard to what's happening to local and
global environments now

The Power of Choking Off Capital

We must see by now that a long-time, self-anointed 'elite'--whom
we must also recognize to be like monsters in both their power and
their lack of feeling--want to expand and tighten their rule over
ordinary, intelligent and compassionate people.

We must also see by now that we human beings in the modern West
matter most to our species' future.

We've seen by how much we who are relatively affluent here are
the most wasteful and destructive consumers of the Earth's resources.

Our consumption is like an addiction. It's like addiction--"habit"--
to a diseasing drug that's bound to kill us.

Suppose, however, that we turned our consumption back on the
Corporate rulers who profit most from it.

Suppose we turned off or turned away our :habits" and thereby cut
off our Corporate rulers' cash-flow.

Suppose that we squeezed them and bent them to our will.

Suppose that we decided to bend the oil-and-gas cartel, for starters,
to our overwhelming will.

Even Polls by Corporate media show that huge majorities of people
in the modern West consider environmental remediation to be our
species' first priority.

We know that drastic measures must be taken to prevent more
icebergs from floating north and south toward Palm Beach.

We know that we must combat global warming to save the air our
children breathe.

We know that the suprnational Corporate Government and in
particular the oil-and-gas cartel (ExxonMobil, ChevronTexaco,
British Petroleum/Amoco, and Royal Dutch Shell among its major
partners or conspirators) has done nothing for decades but subvert
the desires and efforts of the world's people to reduce pollution and
diseases from carbon-dioxide emissions.

So: We choke Chevron.

We target one member of the oil-and-gas cartel for the choking
pressure of a protracted boycott.

We make our boycott of one fat, logoed arm or tentacle of the cartel that itself is choking us as BIG and international as possible.

We make it HURT its target arm or tentacle as much as possible.

Capital is the life-blood of any Corporation.

Any cartel needs all its arms to function with full and necessary strength.

"Oow!" Mr. P. P. (Peoplecare Peopledo) Chevron or Mr. Exxon R. Mobil exclaims to his fellows after a month or two of tens of millions staying away from his pumps.

"My bottom-line is hurting!

"Fellows, we've got to pay attention to what these damned, persistent people are saying! I'm hemorrhaging! My stripes are fading! Soon I won't be able to afford put out any more of those smiley-face toy cars! I won't be able to help you in Kazakhistan or the Timor Sea. Remember--if I go down, I'll take at least some of you with me! My arteries are your arteries! My blood is your blood!"

At the same time as we squeeze one member of the oil-and-gas cartel, we present it with demands that reflect the overwhelming majority of people's concerns

Such demands might be:

1. Reduce your extraction of fossil-fuels from our planet as much as possible and with all possible speed.

A reduction of 10% PER YEAR should be minimal.

2. Turn your thousands of personnel and billions of dollars in budgets toward forms of renewable energy (solar, tidal, wind) as much as possible and with all possible speed.

Results should include a 10% gain PER YEAR in renewable energy for municipal, State and national jurisdictions.

3. Employ in installion of renewable energy those who have suffered most from fossil-fuel energy. That is, employ those who have lived closest to refineries and Power Plants.

4. Restore as much as possible and with all possible speed the wooded, grassy, potable, swim-able environments that preceded refineries and Power Plants.

With such actions we may prevent the rise in asthma-rates among our children. We may prevent Dresden and Venice, Haiphong and Bombay, Christchurch and New Orleans, from going permanently underwater due to global warming.

We can use the same tactics toward any cartel and a targeted partner of that cartel--the pharmaceuticals cartel (Eli Lilly, Merck, Searle, ...), the entertainment cartel (AOL Time Warner, Capital Cities/Disney, Viacom/CBS, ...) the grains-to-market cartel (Cargill, Archer-Daniels-Midland, ...).

All of these cartels are vulnerable--like much else in the intensively industrial, technological and commerical world--due to their concentration and stratification of power.

WE, however, we the majority who remain intelligent and compassionate, HAVE and ARE the crucial power on Earth.

We HAVE the numbers.

Everything depends on OUR choices and consumption.

We CAN compel a new world--one much different, much happier--one more level, cooperative and creative--than the 'New World Order' that our old Lords still try to force upon us.

The Next Generation, the New America

Our order here in the U. S. still is "rapidly changing."

The United States today is like a developing nation in the mix of its races.

Here now is a more colorful "melting-pot" than ever before.

At the same time, an old America of unlocked doors and unspoken trust still exists among the vast majority of people in the Western Hemisphere.

Trust and cooperation necessarily exist throughout most of human societies.

That is, here's still plenty of hope in how the great mass of distinct, normal, intelligent and compassionate people behave toward each other.

Last June I flew to Minneapolis/St. Paul on the way to being the first (and entirely titular) "poet-in-residence" (thank you, Diamond Dave Whitaker of Food Not Bombs and Theresa Marquez of Organic Valley) at the 30th-or-so annual Rainbow Family Gathering.

The Rainbow Gathering this year found its home among National Forest woods on the Upper Penisula of Michigan.

I rented a car and drove into St. Paul. On this sultry Friday night of breeze sashaying through leaves the house where I stayed on

Goodrich Avenue in St. Paul--nearby streets named Pleasant,
Fairview and Summit--kept its front door open past midnight.

 The next morning passersby in the neighborhood volunteered
directions and a girl about ten years old rocked in a porch-swing with
an English sheepdog on her lap.

 Later in this trip--after four days at the Gathering--I read at the
Heartland Cafe in the Rogers Park neighborhood of northeast
Chicago. Pete Wolf, the reading's host, said that he was "4th-
generation Rogers Park." He also said that his Zip Code was now the
most multi-ethnic in the U.S.

 On the evening of July 3, the eve of the 4th of July, feeling again
like Walt Whitman, I walked beside Lake Michigan. Between the
lawns and sand of a beachfront Park were Blacks, Latins, Arabs,
Russians, Jews and tow-headed Wisconsin girls. They were strolling,
pedaling, playing and lounging.

 'Here the luminous smiles and ambling walks commonly seen
outside the States', my notebook says.

 'Here a segmented mural with richly painted images and slogans
fronting Lake Michigan, 8 miles from the Gold Coast.'

 The 'segmented mural' refers to a concrete bench that faced the
Lake--the Lake steaming gray-blue with heat that was still near 100
degrees around 7:00 p.m this July evening--across a paved pathway.

 Separate designs of colors-and-quotes adjoined along this bench
like sections of a skein or storyboard.

  'Make no small plans', one read.

  'Unity, Faith, Service' was drawn on another.

  'Free To Skate' was another's message.

Buddha and Rumi were quoted in other designs.

  'As a mother would risk her life to protect her
  child--even so one should cultivate limitless heart
  toward all beings--Buddha'

  'Let The Beauty/ We Love Be What We Do/
  There Are Hundreds/ Of Ways To Kneel And/
  Kiss The Ground--Rumi'

I also copied this hand-painted message:

  'The Day's Divinity/First thing you see'.

Below a painted trio of girls--one African, one Caucasian and one
Asian--was inscribed:

  'Children should be raised with Open Minds,
  Free Spirits and Clear Hearts'

Here, I thought, was the real, new America to hoped for and worked for, I thought.

Here was the new American rainbow in its mix and promise.

Here was Blake's and Whitman's, Jeanette Armstrong's and Leonard Peltier's wished-for America, the America of Brasilean Bahia's 18th-century Quilombo.

I remembered what Medicine Story, an elder of the Rainbow Family, had said at the Hipstory performance in the Granola Funk Theater the previous night.

Then, as a roaring thunderstorm drummed the tarp strung overhead between the improvised Theater's trussed limbs, Medicine Story-- light-skinned and for decades "on the Rainbow Path", lean, long- haired and like grayed leather in his loincloth, lantern-lit but enshrouded by dark northwoods--addressed the mostly twenty- somethings who were huddled under the tarp to avoid the rain. Medicine Story said that he thought the Rainbow Gathering should be considered "Summer School for a better world."

I also remembered my first time in Chicago, 35 years earlier. Then, age 17, I was hitchhiking back from Montreal's World's Fair to my Senior year of High School in northwest Washington.

Noontime of that day, a salesman from Indiana let me out in the Loop so that I could go to the Art Institute. My jeans, T-shirt and jacket were almost dried by three hours in his car. In the darkling dawn of that morning I'd been woken and rousted out of the Toledo truckstop-motel hall that had been 3:00 a.m. refuge for me and my sleeping-bag--ordered back out into a drenching downpour--by a partly bald manager who was irate at "dirty, goddamn hippies!" in this August 'the Summer of Love'. He cussed me before I cussed him. At the Art Institute I first saw original Matisses and Van Goghs-- their shocks of boldness and beauty across a Gallery themselves supernatural like passages from Rimbaud or Dostoyevsky--before lugging my sleeping-bag and suitcase out along Congress to seek a ride north and west to Interstates 90 and 94.

What a difference between then and now! I thought in Rogers Park.

What a difference over 35 years!

How impossible to imagine then that we would now suffer " 'leaders' " such as George W. Bush!

How impossible to imagine in 1967 that we would look back at a President of the United States named Nixon and lesser, less individual personalities named Ford, Carter, Reagan, Clinton, and George Herbert Walker Bush!

In Rogers Park of July 2002 I thought again about how we of
" 'the '60s Generation' " have been diminished

What losses have come to the idealistic purposes, sharp minds and
warm hearts that were common then!

How HAVE we been so subverted or seduced, degraded and
diminished? I thought again by Lake Michigan.

We once laughed at sex. We once sided with the struggling
majority of Vietnamese, then with the struggling majority of
Nicaraguans. Once tens of millions of our generation wanted to side
with the struggling poor everywhere.

Now: What a lot of sleep-walking into things! What a lot of PBS
programs about otters and operas! What a lot of programs for
spiritual answers and investment-securities! What a lot of funding by
Foundations that are used by the ruling few to evade taxes and
control opinions! What a lot of billions spent on " 'fitness' " (Fit for
what?) What a lot of SUVs! What a lot of manufacturing 'Rebellion'
and 'Revolution' into the consumption that's taking the future from
our children!

And yet ... And yet ... A great deal for hope is still present and still
arising, I thought in Rogers Park beside Lake Michigan.

" '9/11' " must wake us from our sleep, I thought again.

Tens and hundreds of millions and even billions around the world
already know what I hope this book has shown: Parts of the U.S.
Corporate Government committed the atrocities of
9/11/0 to make money from oil and otherwise further their ends.

Think of Dick Cheney. Think of Donald Rumsfeld. Think of what
they've done and said.

Think of Corporate media's and supposedly " 'Left' " media's
shameful lack of investigation (Noam Chomsky, Amy Goodman,
Pacifica Radio, ...) into the glaring holes of the " '9/11' " story.

Think of the Bush and Rockefeller and other families who
have tricked and sacrified working-people into Wars over a century
or over centuries.

You'll realize, I hope, that " '9/11' " is but one more 'pretext' in a
bloody skein of horrors, a skein completely different from the colors
living and painted in Rogers Park.

You'll see, I hope, that we the people of the United States and the
world can only depend on ourselves to make changes.

We must make changes from the ground up.

You'll also know by now, I hope, that conspiracies are not theory. Conspiracies are history.

Conspiracies are how ruling concentrations of criminal exploiters grab more of existing power

Revolutions, on the other hand, are how great masses of people make the changes that are vital for them.

You'll feel, I hope, that resistance unto revolutions is vital for us now.

Fascists of our Corporate Government--I say fascists because their acts deserve the naming--are rolling on with their plans.

A fascist State can ONLY go to Wars to to feed its economic priorities.

Lunging heedlessly--like a blood-starved vampire--and leaving corpses behind it--a fascist State or 'Corpose State' can't EVER take in more than it needs to consume in order to sustain itself.

Thus the fascists for oil must have their " 'Endless War.' "

They must therefore perpetuate more terror to feed their war.

Such is what we have to face, I believe. Such brutal reality, more revealed to me in these past 12 months of my own education, is what I've hoped to convey in this book.

I remember now something my mother said at Chrismastime in the past Winter, the Winter of 2001-2002, when my 3-year-old nephew Aidan bumped his head against a kitchen counter.

She said to him something that must be a familiar in many cultures: "Life is hard, life is real."

Life is hard, life is real--I think of her counsel now and how truly it relates to resistance and possible victory by 'ordinary, intelligent and compassionate people' in the 21st century.

Our resistance will have to be unprecedented.

Our resistance will have to be supranational.

Our resistance will have to be complex and connected as no other resistance before. It will have to involve abandonment, sacrifice and sabotage. And our resistance will have to be rooted in something unshakeable in our hearts and minds: that our effort is based on love and hope for humans' free possibilities.

Such resistance is to me the the most fitting and truthful tribute we can offer against the loss of life on 9/11/01 in the United States--and against the loss of life that has followed in Afghanistan and elsewhere.

We shouldn't be afraid of new reality and resistance.

'Truth is the way to peace,' I realized after citing the Buddhist monk Thich Nhat Han--a friend of Martin Luther King Jr.'s--in my second *San Francisco Bay View* column last September.

We'll have steadily more increasing reasons to fear, I think, if we do not truly face and fight those who are our children's enemy. Fascism, after all, preys on fear as well as war.

And we CAN win.

In the trust that's everyday along St. Paul streets called Summit, Grand and Goodrich--and in the mix of races who are laughing and cross-generating in Rogers Park, the mix of races that's inevitable and everyday in the Hip-Hop Generation--a new America of all the Americas and the world--Blake's and Whitman's, Natives' and Africans' and Indians' and whoever more's (whoever they may be) America-- the next America--can arise.

A new America's of all the 'Americas' around the world MUST arise. It must because there's no other way forward now but to fight for each other and to work with each other.

Only together can we make technology freedom. Only together can let our creativity loose. Only together can we know the richness of our differences. Only together can we see our children shine into possibilities of their generation and the next generations.

Only together can we create the next revolutions.

September 14, 2002

2.25" CIRCULAR BUTTON

Campaign-button in Marie's race for District 10 Supervisor
in San Francisco, 2000

"Whenever this Administration is confronted with some opposition or exposure one of its Old Guard chickenhawks--Cheney or Rumsfeld or another of those guys who look like they eat death for breakfast-- threatens us, the U.S. public, with more terror."

Interview in December 2002
by *San Francisco Bay View* columnist and activist
(*Greenaction, Housing Is a Human Right*)
Marie Harrison

(Marie and I became big friends through work on her year 2000 campaign to be elected Supervisor of District 10 in San Francisco. We and Alma Lark and Malik Rahim then worked with Public Housing residents in the North Beach, Hunters View, and Harbor Road Developments, our organizations Housing Is a Human Right *and* From the Ground Up.
Marie interviewed me in the month that FOFS was published.)

I sat down with Don Paul, frequent *Bay View* columnist, a man of many talents and my friend, to talk about his new book, " '9/11' " ....

Why, considering all the other books that he could have written, did he take on such a task? It's all about information and education, it's a call to action, it will make you stop and think and soon you'll start putting things together.

But most importantly, Don's analysis of 9/11 will remove all doubt from your mind that our government is not the good guy here and that we need to take action now to bring it back in line. If nothing else, it will help us have the courage to say to ourselves, "Never again, not in this lifetime or any other."

Now ask yourself, "Why are we educating and training, not just training but militarily training, those folks who would use their training against us in return?" Read the book, then you tell me have we been too foolish for too long and isn't it time to say no to our governmental machine.

MARIE HARRISON: *Why " '9/11' "?*
DON PAUL: Why the book's title? Well, because I think the crimes of 9/11/01 exemplify where the U.S. Government is at now. I also think--and I think the book shows--that those crimes are only the latest and greatest in a long line of atroctities against ordinary people that the power-elite in this nation have committed. Oh, and the

double quotes around 9/11 are meant to suggest how we the public
are made to repeat what Corporate Media says--how false information
is received and passed along.

M H: *You think it was a set-up?*

D P: Well, Marie, after a year or so of research, I know now that only
forces within the U. S. Government could have committed the crimes
as they actually happened. Only the highest levels of the U. S.
command-structure--I mean the Joint Chiefs of Staff, the North
American Air Defense and their civilian commanders--could have
been responsible for the failure to intercept United
Airlines Flight 175, the second airliner to hit he World Trade Center,
and to intercept American Airlines Flight 77, the Boeing 757 that's
supposed to have hit the Pentagon. Also, I'm sure now that the Twin
Towers and World Trade Center Building 7 were demolished by
explosives set off inside them.

M H: *So you don't have much faith in the investigation the
Government is launching now?*

D P: (laughing with her) Well, I have complete confidence in Henry
Kissinger's will to carry out any intention of the power elite's. This is
the man who bombed Cambodia, who overthrew the democratically
elected regime of Salvador Allende in Chile, who okayed Indonesia's
slaughter of tens of thousands in East Timor. He's a chronic liar and
mass-murderer--so he'll do fine. Seriously, though, the families and
friends of victims of 9/11/01 and the public at large deserves a true
investigation of that day. We should have the evidence that so far is
missing--the flight-recorders, surveillance-photos of the Pentagon,
Trade Center sites--or else we'll remain blinded by this
Administration and its media.

M H: *So how did it happen? How were those planes flown?*

D P: I think all the airliners were flown by remote control. Since the
hijackings of the 1970s commercial airliners in the U.S. have carried
a program that lets ground control take over their operation. Another,
more advanced means of remote control, Global Hawk, flew a
Boeing 737 from Edwards Air Force in California to a Base in
Australia in April 2001--take-off to landing....

M H: *What you're saying is pretty awful. But a lot of people have felt
that 9/11 is being used as a scare tactic. A lot of people have asked
who all this is benefiting.*

D P: Right--pretty cold, pretty awful. Certainly 9/11 is the greatest
scare tactic ever in this nation's history. Certainly it's benefiting the
Bush Administration and the power elite of which the Bush family
and the current Cabinet are a part. It's making them money from oil,
military contracts, and narcotics trafficking. We should never forget
that the most immediate profits from the ouster of the Taliban in

Afghanistan are in the opium trade--production of opium there has
jumped from 173 metric tons last year to 3500 tons this year--which
represents $150 to 200 billion a year--which in turn represents 20
times that value to Banks and Stock Markets when this money is
transferred into legal businesses--that is, 3 to 4 trillion in one year.

Scare tactic is exactly right. Whenever this Administration is
confronted with some opposition or exposure one of its Old
Guard chickenhawks--Cheney or Rumsfeld or another of those guys
who look like they eat death for breakfast--threatens us, the U.S.
public, with more terror. "Al Qaeda is gonna get us with dirty nuclear
bombs in somebody's shoe." "Al Qaeda is gonna get us with anthrax
that somehow comes from Fort Detrick in Maryland. Al Qaeda is
gonna get us with smallpox unless we line up for vaccinations from
unaccountable pharmarceutical Corporations allied with the Bush
Administration".

Don't, please, let your family or your grandchildren take those
vaccinations.

M H: *So what's going to stop them? What is going to stop this
Government?*

D P: We have to stop them. We have to save ourselves. We actually
have to defend ourselves. You see, Marie, I think the White House
gang in power now won't stop till they're materially defeated. I think
we have to engage in economic warfare. Boycotts of vital arms of the
cartels that profit from traffic in oil and/or narcotics are what the
book calls for--starting with Chevron and Citibank. I noticed that
three separate articles in a Bay View of a few weeks ago called foy
boycotts--of Macy's, of radio-station *KMEL*, and of ho's-and-
gangstas rap. That's one way. If we can organize as tens of millions
around the world, we can be felt.

M H: *Finally, what do you hope people will take from your book? Is
what you just said its message?*

D P: Well, first, I think that this nation's salvation can only come
through empowerment of people of color. To repeat, to me, what we
call 9/11 is only the latest and most brazen of crimes in this nation's
history of conspiracies. Theft, slavery and mass murder by elitists,
deceiving and directing masses, built this nation. But the people of
the United States remain well-intentioned, I continue to believe, and
we still can do great things, as we began to do a generation or two
ago. But first we have throw off our old lords, Democrat and
Republican, and organize for our self-defense along the lines of
principles voiced by the Black Panther Party, the Cuban and Chinese
Revolutions, freedom-fighters of Africa, the Communards of Paris,
the Levellers of England, and many other true democrats and

people-loving revoltutionaries--and we have to do it with complete
determination. I guess that's it. Thank you!

"For one fact, bolstering supposition that a secret team within the U.S. government primarily carried out the 9/11 attacks, the FBI is directly connected to the attempt you mentioned, the bombing of the World Trade Center Twin Towers on February 26, 1993, a blast that killed six people and injured more than 1000."

Interview in June 2003
by investigative author
(www.leftgatekeepers.com) Bob Feldman

(Bob Feldman of Boston is also a singer-songwriter. Tracks of his can be heard at http://www.myspace.com/bobafeldman68music. He did this interview for New York Indymedia.)

U.S. anti-war movement writer Don Paul is the author of an anti-war book, " '9/11' ": Facing Our Fascist State. Paul's 9/11 book hasn't been reviewed much by the U.S. academics that generally review books on recent historical events for the U.S. media. Yet Paul's 9/11 book provides anti-war readers with an alternative to the U.S. military-industrial-media-university-foundation complex's version of what happened in downtown Manhattan on September 11, 2001.

Besides being the author of the anti-war 9/11 book, Paul also holds the New York Road Runners Club record for both running 50 kilometers and 50 miles in its Central Park events. In 1980 the 9/11 author finished the 50-mile run event in 5:09:58 and in 1982 Paul finished the 50-kilometer run in 2:50:55. In 1971 he was the youngest winner of a Stegner Fellowship in Creative Writing at Stanford, after Ken Kesey and Tillie Olsen and before Raymond Carver. In the 1990s he produced albums by the jazz artists Glenn Spearman, Lisle Ellis, India Cooke and Paul Plimley.

Anti-war movement writer Paul lives in California's Bay Area and was recently interviewed via e-mail.

BOB FELDMAN: *September 11, 2003 will mark the second anniversary of the collapse of the World Trade Center buildings that killed thousands of New Yorkers. Like MIT Professor Noam Chomsky, you've written a book about what happened on 9/11. Would the New Yorkers who read MIT Professor Chomsky's book on 9/11 learn anything new about why 9/11 happened by reading your book?*
DON PAUL: My view as to the why of the 9/11 attacks differs radically from Noam Chomsky's. His view accords with the U.S. government's line that "Arab terrorists" (i.e., al-Qaeda) committed

those attacks. Chomsky's explanation as to why differs from George W. Bush's only in that he attributes the reason for the attacks to "blowback" from nefarious U. S. Government operations and policies in the Middle East and Afghanistan over the past several decades, while our current selected President attributes the attacks to envy at freedom and prosperity in the U.S. by fanatical followers of a fundamentalist kind of Islam.

Chomsky also limits his explanation to the confines of what's widely known as "structural analysis." That is, he and his followers reject the importance of individual perpetrators of crimes such as the 9/11 attacks and the ensuing invasion of Afghanistan and Iraq--just as they reject the importance of which Government politician ordered which crime in the more distant past--such as Suharto "in" East Timor, Kissinger and Nixon "in" Cambodia, Brzezinski "in" Afghanistan, Reagan and George H.W. Bush "in" Afghanistan, Nicaragua, El Salvador, et cetera. They say that structural realities, structural inequities, are really determinative, not the villains who come and go as heads of State.

So far as such analysis goes, I agree with it. The U.S. Presidency has passed from a Bush to Clinton and back to a Bush with very little variance in the direction that material realities and an elite's drive for profits and power have compelled "U.S. foreign policy." Oil remains the U.S. elite's prime concern and opium from Afghanistan remains a main mover in the world's illegal and legal economies, just as both commodities were 15 years ago.

The failing of analysis such as Chomsky's, I think, is that it stays short of identifying and examining the structures that are really most powerful and determinative in the world. And so it stays short of naming those structures' most consequential criminals. So it doesn't name, of course, the institutions and Foundations that fund and promote the limits of "structural analysis"—I mean institutions funded by Rockefellers, Rothschilds, Pews, et cetera. George Soros and his Open Society Institutes and Human Rights Watch particularly, maintain illusions of democracy and investigation that misleads million of people.

I think these structures and forces and their operators are far above elected governments. They far outstrip governments in their reach and power. At the heart of their structure and operation is, I think, the international financial system—a cruel, abstract system that depends upon more and more exploitation of people and resources—a profoundly irrational system whose failings can only be disguised and whose operations can only be sustained by the kind of "endless war" and Patriot Acts brought to the U.S. public after September 11, 2001.

In my view, a secret team within the U.S. government primarily carried out the 9/11 attacks. The attacks could not have happened without the participation of such a team. In particular this team was responsible for the unprecedented failure to intercept hijacked airliners on the 9/11 morning—one hour and 28 minutes elapsed between 8:15 EDT, the time of the first off-course deviation by American Airlines Flight 11, the airliner that hit World Trade Center Building 1, the North Tower, at 8:48—and the crash into the Pentagon at 9:43.

Noam Chomsky disdains to consider such a conspiracy ("I think such speculations lead us from issues of prime significance, not towards them . . . Personally, I don't think it's worth the effort."). But I find such a conspiracy from the inside of the U.S. government far more likely than the absurd cartoon which is the official story—made up of physical impossibilities, incapable pilots, hard-drinking Muslims, indestructible passports, et cetera—a cartoon that both Corporate and supposedly "Left" media continue to parrot and thereby promote.

Why were the attacks carried out? Why were such mass murder and horror and suffering visited on New York City in particular? The superelites' exploitative, irrational economy needed a pretext to avoid the consequences of its failings—over 1.1 million jobs had been lost in the U.S. between January and August 2001—and needed a pretext to grab control of oil and gas reserves from Central Asia and to regain control of the opium potential in Afghanistan. The Taliban had cut the opium crop there from 4600 metric tons to 173 over the year before 9/11/01, removing $150–200 billion from the world's illegal economy in one year and removing an amount 20 times greater than $150–200 billion from Banks and Stock Markets and other legal institutions through which profits from this opium-traffic are laundered.

Economic vulnerability and the grab for reserves of oil and gas are also leading the U.S. to invasion and occupation of the Middle East—Iraq first—mass murder on top of mass murder. And all these invasions are based on the cartoon-like lies about 9/11 that Corporate and "Left" media refuse to examine and expose.

B F: *What actually caused the collapse of the Twin Towers in Manhattan on September 11, 2001?*

D P: To tell the truth, I'm not sure. My book states: 'Neither jet fuel's fire nor anything else that was in the Towers that morning burns hot enough (1022 degrees Fahrenheit) . . . to deform steel." FOFS also states: "to not topple sideways, but to instead fall straight-down within their foundations, the 110-story Towers had to be imploded by explosives set off against their load-bearing columns and beams."

I remain sure of those statements. I'm also sure that the Twin Towers' must have been severed at their bases, seven stories underground, by explosives comparable to nuclear devices....
Also, temperatures of the rubble at the Towers' sites remained above 1000 degrees Fahrenheit five days after 9/11/01 despite firefighters' regular soaking of the sites, suggesting that some causal force far beyond fire from jet fuel or plastics was still operative there. Also, recent analyses on the Internet suppose that the volume of dust in the Towers' in-air collapses—that volume 3 to 5 times each Tower's diameter—points to explosive causes for the Towers' collapses that we have yet to identify.

I can say for sure, too, Bob, that the U.S. government's explanations for the collapse of both the Towers' and WTC Building 7 are grossly inadequate.

In May of 2002 the Federal Emergency Management Agency (FEMA) issued its "World Trade Center Building Performance Study.' FEMA's group of professorial experts had a budget of only $600,000 to investigate the collapses that killed almost 3000—compared with the $40 million that was spent for investigation of Bill Clinton's activities with Monica Lewinsky in 1998–99. FEMA's Study states: "With the information and time available, the sequence of events leading to the collapse of each tower could not be definitively determined."

FEMA's Study is even more waffling in regard to WTC Building 7, the 47-story Building 7 that fell straight-down in class controlled-demolition fashion at 5:20 on 9/11 afternoon. FEMA's Study states: "The specifics of the fires in WTC 7 and how they caused the building to collapse remain unknown at this time."

WTC 7 and the Twin Towers were owned and heavily insured by Silverstein Properties.

B F: What actually caused the initial fires at the World Trade Center buildings to start on September 11, 2001?

D P: So far as I know, collisions by airliners started the first fires in the Twin Towers on 9/11. Regarding WTC-7, the origin of its internal fires appears more mysterious.

FEMA's Study says that fires burned in WTC 7 for seven hours before its collapse. That puts their start in the same hour as the collapse of the North Tower, WTC 1, which fell at 10:29. There's no evidence I know, however, that debris from Building 1 ignited anything inside Building 7. Video and photographs show that 7 remains wholly upright and scarcely marred at mid-afternoon of 9/11, only small fires visible on the 7th and 12th floors. Its collapse at 5:20 is very precipitous, less than 7 seconds in duration, and it collapses inward from its top-down. It looks like a perfectly controlled demolition.

Before 9/11, no buildings of structural steel had ever collapsed due to fire. In February of 1991 a fire burned for 19 hours in the 38-story building at One Meridian Plaza in Philadelphia, spreading to eight floors and causing the death of three firefighters. But this building stood.

WTC 7 contained offices of the FBI and CIA and then-Mayor Rudolph Giuliani's Command Center. Many people speculate that WTC 7 served as the base for executing operations that took down the Twin Towers. It offers a wide, open view to both Buildings 1 and 2. Evidence of the operations would be largely destroyed with Building 7's demolition.

We're not likely to know for sure what happened to the three collapsed WTC Buildings and their thousands of victims, however, till courageous witnesses offer testimony. Evidence from the Buildings' sites—where more people lost their lives than at Pearl Harbor—was removed and destroyed with unprecedented speed in the weeks after 9/11.

The company responsible for this removal, Controlled Demolition, Inc. of Maryland, also took care of the wreckage that was left after the bombing of the Murrah Building in Oklahoma City killed 168 people (none of them the personnel of the Bureau of Alcohol, Tobacco and Firearms who were the attack's supposed target) on April 19, 1995. This bombing prompted passage of the federal Anti-Terrorism Act.

B F: *Was there any connection between what happened at the World Trace Center on 9/11/01 and a previous 1990s alleged "terrorist" attempt to destroy the World Trade Center?*

D P: Again, you'll have to draw your own conclusions.

For one fact, bolstering supposition that a secret team within the U.S. government primarily carried out the 9/11 attacks, the FBI is directly connected to the attempt you mentioned, the bombing of the World Trade Center Twin Towers on February 26, 1993, a blast that killed six people and injured more than 1000. Israel's counterpart to the CIA, the Mossad, is also connected to this bombing.

The FBI is on record that an Egyptian, Emid Ali Salem, was its informant within this admitted conspiracy. According to a *New York Times* piece of October 28, 1993, Emid Ali Salem secretly recorded talks between himself and his FBI supervisor, John Anticev. Salem's tapes reveal that the FBI's Anticev stopped a plan to substitute harmless powder for the nitrate that eventually exploded the huge bomb under the Twin Towers. Remember that 6 people were killed and more than 1,000 were injured by this bomb. Salem's statement is that he built the bomb and received $1,000,000 from the FBI for his work. We also know that the rental agreement for the truck that

carried the 1993 WTC bomb gives the phone number and address of
a Mossad agent, Josie Hadas.

There are parallels within the official stories for the 1993
and 2001 World Trade Center attacks. The supposed "spiritual leader"
of 1993's group of "Arab Terrorists" and "Muslim extremists," their
name the Gamaa Al-Islamya, was Sheikh Omar Abdel-Rahman.
Sheikh Abdel-Rahman resembles both "al-Qaeda mastermind" Osama
bin Laden and 9/11's supposed "terroriist ringleader" Mohammed
Atta. Like Osama bin Laden, Sheikh Abdel-Rahman was a CIA asset
in Afghanistan in the 1980s. Like Mohamed Atta, Sheikh Abdel-
Rahman received U.S. government assistance in entering this nation.
In 1996 Sheikh Omar was sentenced to life-imprisonment for his part
in planning the first World Trade Center attack.

Attorney Ron Kuby represented one of the 1993 defendants. In
response to the *New York Times* article of October 28, 1993, Ron
Kuby said in the *Atlantic Monthly*: ' "The article on the FBI being
involved in the World Trade Center bombing actually understated the
evidence, believe it or not. The informer, Emid Salem, is actually on
tape saying that he built the bomb that ultimately blew up the World
Trade Center . . . . The mastermind is the government of the United
States. It was a phony, government-engineered conspiracy to begin
with. It would never have amounted to anything had the government
not planned it." '

B F: *To what degree was the U.S. government responsible for the
deaths of so many New Yorkers on September 11, 2001?*

D P: In my view, 100 percent responsible, whether by neglect or
participation.

B F: *Do you see any similarities between what happened on
September 11, 2001 in New York City and what happened on
November 22, 1963 in Dallas, Texas?*

D P: Well, Bob, I see a skein of conspiracies that have benefited a
tiny super elite within the U.S. over at least the past 40 years—from
"Dallas" to "9/11" and beyond.

These conspiracies have caused numberless atrocities. They've
caused assassinations, invasions, massacres; they've started wars with
false pretexts; and they've devastated entire countries and generations
through imported violence, oppression and addictions. These
conspiracies' endgame, I believe, is a "New World Order" that will rob
everyday people of their rights and powers to resist the super elites'
accelerating degradation of once natural environments. By
degradation I mean, in part, the plagues and disasters that are arising
now.

The conspiracies follow a pattern. Lee Harvey Oswald called
himself "a patsy" before he was somehow shot by Mafia nightclub-
owner Jack Ruby in the basement of police headquarters. In the

assassinations of JFK, MLK and RFK a patsy was used, I believe, to distract attention from the real killers. With Oswald, an elaborate history was developed over years, connecting him with Communism and especially with sympathy for the Cuban Revolution. With Atta in particular, of those blamed for 9/11, a similarly elaborate history is shown. But with Atta the fiction is much cruder. Mohamed Atta goes from being an abstinent recluse in Hamburg, averse to touching women, to a coke-snorting regular in strip-clubs in Florida.

The whole story of the 19 "hijackers" seems to me a crude fiction. For one aspect of the degrading cartoon it makes us inhabit, at least five of the 19 who were indicted in the United States District Court for the Eastern District of Virginia in December of 2001, these 19 named by an FBI attachment in the case against Zacarias Moussaoui, had declared themselves alive, after all, in Saudi Arabia or Morocco, in the few weeks immediately following 9/11.

To come back to the subject of your question, the killing of JFK and the attacks on 9/11 both served objectives that the superelites deemed urgent, I think, Bob. JFK was threatening to pull troops out of Vietnam and to dismantle the Federal Reserve Bank and to further arms-reduction treaties with the Soviet Union. He'd already yanked former Wall Street attorney Allen Dulles as Director of the CIA. He threatened financial and militarist superelites' profits and plans. So they took him out.

9/11 is more complicated. 9/11 was planned for many years, as pages in Brzezinski's 1997 The Grand Chessboard and the 2000 *Project for a New American Century* study (Dick Cheney, Donald Rumsfeld, Richard Perle and Zalmay Khalizad among its authors)suggest when they imagine that "a new Pearl Harbor" might be necessary to arouse public support for more military spending and U.S. wars in Central Asia and the Middle East.

The colossal, crude crime of 9/11 is also a far more desperate move than the murder of JFK. By August of 2001 the U.S. economy was foundering even for superelites. 9/11 and the subsequent transfusions of Federal capital gave several months of respite. By July of 2002, however, material vulnerabilities threatened to sink even the biggest capitalists.

Through their holdings in "derivatives", the JP Morgan Chase Bank, Citigroup, and the Bank of America are at risk for a combined amount of over $40 trillion—an amount of liability many, many times greater than their combined amount of assets. On July 23, 2002 —on a single day of trading—JP Morgan Chase lost 18.1 percent of its total value. July of 2002 was also when Government and media drums began to beat for U.S. military action in Iraq and Saudi Arabia.

What I see more comprehensively is a skein of conspiracies and pretexts by which the U.S. elitists have ruthlessly killed people and launched wars and grabbed territories and multiplied their profits since the late 19th century. The sinking of the *Maine*, the sinking of the *Lusitania*, the attack on Pearl Harbor, the fraudulent "Gulf of Tonkin incident" are a few of the conspiracies and pretexts we know.

Why Noam Chomsky and other ostensibly moral critics don't call out conspiracies is a question they'll have to answer. It may be that examination of these conspiracies would reveal the real structures and criminals behind them.

All that said, let me end with hope. Only one force on Earth can directly confront and defeat the U.S. Corporate State and its criminal government. That force is us, the overwhelming majority of the people in this country. Despite the horrors of 9/11, the overwhelming majority in New York City are with that same majority around the world, I think, in opposing any American Empire.

B F: *Have the mainstream or alternative radio show producers in New York City been eager to invite you onto their shows to discuss before a New York City audience the issues you raise in your book on the 9/11 events?*

D P: Well, uh, no--I've gotten no contact from either mainstream or alternative radio producers in New York City about the book. Although it lacks a distributor and exposure of it hasn't been widespread, it has been up on the www.onlinejournal.com and questionsquestions.net sites and orders for it are coming from across the country and around the world. I should also add: Neither has anyone from KPFA or any Pacifica station contacted me about the book, though I gave it last December to Dennis Bernstein and Davey D and others with whom I was allied in "the fight for Free Speech Radio" four years ago.

There's an interview with the warm and wonderful Sue Supriano up at www.suesupriano.com and I understand that more stuff through other outlets is upcoming.

The easiest way to buy books of mine online is through the www.wireonfire.com/donpaul site. Thanks very much, Bob, for the ongoing work that you do.

Issue 9
Heaven & Earth
July 18, 2008

Garlic **& grass**

A Grassroots Journal of America's Political Soul

Home   Subscribe   Discuss   Submissions   Resources   Past Issues   Mission   Feedback

Issue No. 8

The Matrix

UPDATED:

Iraq War Truth

9-11 Truth

The Matrix Hides
Electoral Fraud

Watch the Labels the
Media Uses

The Media Matrix
Hides a Party

When Morpheus
Comes

Examining the
London Bombings

UPDATED MATRIX
NEWS REVIEW:

The 'I' Word

Democrats Better
'Republicans' Than
the Politicians in the
GOP

We're All Paranoid

More Evidence of
Vote Corruption

When Media Dogs
Don't Bark

ORIGINAL MATRIX
FEATURES:

Behind the Veil of
the Bush & Clinton
Years

The Matrix

9-11 Truth: A Story On the Verge of Breaking Through

Slowly or quickly, steadily or abruptly, truth emerges

By Tony Brasunas

It's the story of an irresistible force and an immovable object. The irresistible force of truth is slamming against the dense, thick Matrix. The popular movement to discover and expose what really happened on September 11, 2001 continues to grow apace as more and more of the Bush Administration's lies come to light. This huge story is on the verge, finally, of breaking through the matrix and unraveling a significant section of it. Soon, the complicity or ignorance of the corporate media and the corporate political parties surrounding 9-11 could be known to many more than the millions already in the movement....

*How many millions suspect
a cover-up?*

New Developments

1. **A 571 Page Lie.** Esteemed professor and author David Ray Griffin has discovered that the official report of the Kean-Zelikow 9-11 Commission is full of lies and misinformation. He provides a short list of the 115 most glaring lies. More... >>

2. **G&G Exclusive.** Renowned author Don Paul has examined the official story and the available evidence surrounding the full collapse of three buildings of the World Trade Center. He discovers that the best evidence available on whatever occurred comes from the demolition of World Trade Center Building 7 — because this evidence has been provided by the building's developer right on nationwide television. More... >>

Latest at G&G

06.11 - Your more reasoned tones will hopefully bring many to think and investigate for themselves. more >

06.10 - If the facts are wrong, please tell us where they are wrong using proven scientific information. more >

PARTY NEWS
Green Party
Democratic Party
Republican Party
Libertarian Party

ALTERNATIVE NEWS
Indymedia
IPS International
OneWorld
GNN

CORPORATE NEWS
New York Times
Washington Post
other US dailies

NONPROFIT NEWS
AlterNet
Buzzflash
Common Dreams
Democracy Now
Labor Start
Mother Jones
The Nation
Tom Paine.com
The Progressive
Tikkun
Truth Out

FEATURED NEWS
9-11 Blogger

In October of 2003 Jim Hoffman and I put together an 18-page booklet that was titled <u>" '9/11' "</u> / <u>Great</u> <u>Crimes,</u> <u>a</u> <u>Greater</u> <u>Cover-Up</u>. Chris Carlisle particularly helped with our assembling and editing contents.

The booklet had a lengthy subtitle: 'An Open Letter of Sympathy and Information to Families and Friends of the Victims of Events on September 11, 2001 from Concerned Researchers, Broadcasters and Citizens'. It concluded by urging 'families and friends of the terrible day's victims' toward 'an honest pursuit of truth and justice'. It was signed by 15 other 'Concerned Researchers, ...'

In 2004 Jim and I co-wrote the short, pictorial book <u>Waking</u> <u>Up</u> <u>from</u> <u>Our</u> <u>Nightmare</u> / <u>the</u> <u>9/11/01</u> <u>Crimes</u> <u>in</u> <u>New</u> <u>York</u> <u>City</u>, This book brought out more detailed and inter-related evidence, I think, of the demolitions of WTC Building 7 and the Twin Towers. It further explored 'The Financiers behind 9/11' (the subject of my talk to a 9/11 Truth Inquiry at the University of Toronto in May 2004) and it touched on 'Cooperative Solutions' to the overall predicaments that underlie acts of false-flag terror.

In 2005 the Editor of the online magazine Garlic & Grass, *Tony Brasunas, asked me to write about "the best evidence" I knew for "the 9/11 conspiracy". I wrote about Larry Silverstein and WTC 7. (You can check the piece out online via http://www.garlicandgrass.org/issue8/911_Review.cfm under 'G&G Exclusive' .) The version that follows here is augmented by more information about profits for supranational insurance Corporations and partners of theirs in the oil-and-gas, weapons-making, and banking/money-laundering businesses.*

'The Best Evidence Available on the 9-11 Conspiracy'
(article about WTC 7 for the online publication *Garlic & Grass*, June 2005)

Demolition of World Trade Center Building 7 was admitted by its developer on national television

The most revealing statement about the conspiracy that orchestrated mass murder on September 11, 2001was broadcast across the United States more than two years ago.

On September 14, 2002, the Public Broadcasting System (PBS) aired a documentary on reconstrucion of the former World Trader Center site in lower Manhattan. The show's title was --America Rebuilds--. During this PBS documentary, the developer of World Trade Center (WTC) Building 7, Larry Silverstein of Silverstein Properties, said that he and "the commander" of the New York City Fire Department had decided to "pull" WTC Building 7 late in the afternoon of September 11, 2001.

The developer, then 70 years old, whose Silverstein Properties had become the principal lease-holder of the World Trade Center's Twin Towers just seven weeks before 9/11/01, told PBS: "I remember getting a call from the, er, fire department commander, telling us that they were not sure they were going to be able to contain the fire, and I said, "We've had such a terrible loss of life, maybe the smartest thing is to pull it". And they made that decision to pull and we watched the building collapse."

To "pull" a building, in the lexicon of realtors and Fire Departments, is to demolish it. Thus, in its context, Larry Silverstein's repeated use of the phrase "to pull" means "to demolish." Earlier in --America Rebuilds-- a sequence of quotes about WTC Building 6, a building also brought to ground on 9/11, makes clear that "to pull" means to demolish. First, the PBS documentary plays an official's voice on that horrendous morning: "Hello? We're getting ready to pull Building 6." Then the documentary presents commentary by Luis Mendes of New York City's Department of Design and Construction: "We had to be very careful how we demolished Building 6. We were worried about Building 6 coming down and then damaging the story walls, so we wanted that particular building to fall within a certain area."

Thus the immediately evident meaning of Larry Silverstein's repeated use of "pull" in the PBS documentary, aired nationally in 2002, is that WTC 7 fell due to controlled demolition.

How much time would be required for typical controlled demolition of a building the size of WTC 7, a 47-story skyscraper containing about two million square feet of office-space? Based on precedents we'll see below, several weeks of preparation would be required--that is, several weeks before the tumultuous, epoch-making day of Sept. 11, 2001.

For a Controlled Demolition, Call Controlled Demolition, Inc.

Controlled Demoliton, Inc. (CDI), of Baltimore, Maryland is one of the world's leaders in demolishing large buildings. Owned for three generations by the Loizeaux family, CDI details on its website the 'World Records' that the company holds in demolishing huge structures such as the former Kingdome in Seattle. The CDI website also relates the time-spans that have been required for the company's accomplishments.

We can read on the CDI site about a 17-story building of reinforced concrete in Jeddah, Saudi Arabia (the Sheikh A. Alaki Apartment Building) that collapsed while under construction by the Bechtel Corporation in 1998.

The CDI site recounts: 'At the request of Bechtel, Controlled Demolition, Inc.'s team mobilized to the site in less than 24 hours, prepared the central-core, flat slab, reinforced concrete structure in another 27 hours, and put the balance of the building on the ground with absolute safety just 96 hours after the start of demolition preparations.'

So: 96 hours--or four days--was the time needed for emergency demolition of a 17-story building of reinforced concrete by a CDI team in Jeddah, Saudi Arabia.

We can read on the CDI site about its work to bring down the J. L Hudson store, a building that stood 35 stories tall and that contained 2.2 million square-feet of space in downtown Detroit, Michigan, in 1998.

The CDI site reports that after four months of study by associate contractors:

'CDI's 12-person loading crew took 24 days to place 4,118 separate charges in 1,100 locations on columns on nine levels of the complex. Over 36,000 ft of detonating cord and 4,512 non-electric delay elements were installed in CDI's implosion initiation system, some to create the 36 primary implosion sequences and another 216 micro-delays to keep down the detonation overpressure from the 2,728 lbs of explosives which would be detonated during the demolition.'

So: four months and 24 days were needed to plan and place the charges necessary to demolish, within its 420-foot-by-220-foot footprint, a building 12 stories smaller than WTC Building 7.

How, then, could the preparation and emplacement of charges to "pull" WTC Building 7 be accomplished in a single afternoon--in particular the afternoon of Sept. 11, 2001?

Where the Most Obvious Evidence Leads

Let's review features of WTC 7's collapse. The 570-foot tall building and its 25 central columns and 58 perimeter columns of structural steel fell to ground-level in Lower Manhattan in 6.5 seconds--a span of seconds equal to unimpeded free-fall from 570 feet. WTC 7 fell with its roof caving inward. It fell with with explosive "squibs" jetting from its facades. It fell in a precisely symmetric implosion. It fell into its own footprint and scarcely damaged adjacent buildings. Its destruction--which can be seen on many Internet sites--remains a textbook example of controlled demolition.

Upon reflection, the obvious evidence of WTC 7's demolition and Larry Silverstein's statement on PBS of the decision to "pull" the building means that al Queda could not be at all involved in this part of the 9-11 crimes. Al Queda COULD NOT have had the access to WTC 7--a building containing the Mayor Rudolph Giuliani's Emergency Command Center and offices of the CIA, the IRS, the U. S. Secret Service, and more than a one million square-feet of office-space leased by Larry Silverstein to Citigroup's Salomon Smith Barney investment-banking firm--necessary to place the thousands of pounds of more thousands of charges in more than one thousand locations, over a span of days unto weeks, that would be required for the conventional controlled demolition of a skyscraper this size.

Upon further reflection, this obvious evidence means that only those with secret access to WTC Building 7's 25 central columns and 58 perimeter columns could have been responsible for placing the charges necessary for conventional controlled demoliton.

This obvious evidence and his statement on national TV suggests strongly to me that the building's developer and lease-holder, Larry Silverstein, must be integral to a murderous conspiracy that was carried out in Lower Manhattan on September 11, 2001.

The obvious evidence of serial demolitions in Lower Manhattan on 9/11/01 also suggests to me that WTC 7's mortgage-holders as of that day--the Blackstone Group, Banc of America Securities, and the General Motors Acceptance Corporation--must have known on

that day or soon after it of the extreme likelihood that
internal explosives collapsed Building 7 into its own footprint..

The combined evidence thus suggests to me that these three pillars
of the United States' financial establishment may be integrally
involved in a conspiracy to both commit the terrible crimes of 9/11
and to reap enormous profits from the "War on Terrorism" that
ensued from 9/1.

When we look at the different but also obvious demolitions of the
World Trade Center's Twin Towers, and consider the amount of time
needed for the planning and placement of charges to collapse these
gigantic structures as they too fell (straight down into their
footprints), we see that the entity which controlled the Twin Towers
for decades and which awarded the lease of the Twin Towers to the
consortium of realtors headed by Silverstein Properties in April
2001--the Port Authority of New York and New Jersey--must also
come under suspicion as to emplacement of the charges that were
necessary for the demolitions and the attendant murder of more than
two thousand people.

Connecting the Dots

The Blackstone Group. Banc of America Securities. The General
Motors Acceptance Corporation. The Port Authority of New York
and New Jersey....

We're led deeper into the heart of the United States' financial
establishment, as the Port Authority of New York and New Jersey
has long had close ties to service for the Rockefeller family, a family
long powerful and manipulative with Manhattan real estate.

Let me now detail principal people and relationships. See if
they do not make a picture from a puzzle.

David Rockefeller, an international banker who headed both the
Chase Manhattan Bank and the Council on Foreign Relations from
the late 1960s into the 1980s, was the main mover behind
construction of New York City's World Trade Center from the late
1950s onward. His main instrument for establishing the WTC project
was the Downtown-Lower Manhattan Association.

The Downtown-Lower Manhattan Association was nominally
headed by S. Sloan Colt, a financier who succeeded W. Winthrop
Aldrich, the uncle of David and Nelson Rockefeller, as nominal head
of Banker's Trust in 1931. In 1961 S. Sloan Colt was also Chairman
of the Port of New York Authority. which soon became the Port
Authority of New York and New Jersey..

Nelson Rockefeller was Governor of New York from 1959
to 1973. He used his position to have "the billon-dollar baby" that
was the WTC built with bonds funded by the public. He also used
his position to have 20,000 State of New York employees occupy
office-space in the Twin Towers soon after their completion in 1973,
their occupancy making up the then unprofitable Towers'
largest tenancy.

Let's jump to the year of " '9/11' ".

By 2001 the Twin Towers in particular of the WTC complex
contained costly liabilities.

Eric Darton's excellent study of New York City's WTC, *Divided We
Stand*, published in 2000, summarizes one of the property's problems
as real estate: 'To maintain the trade center as class-A office space
commanding top rents, the [Port Authority] would have had to spend
$800 million rebuilding the electrical, electronic communication, and
cooling systems.'

The Towers also needed removal of asbestos that would have cost
hundreds of millions of dollars. In February of 2001 U. S. District
Judge John W. Bissell ruled against the Port Authority's contention
that insurers must pay for asbestos-removal. According to Douglas
McLeod in the May 14, 2001 issue of the trade magazine *Business
Insurance*, Judge Bissell 'threw out the Port Authority of New York &
New Jersey's final claims in a longstanding suit against dozens of
insurers over coverage of more than $600 million in asbestos
abatement costs at the World Trade Center, New York's three major
airports and other Port Authority properties.' Judge Bissell found that
' "The express purpose of (a Port Authority abatement project) was to
stem lost revenue resulting from a loss of new tenants who wished to
'rebuild office space to their desired specifications but who would not
do so unless (asbestos-containing materials) were abated.' " '

Despite these liabilities intrinsic to the WTC, Larry Silverstein
and his partners pursued their bid and outlasted several seeming
competitors. On April 26, 2001 the Port Authority of New York and
New Jersey awarded a 99-year lease for the Twin Towers and much
other WTC property to the winning group, all of whose lead
members were substantial donors to Republican or Democrat Parties.
JP Morgan Chase, the flagship of Rockefeller-controlled Banks,
advised the Port Authority in this transaction. The Port Authority's
Chairman at this time was Lewis M. Eisenberg. The *New York Times*
wrote about Lewis M. Eisenberg in January of 2001 that Mr.
Eisenberg, an investment-banker, had founded Granite Rock Capital
'a decade ago after leaving Goldman, Sachs & Company, where he
made his first dozen millions and forged his initial rapport with the
Republican elite in the Rockefeller era.'

Silverstein Properties and its partners immediately took out extraordinary insurance-policies on their nominal $3.2-billion-dollar investment. (Silverstein Properties itself invested only $15 million). Coverage more than doubled. According to Alison Frankel in *The American Lawyer* of September 2, 2002: 'The Port Authority of New York and New Jersey, which finished building the complex in 1972, carried only $1.5 billion (per occurrence) in coverage on all of its buildings, which, in addition to the Trade Center, included the three New York City area airports. Silverstein's lenders insisted on more coverage, first demanding $2.3 billion, then $3.2 billion, and then, right before the lease deal closed, $3.55 billion.' The new lease-holders' insurance also contained extraordinary clauses. Quoting the British *Financial Times* of September 14, 2001, the *American Reporter* wrote that 'the lease has an all-important escape clause: If the buildings are struck by "an act of terrorism", the new owners' obligations under the lease are void. As a result, the new owners are not required to make any payments under their lease, but they will be able to collect on the loss of the buildings that collapsed or were otherwise destroyed and damaged in the attacks.'

Silverstein Properties and its partners claimed that the attacks of 9/11/01 constituted two 'occurrences' and so they should be awarded the total value of two, not one, of their insurance-policies on the property. They sued for more than $7.1 billion in losses on their new WTC holdings. The obvious nonsense of the claimants' premise (if a property is destroyed by fire that starts in two places, is the property then worth twice as much?) somehow persisted through more than five years of legal wrangling. Megan Barrett in *Portfolio* magazine of May 23, 2007 reported on a final pay-out. 'More than five and a half years after the attack on the World Trade Center in New York, a final insurance settlement has been reached. New York governor Eliot Spitzer announced today that seven insurance companies have agreed to pay $2 billion to settle all outstanding claims. When joined with the $2.55 billion insurance companies have already paid out, the settlement means that $4.55 billion is now available to begin financing the redevelopment of the site for retail and office buildings. The new construction, which will include skyscrapers, a memorial, and a train station, is expected to cost more than $12 billion.'

Parties to the lease on World Trade Center Building 7 also made large profits due to its destruction. The most recent of these parties was the Blackstone Group, akin to the Carlyle Group in the multifarity of its investments, headed by Peter G. Peterson, then the Chairman of both the Federal Reserve Bank of New York and the Council on Foreign Relations and for decades a close associate of

David Rockefeller's. In October 2000 the Blackstone Group bought the portion of the mortgage on WTC 7 that was held by Traveler's Group. In February of 2002, the Blackstone Group, Banc of America Securities, the General Motors Acceptance Corporation, and Silverstein Properties shared in a award from Industrial Risk Insurers of $861 million for loss of the obviously demolished WTC Building 7. The total investment of the lease-holder and mortgage-holders for WTC 7 was $386 million. Thus they shared in a profit of $475 million from classic demolition of Building 7.

Other insurance-related profits followed from the mass destruction and death in lower Manhattan on 9-11.

There were huge increases in the premiums subsequently paid to the largest surviving insurer Corporations. In this regard, an interview that Controlled Demolition, Inc. executive Mark Loizeaux gave to *New Scientist* in July 2004 is instructive. The CDI executive was asked: 'But 9/11 has also sent your insurance up, hasn't it?' Mark Loizeaux replied: 'It's gone up about 2000 percent since 9-11. Not only because of 9-11 but because insurance companies lost a great deal of money in the stock market collapse just preceding 9-11 with the collapse of dot.coms.'

The amounts of revenue and profit for two of the largest US insurer Corporations, Warren Buffet's Berkshire Hathaway and Maurice Greenberg's American International Group, between 2002 and 2004 have been colossal. These Corporations' gains were set into motion immediately after the 9/11 tragedy.

The 30-page Morgan Stanley *Special Report on 9/11* of September 17, 2001 anticipates that the 'largest reinsurers'--including Swiss Re, Munich Re, and Warren Buffett's Berkshire Hathaway--would raise premiums to withstand losses most readily. Morgan Stanley estimated Berkshire Hathaway's losses from 9/11 to be 'around $1.5 billion or roughly 11 percent of premiums.'

So: 'Looked at very simply therefore, a price increase of 11 percent on unchanged volume would recoup Berkshire's entire loss from the World Trade Center.... We expect Berkshire's volume to increase significantly -- probably more than 25 percent. We expect rates to rise considerably more than 11 percent. Without trying to be overly precise, therefore, it's clear that the largest reinsurers should fare better as the flight to quality steers customers back to reinsurers who can, without question, pay claims.'

Huge profits for the biggest insurers thus were evident to analysts six days after 9/11,

On October 10, 2001 the *New York Times* quoted Maurice Greenberg, CEO of the American International Group, as being pleased with prospects. 'Mr. Greenberg, whose company is one of the world's largest insurers, said that prices for some kinds of commercial insurance were doubling, up from expected increases of 20 percent to 60 percent as the industry emerged from a long period of cutthroat pricing. . . . "It's a global opportunity. It's not just in the United States, but rates are rising throughout the world. So our business looks quite good going forward." '

(It's worthwhile here to look at connections between principals whom we've been examining.

Maurice Greenberg is a former Chairman of Federal Reserve Bank of New York and a former Chairman of the Council on Foreign Relations.

In 1998 AIG invested $150 million for a 7% interest in Peter G. Peterson's Blackstone Group.

In February 2000 AIG, the Blackstone Group and Kissinger Associstes announced a partnership that would--in the words of Peter G. Peterson--offer their expertise as international consultants to the 'new global economy' in the wake of 'the recent global financial crisis' to 'capitalize on these opportunities.'

In March of 2005 AIG and the General Re reinsurance component of Warren Buffett's Berkshire Hathaway were revealed to be under investigation by the State of New York for collusion in sham transactions that 1) bolstered AIG's credibility and 2) paid General Re at least $5.2 million in fees.

In June of 2005 AIG adjusted its 2004 profits downward by 12%-- to an unprecedented height of $9.73 billion for the year!)

Comparable to the multi-billion-dollar post-9/11 gains for major insurers are those for oil-and-gas corporations such as Chevron, Exxon, British Peteroleum and Royal Dutch Shell; weapons-making corporations such as Lockheed Martin, Northrup Grunman, and General Dynamics; and money-laundering banks and stock markets through which the post-2001 $180-billion-per-year in profits from Afghan-grown opium are flowing.

These profits are charted or noted on pages 46 to 49 of *Waking Up from Our Nightmare: The 9-11 Crimes in New York City*, Jim Hoffman's and my 2004 book.

All of these corporations are connected in multiple ways through their interlocking Boards of Directors and major stock-holders.

'In 1972, long before the enormous corporate mergers of the past decade,' *Waking Up from Our Nightmare* relates, 'the then Chase Manhattan Bank held 5.2% of the voting stock of Mobil Oil and 4.5% of Atlantic Richfield (now Arco). As of 1993, the Rockefeller family was among the top five vote-holders in 93 of the United States' 122 largest corporations. As of 1997, the Chase Bank and

Citigroup controlled more than half the stock of the privately owned Federal Reserve Bank of New York.

All of these corporations have vital connections to the heart of the US financial establishment, an establishment represented among the financiers who constructed or controlled the World Trade Center before the demolition of the Twin Towers and WTC Building 7.

Such a nexus of financiers currently controls master plans for rebuilding at Ground Zero.

Founding Chairman of the 21st-century's Lower Manhattan Development Corporation is long-time Rockefeller associate John C. Whitehead, a former Chairman of the Goldman, Sachs investment-banking firm and a former Chairman of the Federal Reserve Bank of New York. According to its website, the current LMDC 'was created in the aftermath of September 11, 2001 by then-Governor Pataki and then-Mayor Giuliani to help plan and coordinate the rebuilding and revitalization of Lower Manhattan, defined as everything south of Houston Street. The LMDC is a joint State-City corporation governed by a 16-member Board of Directors, half appointed by the Governor of New York and half by the Mayor of New York.'

Another Member of the LMDC Board is Robert Douglass, who was Counsel and then Secretary to Governor Nelson Rockefeller between 1965-72. Robert Douglass, the LMDC website writes with typically headlong corporate-diction, 'also serves as Chairman of the Downtown-Lower Manhattan Association founded in 1958 under the leadership of David Rockefeller representing the interests of over 90 members of most of the major businesses Downtown.'

But back to Larry Silverstein, spokesperson for the group that assumed such advantageous, nominal control of the Twin Towers less than seven weeks before 9/11.

His statement on national TV in September 2002 allows us access to the nexus of financiers I've began to trace here, a nexus whose principals must have known about the demolitions of 9/11/01 not later than soon after these obvious demolitions occurred.

Their secrets remain our plague.

Following Silverstein's "pull it" and the comparably in-your-face demolitions to logical conclusions as to their sources in a a deeply interlocking conspiracy--a conspiracy most certainly not orchestrated by Arabs--may be our cure.

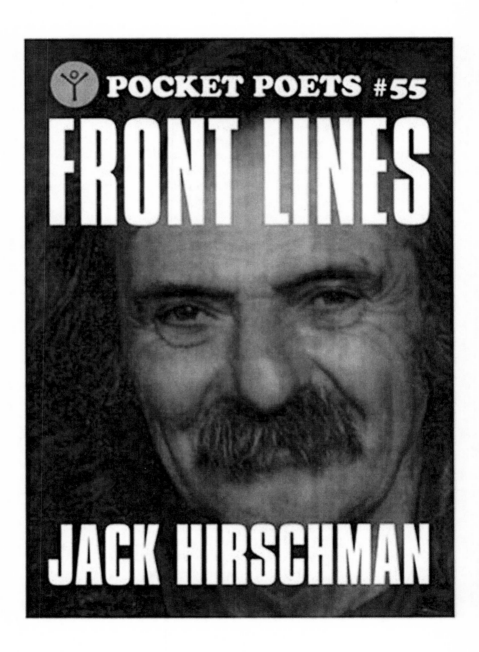

On Jack Hirschman's <u>Front</u> <u>Lines</u>: <u>Selected</u> <u>Poems</u> <u>1952-2001</u>

(In 2002 a collaborator and friend of mine for about 15 years,
Jack Hirschman ((included in both <u>Rebel Poets</u> *cassette-albums*
and the <u>Havin' A Riot</u> *mini-CD)) published a selection of his poems*
that spans four decades. This review was printed online in the
the sfcall.com publication edited by Betsey Culp.
  How it relates to subjects of this book may be evident to you.)

To observe the development of a strong, ardent, creative
personality is always compelling.
  How will he or she turn out? What turns will his or her expression
take? How will he or she resolve the conflicts and desires that
animates any intense lifetime of personal creation?
  Jack Hirschman's selection of poems over a 49-year period, *Front
Lines,* published by City Lights in late 2002, lets us discover and
enjoy his development.
  We can see that Jack wanted to be a righteous warrior early on. Still
a teenager, not yet out of New York City, before the Cuban and
Algerian Revolutions, he wrote "Guerrillas" in 1952: 'In the mountain
caves they sleep:/ The Stubborn Men./ Without the quench of water,/
Without the warmth of woman or child./ Bedpost of bayonet,/ Pillow
of steel.'
  We can also see, early on, that Jack insists whole truth must have a
mystic element. We can see that his open-hearted engagement with
subject, his Romantic surrender to feeling through language and
music, can tend to overstep its grounding in authenticity. His
homages to Allen Ginsberg (1957) and to the burnt-at-the-stake
philosopher Giordano Bruno (1960) contain lines of fine insight and
lyricism, but might speak more if they didn't try to tell so much.
  We see early on that Jack is an advocate of the dithyramb, the
Dionsyian song/dance that values passionate sincerity as primary
virtue, but we also see his care for exact detail, his skill in many
forms, and his tremendous range of appreciations (W.C. Fields, Dylan
Thomas, Franz Kline, Jackson Pollock, Hemingway, Ray Charles, and
Johann Sebastian Bach are some through 1967). We see that he has
the courage and sensitivity to render moments of uplifting or heart-
wrenching love with his first wife, Ruth, in simple, elemental lines.
  We can see that this Jack is unmistakably a poet.
  We trace him into the late 1960s and middle 1970s and we wait,
really, for this poet's voice to find its fulfilling identity. The decade

1965-75 is least represented in Jack's selection and holds the group of poems that I find to be least sure-footed. They're more about the past and abstractions and they're more imitative of passing fashions than those of his other periods. They give off the sense of desperate effort to regather an unraveling center.

Jack then settles in North Beach and commits to regular, communist activism. He'll be a poor poet (he'd lost his post at UCLA in 1966 for helping students resist induction into the Vietnam War), but one who is free and wholly devoted. Here the poetry becomes both more of everyday experience and magical transmutation. From "A Village Poem" onward there's some fantastically good stuff. It's of robust verbs and nouns, non-linear connections, illuminating visions, and profound sentiments. Check out these passages.

From 'Running Poem': 'I want to ride the prairie of your eyelids/ like a pinto of kiss/ and beat on the drum of a river/ till its time gives way/ and run like a small child with a squirrel for a head/ ...

From 'Spirals': 'Onward and upward./ the smoke from the chimneys/ spirals/ spirals even today./ A generation and more/ of clouds/ made of Communists, Catholics/ Jews, Gypsies, Witnesses,/ Gays./ Jet planes fly through/ them. They/ are all over the world/ ...

From 'This Neruda Earth': 'Sitting against a treetrunk in Dolores Park/ amid the Chilean solidarity gathering,/ my eyes beheld three tiny daisies/ in the grass, their little pollen hearts/ attacked by flies. Nearby, yellowjackets/ were flying over a jungle of blades/ of grass and brilliantly green-backed/ horseflies were making merry on a flute of dogshit./ ...'

From 'The Unnameable': ... /O simple sleep of the sitar/ of body./ I play you with my eyelashes/ the way the feelers/ of a cockroach/ writes its brown verse/ to a breadcrumb in the pantry./ ...

From 'Home': '... /O murderous system of munitions and inhuman rights/ that has plundered our pockets and dignity/ O enterprise of crimes that calls us criminals/ terrorism that cries we are fearful,/ greed that evicts us from the places we ourselves have built,/ ...'

From 'The Love Poem' : 'Bliss of all blisses/ lightly you do declare/ intimacy by putting your/ lips right here./... / there is a language called/ Soul, a tongue that is/ the kiss that's the bliss/ of all blisses. Untranslatable.'

From "The Twin Towers Arcane" : .../The rule of nothingness/ is
complete now/ God murdered on one hand./ God suicided on the
other./ The triumph of fascism,/ We're ordered to live out/ our non-
violent lives/ buying and selling/ and praying to violence/ despite
ourselves/ because there's nothing else,/ nothing's changed,/it's only
standing more revealed.'

    You see? You feel him? From just the passages above you may get
how Jack has done poetry's job (the unspoken articulated, the
disparate bridged, the beautiful and monstrous revealed, the
mysterious and tender elicited) with great earnestness, strength and
charm and grace, his unfinished lifetime's long.

On Lawrence Ferlinghetti's Americus I

(In 2004 my neighbor in San Francisco's North Beach, Lawrence Ferlinghetti, published a book-length poem that spoke again of his career's concerns for the United States. The review that follows was printed in the online publication Beyond Chron. *I reprint it here as a kind of breather, a sidelight, and a reminder.)*

Loosely--and musically--for we must both see and hear lyricism that has signs in it--semiotic lyricism, say--the form of Lawrence Ferlinghetti's latest, ambitious and throw-in-banners-of-morning-headlines-from-the-1890s-onward-along-with-whiffs-of-Bronksville-basepaths Big Poem about America unfolds.

In part this book prompts pleased wonder.

How remarkable that someone 84, Lawrence Ferlinghetti's age now, can write with the vibrant detail and liltling flow of many passages in Americus I.

How wonderful that he remains aroused enough to try this kind of epic--and remains untrammeled enough to freely digress within its form. How valuable that we get to see and hear through a poet's raised perceptions ways of life that are long-gone or going fast. How good it is that Lawrence Ferlinghetti is still singing and still swinging to hit home-runs in this year of our Empire 2004.

Americus I spans the 20th century from France's Dreyfus Trial (' "J'Accuse" Screams Emile Zola') through the first Kennedy assassination and the mass coming of Hip.

It's an autobiographical, historical, poetical and fundamentally spiritual survey. Like Whitman's 'Song ...' and Leaves ... and like many other precedents it cites (Pound's Cantos, Thomas Wolfe's novels, Olson's Maximus, Kerouac's Legend), Americus I wants to make sense of our United States of America as the same time as it presents and illuminates its wayfaring teller, its experience-celebrating I-voice, as everyday but mythic and emblematic character ('a wop and a yid in one/ A kind of Don Quixote/ tiliting at sawmills and ginmills/ A Euro man indeed/ ...'),

The poem of 12 sections is for me most effective when it's detailing autobiographical experience or when it's lyrical to a songlike, abstract extreme. Its passages about boyhood stickball in Bronxville ('And the kids playing stickball/ Their far cries echoing/ In this green meadow/ with its worn baseball diamond/ with rocks for bases/ ...') and young-manhood command of a 'diesel-powered wooden-hulled subchaser' on the English Channel late in the night before D-Day ('And in the very first light on the western horizon astern, they were just begining to see a forest of masts rising up, ... a huge armada of great ships and troop transports and escort vessels ...') are vivid. And its lines like song--combining personal romance with general history in poets' intrinsic tendency--embed in consciousness like the remembered waves of Joycean dream: 'While we made love/ Late that night/ In the fall of that year/ Among the yellow fallen leaves/ Under the linden trees/ In Boston Common/ In the fall of that year/ Where now they are marching again/ Wearing colored rags of flags again/ ...'

The book's empathic sensitivity also stands out. Lawrence Ferlinghetti (Americus) registers as 'felt life' the trench-bound impasses of World War I, the first World War in which artillery shells decimated men and horses. 'Look look the horse has lost its head ... They keep coming and coming the brown troops the gray troops the black uniforms in steel helmets pointed helmets my god we're being run over...' He registers also the enduring hopefulness of our public's wishes just after World War II. 'There was still a garden/ In the memory of America/ .../ In the sound of a nightbird/ outside a Lowell window/ In the cry of black kids/ in tenement yards at night/ In the deep sound of woman murmuring/ a woman singing broken melody/ in a shutted room/ in a wood house ...'

The book works much less well when it digresses from tactile experience into cultural survey. While sometimes clever, its notes on German Expressionists ('And Rotliff painted his rusty lust/ And Otto Mueller ate cruellers as his paintings grew crueler'; and on New York Abstract Expressionsts ('with their primal nonobjective images/ destroying the fine arts tradition/ of their Euro fathers'; and on Proust ('a whole belle universe where we did wander enchanted within a budding grove along Swann's Way to a Germantes soiree'; and on Mannahatta's motley mix ('Irish micks and potato farmers/ dustbin pawnbrokers/ dustbin pawnbrokers/midtown clothing-district rabbis/ ...'); and on 'alienated generations' who 'lived out their expatriate visions/ here and everywhere'; and on the national totems fused into the mythic being of L. F./ Americus himself ('He the journeyman poet/ On the Open Road/ He Abe the Railsplitter/ And Ahab the Whaler/ And Sinbad the Sailer/ ...) are notes that often run to superficiality and cliche. They're strangely disconnected. They lack exact, spiritual or physical sensation. Their palimpsest of selectively shared experience misses the 'felt life ', in short, that makes other passages in the book affecting.

<u>Americus</u> <u>I</u> (let's hope for a <u>II</u> and even a <u>III</u>) closes
chronologically with the pall that followed the killing of JFK--that
murder the trigger for violence which provoked hopeful rebellion
later in the 1960s.

From its first section to its last <u>Americus</u> <u>I</u> poses choices for the
public here. What are we to have? What are we to make? Are we to
make and have the embracing, egalitarian freedoms of Whitman and
Chaplin that are beloved by L F? Or are we to have 'totalitarian
plutocracy' under 'Bush League Presidencies'?

Will our every day's subliminal headline continue to be:
'OUTMODED CAPITALISM/ THREATENS HUMANITY/ WITH
MULTIPLE PERILS'?

Will our oil-based, air-conditioned, everything's-gonna-be-made-
out-of-plastic America be Olson's 'foul country where/ human lives
are so much trash'? Will we continue to look back on
something largely like Langston Hughes' 'past a mess of blood and
sorrow'?

Or can our America yet be Lawrence Ferlinghetti's assertive hope
for it: 'the greatest experiment on earth/ with the greatest chance to
create/ a higher human being/.../ at home on the two continents of
America/ made of many cultures and calamities'?

In short, can we let the world dance by joining its potential rather
than destroying its potential? Can we like lightning yet leap forth?

<u>Americus</u> <u>I</u> closes finally with lyrical celebration through the verity
of spontaneous writing.

In this closing passage L F again sides with ... life.

'Yet still endless the splendid life of the world/ Endless its lovely
living and breathing its lovely sentient beings seeing and hearing
feeling and thinking laughing and dancing ...', he writes.

'No end to the making of love to the sound of bedsprings
creaking ... The waiting of lovers on station platforms the cawing of
crows the myriad churning of crickets the running seas the crying
waters rising and falling ... No end no end to the withering of fur and
fruit and flesh so passing fair and neon mermaids sing each to each
somewhere ... For there are hopeful choices still to be chosen ... And
there is no end no end to the doors of perception still be be opened
and the jet streams of light in the upper air of the spirit of man the
outer space inside us/ Shining! Transcendent!/ ...'

"Bravo! Viva! Ride on!" So some young audience may respond to
Lawrence Ferlinghetti, our good, gray, young-at-heart poet, now.

VS

Bessie Smith

Warren Buffet, Arnold Schwarzengger, and Lord Jacob Rothschild
at Rothschild's English estate, September 2002

TO PREVENT THE NEXT
" '9/11' "

ABANDONING
THE 'NEW WORLD ORDER'
OF FINANCIERS'
CORPORATE STATE
(featuring, for 2008,
Auld Crow
and
Sid the Elephant)

SOME POST 9/11/01 FACTS

SECTION 802 (a) (5) of 2001's Patriot Act defines 'domestic terrorism' as 'activities that appear to be intended to intimidate or coerce a civilian population; or 'to influence the policy of a government by intimidaiton or coercion.'

SECTION 304 of 2002's Homeland Security Bill allows the U. S.   Secretary of Health and Human Services to order forced vaccination of anyone in the nation.

CORPORATIONS exclusively licensed to supply vaccines for smallpox and anthrax in the U. S. (BASF, Bayer, and Hoechst) descend directly from Nazi Germany's central cartel, I. G. Farben, a partner of Standard Oil's and General Electric's into 1944. Farben, Standard Oil, and G. E. were or are controlled by interlocking, international financiers, uppermost of whom are the Rothschild and Rockefeller families.

BETWEEN September 2001 and March 2005 more than 30 of the world's leading microbiologists--researchers whose knowledge might combat or refute supposed sources of a new " 'Plague' " from a virus or other bacteriaphage--have died due to causes termed 'suicide' or 'accident.'

THE INTELLIGENCE Reform and Terrorism Prevention Act. passed by huge majorities of the U. S. House of Representatives and Senate in December 2004, 'requires the Department of Homeland Security (DHS) to assume from aircraft operators the function of conducting pre-flight comparisons of airline passenger information to Federal Government watch lists for international and domestic flights', an assumption that may result in the DHS banning any individual from domestic or international air-travel.

SOME QUOTES

'Forcing the states of Europe to borrow at twenty or ten per cent, making up this ten or twenty percent from public funds, holding whole industries to ransom by monopolizing raw materials, ... such pecuniary warfare constitutes the high politics of money.'
> HONORE DE BALZAC on the private financiers of Europe, circa 1829, in his novel <u>A</u> <u>Harlot</u> <u>High</u> <u>and</u> <u>Low</u>.

'I see in the near future a crisis approaching that unnerves me and causes me to tremble for the safety of my country. Corporations have been enthroned, an era of corruption in high places will follow, and the money power of the country will endeavor to prolong its reign by working upon the prejudices of the people until the wealth is aggregated in a few hands and the republic is destroyed.'
> ABRAHAM LINCOLN, letter, November 21, 1864, one year before the Civil War ended and he was assassinated; evidence shows that both the Civil War and Lincoln's assassination were orchestrated by European financiers.

"I think that all of us were really fascinated by the way the U. S. Government intersects with such an extraordinary intimacy with multinational corporations that profit from war and chaos, ..."
> JONATHAN DEMME, director of 2004's "The Manchurian Candidate", interviewed on the movie's DVD

"We're going to have something in the way of a major nuclear event in this country. It will happen."
> WARREN BUFFETT, financier with major holdings in insurance and reinsurance, on May 6, 2002.

"Instead of losing thousands of lives, we might lose tens or even hundreds of thousands of lives as the result of a single attack, or a set of coordinated of attacks."
> DICK CHENEY, U. S. Vice-President, former Chief Executive Officer of the Halliburton Corporation, on the potential use of chemical, biological, and "even nuclear weapons" by terrorists, to the World Affairs Council in Los Angeles, January 14, 2004

SOME HISTORY OF FINANCIERS, FAMILIES, DEBTS AND WARS: HOW TO USE MONEY-LENDING TO CONTROL COUNTRIES AND PEOPLES AND IMPERIL ALL HUMANITY

Between 1818 and 1832 Nathan Rothschild handled 39% of the loans taken in London, England by the Governments of Austria, France and Russia. **In 1868** the annual income of James de Rothschild of Paris, $40 million U. S. dollars (equal to about $40 billion per year in 2005) exceeded the total wealth of any family in the U. S. **From 1857 onward** European Rothschilds lent millions of Pounds and Francs to Morgan and Rockefeller interests in oil, railroads, mining and banking in the U. S. as well as to Cecil Rhodes in Africa. **In 1913** private bankers gained control of the United States' money-supply through Congress' approval of the Federal Reserve System; Rothschilds' relative Paul Warburg went on to control the Federal Reserve Board at the same time as his brother Max headed Government finances in post-World War I Germany. **By 1993** the Rockefeller family was among the top five vote-holders in 93 of the 122 largest U. S. Corporations. **In 1995** the Kuhn, Loab investment-bank, funded by Rothschilds and headed by their relatives since the 1880s, had a member on the boards of ABC, CBS and NBC TV Networks. **In 1997** more than 52% of the stock in the United States' interest-setting Bank, the Federal Reserve Bank of New York (decisive Bank in the Federal Reserve System), was owned by the Chase Bank and/or by Citigroup--that is, it was owned by Rockefeller and Morgan interests and these families' long-standing benefactors in Europe, Rothsichilds principal. **In 2002** the total risk in debts from derivatives held by JP Morgan Chase, Bank of America, and Citibank exceeded $23 trillion. **In 2003** the U.S./British war in Iraq began.

THE 'NEW WORLD ORDER' OF FINANCIERS' CORPORATE STATE HAS NOWHERE TO GO BUT TO TERROR AND WAR

TO PREVENT ...

THE RULING FEW AND WE MASSES
What more to tell? Three major moves against We Masses since September 2002: the war in Iraq, The 9/11 Commission Report, and the vote-fraud and 'psy-op' of November 2, 2004. Introducing Auld Crow and Sid the Elephant. Clubs of the Ruling Few.

BURNING ALL ILLUSIONS/ THE CORE OF THE CRIMES
Advances in knowledge about 9/11/01 over the past three years. Blinders of the " 'Left' " and " "Right' ". Perils of credit and debt that threaten us all.

BANKERS. WARS, SECRET SOCIETIES, THE 'NEW WORLD ORDER', AND ... WE MASSES
More than 200 years of conspiracies by financiers, nobility, and politicians to gain profits and power from wars, revolutions and assassinations. Behind the scenes. Secret bodies for 'population control'. How to become an elitist: the uses group masturbation and secret societies. And the enemy is ... us.

RACE, ECOLOGY, AND THE NEXT "TERRORIST ATTACK"
Divide and conquer. Our boiling pot. The World Wildlife Fund, the World Bank and That Old 'New World Order'. Clubs Wielding Clubs. The next terrorist attack is ' "a virtual certainty." '

SEEING THROUGH OUR CAPTORS' EYES

RENEWABLE ENERGIES AND RIGHTEOUS MOVEMENTS
Abolish the Federal Reserve System1Our own banks. Our own currencies. Our own food. Our own power. What genuine revolutions have done and may do. An 'America' of all the world and of equality for every compassionate person's hopes.

THE RULING FEW AND WE MASSES

'To Prevent ...' begins with what may seem an obscure source.
It begins during the United States' Civil War with a letter from the
Rothschild Brothers investment-banking firm to its associates at
Iklheimer, Morton and Vandergould of New York's Wall Street. The
letter quotes 'A Mr. John Sherman' of Ohio on the 'profits that may be
made in the National Banking business under a recent act of your
Congress', an act that 'Apparently' had been 'drawn upon the plan
formulated here last summer by the British Bankers Association', an
act that 'would prove highly profitable to the banking fraternity
throughout the world....',.

This act was, in fact, European financiers' third attempt to impose a
central banking system on the United States for their own profits. The
same financiers (a Ruling Few of their era) provoked the U. S. Civil
War by manipulating cotton prices.
The excerpt from the letter below uses a third party (the 'Mr. John
Sherman', later author of the Anti-Trust Act) to state cynical
assessments of the ethical or mental capacities of the folk (that is,
We Masses) who are meant to be manipulated by 'the system'. Less
than two weeks after the date of this letter, June 25. 1863, the Battle
of Gettysburg killed more than 70,000, none of them active bankers.

' 'The few who can understand the system,' he says 'will either be so
interested in its profits, or so dependent on its favors, that there will
be no opposition from that class, while on the other hand, the great
body of people, mentally incapable of comprehending the
tremendous advantages that capital derives from the system, will bear
its burdens without complaint and perhaps without even suspecting
that the system is inimical (adverse) to their interests.' '

The quotes that immediately follow the Rothschild Brothers letter
concern the modern Corporate State, terror, war, and ecological
peril.

"Everything in the State, nothing outside the State, nothing against
the State."'
Benito Mussolini, Italian Fascist, speaking in 1925 about the
society that Western media later lauded as the Corporate State.

"The people can always be brought to do the bidding of the
leaders. That is easy. All you have to do is tell them they are being
attacked and denounce the pacifists for lack of patriotism and
exposing the country to danger. It works the same in any country.'
        *Hermann Goering, Nazi leader, interviewed by Dr. Gustave
Gilbert for his Trial at Nuremburg as a war-criminal*

"We remain a nation at war, and intelligence is our first line of
defense against the terrorists who seek to do us harm.'
        *George Walker Bush, 43rd U. S. President, welcoming
passage of the Intelligence Reform and Terrorism Prevention Act of
2004 by huge majorities in the Senate and House of Representatives,
December 8, 2004; the Act requires domestic passports and
checkpoints for all within the U. S. during a state of national
emergency.*

"It's the end of the goddamn world. I keep sayin' it. The animals
know it.... The elephants know what's up."
        *Paul Mooney, African-American comedian, speaking
on his cassette album* Masterpiece, *1995*

What More To Tell?
Introducing the second edition of a topical book that one has
written--and thank you to John Leonard and others for urging that a
second edition of " '9/11' " / Facing Our Fascist State come out--lets
one look back at both the book's contents and at events that have
occurred during the passage of time between editions.
   One gets to check what and how one has done.
   How do subsequent events reflect on the first edition?
   What more does one have to tell?
   Now, February of 2005, three years and five months after the
traumatic horrors we know by their shorthand for alarm, " '9/11' ",
and two years and five months after completion of FOFS, I must say
that 'Our Fascist State'--that is, the fascist State of us living in the
United States--appears to me far more evident than it did in
September 2002.
   Said State in fact appears so inescapable as to be undeniable unless
we--the you and I who live in the U. S., We Masses--become blinded
by the very thoroughness of its agencies. It surrounds us as much as
the " 'reality' " of Corporations' Network TV.

How may we better identify a fascist State?

Benito Mussolini, the leader of Fascist Italy, much-lauded by Western Corporations' media during the middle 1930s, defined in 1932 his totalitarian society 's inclusiveness. Bald-headed Benito said: 'The Fascist conception of life stresses the importance of the State and accepts the individual only insofar as his interests coincide with the State.' (1) 1930s' State Fascism in Italy meant its propaganda/advertising to merge its people with participation/consumption in the society that it called 'the Corporate State'.

We now have the same thing in more subtle fashions, I think.

Who now doubts that the nominal 'democracy' of the U. S. and all Western Governments serves Corporations above all?

Legislators are funded mainly by Corporations. Elections are tabulated by Corporations. Nations' budgets are decided and devoured by Corporations even when these Corporations appear to not be the entities at work in nations' budgets.

One such entity is the United States' Federal Reserve System, a central banking system owned by a relatively few private Banks (JP Morgan Chase and Citbank principal among them) for the private profit of a relatively few families (Rothschild, Morgan and Rockefeller principal among them), the Ruling Few families whom I've come to study and detest more over the past two years. (2)

(Let me now offer a contemporary, 2008 accompaniment to the 2005 text of To Prevent ....

You recall the elephants mentioned by Paul Mooney above?

Can you imagine a crow? Good. A crow perched upon the broad and wrinkled brow of an elephant? Good.

Can you further imagine crow with a Scots accent? That's right--oow, this one is going to hurt--Auld Crow ....

Auld Crow and Sid the Elephant will from hereon wander ((in the Scotch-Irish sense of wander as a noun--"Let's go for a wander and see what we can see")) in and out of the To Prevent .... *text, adding Folk Commentary to the whacky times we inhabit. They'll wander in from their pub, the--oow and oow again!--thee Crow and Elephant.)*

The increasing uniformity between utterances of Government officials and Corporate media--the increasing 'echo-effect' of a de facto 'Corporate Government' that FOFS observed in its first few pages--is only natural within the needs of our whole Corporate State.

Three Major Moves

Since September 2002 there have been three major moves, I think,
to compel 'ordinary, intelligent and compassionate people' FOFS) of
the United States further into an outright fascist State and further into
the imminent, financial and environmental ruin that's evidently
wanted for us, We Masses, by the Ruling Few. .

First was the U. S./British invasion of Iraq in March 2003.

Massive fraud, allowed or promoted by Corporate media, led to
this invasion. Bush and Blair Administration claims that Iraq
possessed " 'weapons of mass destruction' " and both Adminstrations'
suggestions that Iraq figured in " '9/11'" weren't significantly
investigated, much less debunked, by ABC, BBC, CBS, NBC, *New
York Times, Los Angeles Times, Washington Post/Newsweek*
'journalists'. Corporate channels for informing their publics
maintained, instead, the crude fiction of the supposedly threatening
weapons--just as they still maintain the crude and ever more-
debunked fiction that 'al Queda' carried out " '9/11' ".

By early 2005 the U.S./British war of occupation has become an
increasing bog of bloodshed. Every day, still, Corporate media
channels faithfully maintain lies behind war that profits their
advertisers. As Germans, Italians and Japanese were told in the 1930s
and 1940s that they were bringing security to themselves and
freedom, pride, and prosperity to the dangerous peoples whom their
States invaded, so we in the West are told by TV. And the same
Corporations that profited from German troops' invasion of Poland,
Italian troops' invasion of Ethiopia, Japanese troops' invasion of
Korea and China--Corporations based in the U. S. and England such
as Standard Oil and Royal Dutch Shell--now sell 'Support Our
Troops' decals through the very gas-stations that are also selling oil
stolen from Iraq--the latter theft another crime which Corp. Gov.
media never admit.

FOFS stated toward its end: 'A fascist State can only go to Wars to
feed its economic priorities ... The fascists for oil must have their "
'Endless War' " '. Among families, Rockefellers and Rothschilds are
first in ownership of Big Oil Corporations.

(Auld Crow: And a high-flying bunch of nabobs they be!
Zoom! Zip! Helicopters! Lear jets! Next Jets!

Sid the Elephant: They fed me. They rode me. They put tassels
on my tail and a fez upon my head. I wanted to believe them!)

Continuing chronologically, the second major move that I see
against We Masses since 2002 is The 9/11 Commission Report.
Released in July 2004 under the nominal authorship of an 11-
member National Commission of Terrorist Attacks which had as its
heads Republican Thomas Kean and Democrat Lee Hamilton, this
567-page 'instant bestseller' was later nominated for a Pulitzer Prize
in Non-Fiction and other national honors.

The 9/11 Commission Report is, however, more of crude fiction. It
adds elaborate hair to bald lies told by Government officials and
Corporate media prior to it. It advances an agenda of blame with the
prejudicial prose of a low-grade Airport Top-10 paperback. As one
instance, it has this to say about 'procedures' after the 1993 WTC
bombing, a bombing for which the F B I was provably guilty (5):
'Neither President Clinton, his principal advisers, the Congress, nor
the news media felt prompted, until later, to prress the question of
whether the procedures that put the Blind Sheikh and Ramzi Yousef
behind bars would really protect Americans against the new virus of
which these individuals were just the first symptoms.' (6)

Most fundamentally, the Commission Report tries to hide in
sensationalistic narrative the crucial facts of the crimes of 9/11/01
that it misrepresents or ignores.

Regarding the explosive, straight-down collapses of World Trade
Center Buildings 1 and 2, the Twin Towers' collapses that killed
more than 2000 people on the morning of 9/11/01, the Report
simply fails to consider the 47 central columns of structural steel, all
more than 3 feet thick at their base, that should have stood despite
any " 'pancaking' " in each 110-story Tower.

Regarding the collapse of the 47-story World Trade Center
Building 7, a skyscraper that fell straight-down into its own footprint
at 5:20 in the 9/11/01 afternoon, the Report simply fails to mention
this Building at all, much less question why it fell.

Regarding the failure of U. S. fighter-jets to intercept wildly off-
course Boeing airliners that were aimed straight at New York City
and then--50-some minutes later--the Pentagon, the Report fails to
question why North American Air Defense (NORAD) changed its
explanation for these failures three times and why NORAD's
explanations still do not account for F-16s and F-18s being flown at
1/3 to 1/5 of their top speeds toward New York City and
Washington, DC.

The second book by David Ray Griffin, he a valuable 2004 addition to researchers of the 9/11/01 crimes, <u>The</u> <u>9/11</u> <u>Commission</u> <u>Report</u>/ <u>Omissions</u> <u>and</u> <u>Distortions</u>, lays out many of the best-seller's shortcomings. A chart at Joyce Lynn's Website, www.joycelynn.com, depicts the many-layered connections between members of the Commission and members of the Bush Administration. The chart traces Commission members' shared financial interests in Corporations that have prospered from oil and gas, weapons-making, and Banks' money-laundering of profits in opium and heroin due to the invasions of Afghanistan and Iraq since " '9/11' ". Jim Hoffman's main Website, 911research.com, provides more information about these colleagues in criminality.

Despite its bald lies and leaden prose, the <u>9/11</u> <u>Commission</u> <u>Report</u> received glowing praise from more than 30 large-circulation newspapers.

That all these newspapers are owned by Corporations that have profited from the " 'War on Terror' " may not surprise you.

(Auld Crow: Then came the Election. Lovely game, that. Had us poo'ur Believers looking again for the ground beneath our faith, I count m'self, and you, too, faithful bearer, Sid. What a beautiful tool, the computer, when you control its results! Whir! Whip! What you saw is not what you got! Lovely game!

Sid the Elephant: Tassels on my tail and a fex upon my head. They let me vote. And I'm part-Jewish and part-Black. I'm an Indian and an African elephant.)

The third major assault on people's ability to withstand the Corporate State, as I see events since 2002, is the astounding vote-fraud of November 2, 2004.

Never before has the theft of a U. S. Presidential Election been so obvious. Five minutes' scan of the differences between exit-polls and machine-tallies in nine States on 11/2/04 shows starkly the likelihood of massive fraud. In three States that had paper ballots--Illinois, Maine and Wisconsin--results of exit polls and machine tallies of the votes for John Kerry and George W. Bush are identical or closely alike. In six States that had electronic, inauditable voting--Florida, New Hampshire, New Mexico, North Carolina, Ohio and Pennsylvania--the results show gains for Bush of 2% (New Mexico) to 15% (North Carolina). In the two decisive States of Florida and Ohio the difference between exit polls and machine tallies is at least 5% for Bush, making him the winner.

Side-by-side bars of the exit polls and official tallies are at http://www.whatreallyhappened.com/IMAGES/exit_poll.gif .

Exit-poll results were so clear that at 7:00 p.m. Eastern Standard Time on 11/2/04 both the Harris and Zogby polling companies foresaw a 3% national Kerry victory. (7)

Between 1952 and 2000 exit-polls have predicted the results of U. S. Presidential elections within a margin of less than .09%, their margin of difference equal to chance. In 2004 the same swing between exit-polls and official results exceeded 5%. (8)

Later in November 2004 Steven F. Freeman of the University of Pennsylvania computed that the odds for Ohio, Florida and Pennsylvania together showing their respective discrepancies between exit-polls and inauditable, computer-generated tallies (6.7% for Ohio, 5% for Florida, 5% for Pennsylvania) were 250 million to one. (9) U. S Vote Counts found in January 2005 that the differences between exit-poll against official results in the 2004 Presidential election were as follow: paper ballot 0.9%; mechanical voting-machine 10.3%; touch-screen 7%; punch cards 7%; and optical scan 5.5% (10)

What explains the more-than-suspicious official results?

In the United States now 80% of all votes are counted by two Corporations, Diebold and ES&S. The Chairman and Chief Executive Officer of Diebold, Walden O'Dell, wrote in August 2003 that he was 'committed to helping Ohio deliver its electoral votes to George W. Bush.' (11) Executives Bob Urosevich of Diebold and Todd Urosevich of ES&S are brothers and Republicans. Ohio's Secretary of State, Kenneth Blackwell, co-chair of the Bush/Cheney campaign in Ohio, still refuses to acknowledge more than 140,000 votes that should count for Kerry. In Florida all of the discovered errors in electronic voting favor Bush or Republican candidates. In Ohio's Marion County the Courthouse was closed and votes removed from inspection due to orders from the Department of Homeland Security. (12)

In 2004, as in 2000, flagrant racism also figured in the vote-fraud that made George W. Bush the U. S. President In Ohio 2004, as in Florida 2000 and 2004, African-Americans were particularly denied their vote due to State machinations. (13)

Many groups, Websites and researchers have bravely pointed the flaws and/or likely vote-fraud in the 2004 U.S. Presidential election. Some figure in the endnotes here. Others are Bev Harris and blackboxvoting, www.wheresthepaper.org, Verified Voting,

Jonathan Simon, Thom Hartmann, Michael Hout and his team at the University of California at Berkeley, and--I'm sure--more.

And yet--despite the obvious discrepancies and abuses surveyed above--the Democrat Party failed to substantially protest 2004 Presidential election results. The day after the " 'election' " John Kerry conceded to George Walker Bush, his lifelong "brother" in their secret-society of Skull and Bones at Yale University.

And so more than 55 million Kerry voters had to accept defeat from results that overwhelming evidence showed to be fraudulent.

And so these voters were made accomplices to Democrat leaders' acceptance of crimes against democracy. As with " '9/11' ", traumas and then lies were visited on We Masses.

Subsequently all Corporate media and most " 'Left ' " (Pacifica radio, the *Nation* magazine, etc.) media spun the Offical results as coming from a swell in Christian values that somehow gave George W. Bush 9 million new voters despite mass-media Polls that showed less than 50% of the nation's voters approved of his performance as President. To reverse "our defeat", media told us, Democrats and the " 'Left' " needed to organize better for 2008.

And so further acceptance of lies, further denial of abuses, and further perpetuation of illusions were put on us. We were treated as if we were meant to be made stupid and weak.

(Auld Crow: 'Tis hard, Sid. Tis hard to have worked many months from dawn till dark and lost through na' fault a' yer ou'wn,

Sid: It did not feel right. I can tell you that from down here. It felt wrong.

Clubs of the Ruling Few

The vote-fraud of 11/2/04 resembled " '9/11' " in its blatancy and intended effects, I think. Such a massive psychological operation or "psy-op" has been the study and practice of private institutions (England's Tavistock Institute and its U. S. beneficiaries such as the Stanford Institute and Rand Corporation) and Government agencies (such as England's M-6 or the U.S. Central Intelligence Agency) since middle of the 20th century.

All of these private Institutes and Government agencies share leadership who come from the most endowed of colleges and the most subsidized and inbred of families: the Ruling Few. Their leadership also belong to organizations outside State Government whose rules swear members to secrecy. These same organizations (among them the Council on Foreign Relations and the Bilderberg Group) also contain and provide leaders of the United States' Democrat and Republican Parties.

John Kerry, George W. Bush, Al Gore, and George H. W. Bush come from private clubs at Ivy League colleges. Earlier, Democrat W. Averill Harriman, a beneficiary of Rockefellers and Rothschilds, and Republican Prescott Bush, grandfather of GWB, both of them investment-bankers whose mutual partnership with Nazi Germany extended into 1942 (as FOFS observes), Harriman later Governor of New York and Prescott Bush later U. S. Senator from Connecticut, were also brothers in Skull and Bones.

It's about these imperious, ruthless Few and their larger, deeper plot--a plot combining financiers, so-called nobles, and politicians across more than 250 years---that I have here, three years after FOFS, more to tell.

Against these Ruling Few we who make up great majorities, We Masses, have our courage and compassion to mount as virtues or weapons in opposition

The very obviousness of the criminal Corporate Government that we face may compel the resistance we need.

BURNING ALL ILLUSIONS / THE CORE OF THE CRIMES

"Burning all illusions tonight!"
Bob Marley, "Burning And Looting", 1973

Advances in Knowledge about 9/11/01
We have less grounds for illusions and more grounds for hope due to work that's been done since September 2002, I think.

For one thing, we know a great deal more about what actually happened in New York City on the morning of 9/11/01. While FOFS made the common-sensical assertion that 'the 110-story Towers had to be imploded by explosives set off against their load-bearing columns and beams' to not topple sideways, Eric Hufschmid's brilliantly illustrated book Painful Questions and his later Painful Deceptions VHS/DVD tapes made clear explosive phenomena and particulars of the collapses that I hadn't seen.

Websites by Jeff King (plaguepuppy.com), Peter Meyer
(serendipity.li), and the Guardian generously added to knowledge. In
June of 2003 my subsequent friend and colleague Jim Hoffman
contributed his paper 'The North Tower's Dust Cloud: Analysis of
Energy Requirements for the Expansion of the Dust Cloud Following
the Collapse of 1 World Trade Center', calculating that the energy
required to 1) pulverize each Tower's 90,000 tons of concrete into
60-micron particles and 2) to expand their masses into the dust-clouds
that roiled over lower Manhattan was either considerably 1) or vastly
2) greater than 'the entire potential energy of the tower's elevated
mass due to gravity.' (13) His website, 911research.wtc7.net, has
become most comprehensive.

In October 2003 a group of 17 'Concerned Researchers,
Broadcasters and Citizens' addressed a booklet to the Family Steering
Committee for the 9/11 Independent Commission. The booklet, '
"9/11' " / Great Crimes / A Greater Cover-Up, asked why the U. S.
Military failed to intercept any of the airliners that struck targets on
9/11/01; why the F. B. I. and almost all U. S. media continued to
present as dead and guilty the five of the 19 alleged " 'hijackers' "
who had shown themselves to global media as alive and innocent
soon after 9/11/01; why the initial damage to the Pentagon was far
smaller than the dimensions of American Airlines Flight 77's Boeing
757-200; why the Twin Towers exploded as violently and collapsed
as precipitously and vertically as they had; and why World Trade
Center Building 7, isolated and scarcely affected into the late
afternoon of 9/11/01, fell at all. The booklet sold out all but 50 of its
5000 copies within six months.

In Spring of 2004 David Ray Griffin's excellent summary of
evidence and arguments against the Official Story, The New Pearl
Harbor, reached more of " 'Left' " media and mainstream outlets.

In September 2004 Michael C. Ruppert's 674-page Crossing the
Rubicon highlighted the far-flung war-games that Barbara
Honegger, Richard Clarke and *USA TODAY* had earlier raised as
distractions of U. S. air-defenses on the 9/11/01 morning. Ruppert's
Crossing ... charged Vice-President Dick Cheney with orchestrating
at least part of the U. S. Military's failure to intercept airliners from
the White House basement in the presence of the U. S. Secretary of
Transportation Norman Minetta. If you find this Cheney/Minetta
scenario credible you may additionally want to look for Ocean-front
property in Utah.

Also in September 2004, Jim Hoffman's and my <u>Waking</u> <u>Up</u> <u>from</u> <u>Our</u> <u>Nightmore</u> / <u>The</u> <u>9/11/01</u> <u>Crimes</u> <u>in</u> <u>New</u> <u>York</u> <u>City</u>, a 77-page book with 91 illustrations, presented proofs of the demolition of W T C Buildings 1, 2 and 7. These demolitons, we asserted, are the crucial core of the 9/11/01 crimes. Our book's third section, 'The Financiers behind " '9/11' " ', investigated the Who and Why of that day's crimes--examining who had the greatest means and motives for carrying out the unquestionable demoltions, who had a history of most profiting from the United States' wars, and why the murderous attacks of 9/11/01 and the far more murderous invasions of Afghanistan and Iraq that ensued from " '9/11' " were essential enablements for sustaining the West's most major, money-laundering, debts-ridden financial institutions.

Throughtout the months and years since " '9/11' ", too, the Websites globalresearch.ca, headed by Michel Chossudovsky, and questionsquestons.net, edited by Brian Salter, and ratical.org edited by Dave Ratcliffe, and leftgatekeepers.com, edited by Shiu Hung, have advanced our knowledge with ground-breaking articles. Victor Thorn's and Lisa Giulani's wingtv.net has been vigorous over the past year, as has the essayist John Kaminski. Alex Jones' radio show and inforwars.com site have reached a wide audience.

Researchers with emphases different from mine have also raised awareness about the crimes of 9/11/01. Rather than stressing possible pods and flashes re. the aircraft that struck the Twin Towers (as Dave von Kleist's dvd "In Plane Sight" and Phil Jayhan's Website letsroll.com do), or the reptilian otherworldlienss of a 'Global Elite' (as the gatherer and sythesizer of information David Icke does), or pointing out ostensibly 'Zionist' members among gangsters in the world's Corporate Government, we should focus. I think, on provable facts of the 9/11/01 day's crimes and on the most fundamental, human criminals behind our predicament.

To me these criminals' only certain shared characteristic and ideology is a pathology for profit and power.

Exposure of the 9/11/01 crimes has also been helped by activism. The 2004 '9/11 International Inquiries' in San Francisco (organized mainly by Carol Brouillet), in Toronto (organized mainly by Barrie Zwicker and Ian Woods), and in New York City (organized mainly by Nick Levis and Kyle Hence), and the '9/11 Citizens' Grand Jury' in Los Angeles (organized mainly by Lynn Pentz and Kathleen Rosenblatt,) brought hundreds together in each location. During the same span, hundreds of thousands gathered in actions that also opposed the war in Iraq, and millions more of 'Deception Dollars' went into people's hands.

Alternative information has evidently registered with masses of the public. A Zogby Poll in August 2004 found that 49% of New York City residents believed that the U. S. Government 'knew in advance that attacks were planned on or around September 11, 2001, and that they consciously failed to act.' 66% of the poll called for a fuller investigation of 'still unanswered questions' about the attacks. (16)

Doubts about our Government's accounts of crimes have long, however, been widespread in even Middle America. In April 2002 the *Atlanta Journal Constituion*, that city's mainstream newspaper, ran an online Poll on the question raised by Congressperson Cynthia McKinney as to whether the Bush Administration had foreknowledge of the attacks of 9/11/01. Of the 23,145 responses between April 12 and 13, 2002, 46% said that 'officials knew it was coming.' In November 2002 the *St. Paul Pioneer Press*, that Minnesota city's mainstream newspaper, ran a Poll on the question of what or who caused the death in a plane-crash of campaigning Democrat Senator Paul Wellstone. 13% blamed weather conditions, 14% blamed mechanical failure, and 69% blamed Republicans.

Since the late 1970s a great majority of the U. S, public has registered disbelief of our Government's lone-assassin explanations for the murder of John F. Kennedy. In 1996 a poll of 800 respondents in the U. S. by *George* magazine (published by JFK's son John, himself killed in a plane-crash) found that 74% believed 'that the U. S. Government regularly engages in conspiratorial and clandestine operations.' (17)

And yet our widespread suspicions of conspiracies--or our recognitions that 'Conspiraces are history', as FOFS asserts--have not yet seen a single prosecution over more than 30 years in regard to any one of the crimes that are noted above.

The U. S.-Government-connected 'secret teams' (the term of L. Fletcher Prouty, a former U.S. Air Force Colonel) likely responsible for the killings of JFK, RFK, Martin Luther King Jr. and many others (18)--and likely responsible for the bombings of the WTC Twin Towers in 1993 and Oklahoma City's Murrah Federal Building in 1995--have so far escaped the kind of mass exposure that might lead to mass awareness and mass outrage among us.

Blinders of the " 'Left' " and " 'Right' "

One reason that these likely teams and the ultimate shot-callers behind them remain unprosecuted is that the edgiest, truth-seeking groups in our society are divided between " 'Left' " and " 'Right' ".

Why and how has this division been imposed on opponents of a tyrannical Government?

And why do " 'Left' " icons avoid the obvious evidence of conspiracies that have transformed the Western world.?

Why does Noam Chomsky still say that only Lee Harvey Oswald and a " 'magic bullet' " (The Warren Commission Report, CBS News, et cetera) killed JFK? Why does Michael Moore's "Bowling for Columbine" not examine the actual wreckage of the Murrah Federal Building bombing, a bombing that killed 168 civilians and that could only have been caused by internal explosives, not by a truck-bomb, when Moore presents as fantasy-ridden gun-nuts some of the " 'Right-wing' " militia who are blamed for the Murrah bombing? Why does Moore's wildly popular "Fahrenheit 911" not examine the explosions of the Twin Towers and the implosion of WTC 7? Why has Amy Goodman's "Democracy Now" balked at airing decisive evidence for demolition of the Twin Towers even though those Towers fell within the very neighborhood of her program's studio?

Do these failures of journalism or simple rationalty owe to material connections? Do they owe to Moore, our baseball cap-wearing "rebel", working for Rupert Murdoch (the owner of his publisher, Harper/Collins) and for NBC (his TV series' Network, owned by General Electric) and for Viacom and TIME/LIFE (the distributors of his movies)? Do they owe to Goodman's receiving tens of thousands dollars from financier George Soros and the Ford Foundation and negotiating a contract worth more than $1 million-per-year for her team's own pay? Do they owe to Noam Chomsky's office at the Massachusetts Institute of Technology, a central contractor of U. S. military and intelligence projects, being in the same building as the office of former C. I. A. Director John Deutsch?

For whatever reason or reasons, these iconic voices of the " 'Left' " appear somehow circumscribed from going to the core of crimes and from naming names of the Ruling Few.

Noam Chomsky impressively details Israel's misdeeds against Palestineans and yet scarcely mentions that Israel's " 'Jewish homeland' " itself came out of maneuvers in 1917 by two English Lords named Rothschild (Victor and Lionel Walter) through their secret-society Committee of 300 fellows Lord Balfour and Lord Milner. The creation of " 'Israel' " at that 1917 juncture assisted the United States' entry into World War I and established a base for Western Corporations (Royal Dutch Shell, Standard Oil et cetera) against Arab control of Middle East oil riches. (20)

Pacifica radio hosts such as Goodman and Larry Bensky welcome "experts" from the Council on Foreign Relations and the Institute for Policy Studies but never investigate how and why the C F R and I P S are instruments long-funded by Rothschilds', Warburgs' and Rockefellers' money (21).

Most crucially, I think, these and other voices of the " 'Left' " never speak as to how We Masses (the hard-working " 'Right' " included) might effectively unite. Although vociferous in "muck-raking" within their apparently circumscribed bounds, they always stop short of urging actions that could have vital, material effect (see 'The Power of Choking Off Capital' in FOFS.).

Instead, they keep followers marching in circles and marching outside normal business-hours.

And so thousands unto millions of well-meaning people on " 'the Left' " are made to feel righteous but powerless, their energies, commitment and courage wasted on tactics that *can't* deal material consequences.

The " 'Right' " has, I think, its own illusions.

Media of the " 'Right'" (such as the *American Free Press* and the online Liberty Lobby and Freedom Forum) often refer to 'freedoms' of the early United States as ideals that should be restored.

They cite statements by 'Founding Fathers' Washington, Jefferson, Madison, John and Samuel Adams (22).

They fail to note that all the signers of the U. S. Constitution were White and male and from a from small, land-owning 'elite' within the 13 former colonies and that at least 1/3 of them belonged to the secret society of Freemasons. (23)

The Constitution of these 'Founding Fathers' denied the vote to women, to Negroes, Indians and all non-Caucasians, and to anyone who didn't own land. (24) Our 'Founders' also set up the Electoral College to assure that a selected few would ultimately decide who became the U. S. President.

The United States thereafter expanded its territory and wealth through more slavery and indentured servitude, more theft of land, and more mass murder--mass murder that was sometimes genocidal.

While Thomas Jefferson and Andrew Jackson did resist European financiers' imposition of a private central Bank on the United States and did act to protect farmers' and other producers' control of the fruits of their labor, as " 'Right ' " media cites, these dead Presidents also owned Negro slaves, stole Indians' homelands, and promoted the United States' intervention anywhere in the Western Hemisphere (Haiti, Florida, Mexico, ...).

Media of the " 'Right' " also extol the 'free market' of capitalism as the agency for producing social equity and individual liberty.

Capitalism, however, *can't* fairly share the fruits of labor's toil.

In even its purest form--leaving out the inequities imposed by Banks' and other Corporations' usury--capitalism is based on the exploitation of exacting surplus value from labor. Capitalism--or 'Capital'--*must* take more from workers than their compensation for work is. As Karl Marx's monumental portrayals make readers feel, 'Capital' as a means for profit *must* deform equity between producers and managers in the economies and societies its mechanisms invade.

It *must* impoverish or devour an ever wider swath of labor to maintain profits' upward spiral and its own (Capital's) intrinsic overproduction and overconsumption.

It *must* corrupt and bloat the whole of the societies it invades.

Inevitably, too, capitalism's mechanisms must crash.

Further giantized in the 20th-century through steroid-like supplements of multinational debt and accounting fraud, Capital's imbalancing mechanisms must bring its dominated societies to 'corrections' that are also called 'Crashes.'

Then Capital's 'bubbles of Credit' are burst, then 'Boom times' are gone, and then large numbers of *lumpen* proletariat, working-class, middle-class, and even *bourgeoisie* are wrecked. And workers' helplessly indebted ruin becomes a field for super-rich financiers--that Ruling Few again--to pluck for holdings.

Thus the 1929-1940 " 'Depression' " was a field of bankruptcies and desperation for Rothschilds. Rockefellers, Warburgs, Kennedys, et cetera to sweep and pluck in the United States, Germany, Britain, Italy and elsewhere.

Perils of Credit and Debt that Threaten Us All

We Masses are in such a state of peril now.

In January 2005 mainstream U. S. publications such as the *St, Petersburg Times* and *Forbes Magazine* ran the columns 'Debt Game Could Sink Homeowners' and 'World on Brink of Ruin' respectively. (25)

FOFS reviewed the growth and burst of speculative bubbles from the 1990s into July of 2002, underscoring the high-risk debts of the most major Banks (JP Morgan Chase, Citibank, Bank of America) above all. FOFS then wrote about U. S.-based financiers that 'their present and the present of the whole of humanity is an unprecedented, perilous mess.'

Jim Hoffman's and my Waking Up ... book offers a broader survey of how Federal, State, and individual consumers' debt in the U. S. has mounted over the past three decades. One more recent, revealing statistic is that mortgage-holders' debt in the U. S. has risen from $6 trillion in 1999 to $9 trillion in 2004. (26)

Such mountains of debt and and the bubbles of credit inside them threaten us all--" 'Right' ", " 'Left' ", Middle, Black, Brown, White, Yellow and Red....

At the same time, too, we can see remedies directly in front of us. We need only the courage to carry out the remedies we can see.

If we proceed with courage from compassion, we'll come back again to the ancient, simple, universal truth that one for all does one most good.

(Sid the Elephant: I had a trainer like this fellow once. This other fellow would go around the ring, tell the lions and tigers and monkeys and sheep and us elephants we should all work together.

Auld Crow: Oh, this fellow! Like a falcon shot from a cannon after sniffing a bottle of shellacv. Myself, being what and who I am, give me facts. I want meat for a good peck-and-chaw. That's who I am. That's Auld Crow!

BANKERS. WARS, SECRET SOCIETIES,
THE 'NEW WORLD ORDER'. AND ... WE MASSES

'I believe that banking institutions are more dangerous to our liberties than standing armies....The issuing power (of money) should be taken from the banks, and restored to the people to whom it belongs.'
Thomas Jefferson

'People who will not turn a shovel full of dirt on the project, nor contribute a pound of material, will collect more money from the United States than will the people who supply all the material and do all the work. This is the terrible thing about interest.
If our nation can issue a dollar bond, it is capable of issuing a dollar bill.... The difference between the bond and the bill is that the bond lets the money broker collect twice the amount of the bond and an additional 20%.... It is absurd to say our country can issue bonds and cannot issue currency. Both are promises to pay but one fattens the usurer and the other helps the people....
It is a terrible situation when the Government, to insure the National wealth, must go in debt and submit to ruinous interest charges at the hands of men who control the fictitious value of gold. Interest is the invention of Satan.'
Thomas Edison, writing on a public-works project that would be funded by Government bonds issued by private Banks.

'The function of money is not to make money but to move goods.'
Henry Ford

'Compound interest is the eighth wonder of the world.'
Albert Einstein

'We are completely dependent on the commercial banks. Someone has to borrow every dollar we have in circulation, cash or credit. If the banks create ample synthetic money, we are prosperous; if not, we starve.... When one gets a complete grasp upon the picture, the tragic absurdity of our hopeless position is almost incredible--but there it is. It (the banking problem) is the most important subject intelligent persons can investigate and reflect upon. It is so important

that our present civilization may collapse unless it is widely
understood and the defects remedied very soon.'
       *Robert Hemphill, former Credit Manager for one of the 12
regional Federal Rserve Banks of the United States' privately owned
Federal Reserve System*

'Here please note that the money supply of every country in the
world today is dependent on banks and financial institutions taking
ownership, essentially, of an ever-growing proportion of the housing
stock—as well as holding I.O.Us in different forms against an ever-
increasing proportion of the revenue of industry and commerce and
government tax revenues.'
       *Boudwejerin Wegerif, 'U. S. Debt Pyramid Scam',
       March 2000*

'None of our problems will disappear until we correct the creation,
supply, and circulation of money.'
       http://americaondebt.com/earthplusfive.html

'Henceforth be masterless.'
       Walt Whitman

More than 200 Years of Conspiracies by Financiers, Nobility, and Politicians to Gain Profits and Power from Wars, Revolutions and Assassinations

The main education I've received since finishing <u>FOFS</u> in 2002
concerns banking and bankers' creation and manipulation of the
most murderous pretexts, deprivations and conflicts that have
ravaged humanity from the mid-18th century to " '9/11' " and
beyond.
    Among the prime objectives of these private bankers has been
control of nations' money-supply and currencies. While waging
vicious wars of economic conquest throughout the world, these
financiers have kept themselves even more removed from physical
danger than the politicians who have advanced their interests.
    Let me here try to give an overview of this deeply layered history.
    Financiers' conspiracies in the West over the past two and one-half
centuries may be traced through the growing wealth and power of
one family, the Rothschilds, and this family's accumulated and often

inbred allies, criminals equal to them, whether nominal Jews, Protestants, Catholics, Moslems, or other.

Mayer Amschel Bauer was the founding father of the Rothschild family's supranational empire. Born in 1743, the money-lender Bauer became a close associate of the Elector of Hesse, William IX. Bauer/Rothschild profited by lending of the Elector's fees for supplying Hessian troops to King George III of England during the American Revolutionary War. He changed the family's surname to Rothschild (meaning 'Red Shield', their subsequent insignia) to accord with the sign he'd put up for his business: an eagle on a red shield with a golden arrow extending from each of the bird of prey's five talons.

In the late 18th century Mayer Amschel sent one son each out to begin banking business in five European capitals: London, Paris, Frankfort, Vienna and Venice. Nathan in London and James in Paris especially flourished, Nathan most due to Napoleon's last war and James most due to the induced 1819 Panic across France.

The brothers' profits let them gain shared control of the Bank of England and Bank of France and the issuance of these nations' and Austria's currencies. In a partnership that would be often repeated over the next 180 years, they shared controlling interests in these Banks with families of so-called nobility--Tudors, Bourbons, Hapsburgs, et cetera, families who were themselves much inbred.

During the same late 18th century to middle 19th century span, Rothschilds reached into the riches of 'America'.

Associates of theirs and of Illuminati theoretician Adam Weishaupt (Alexander Hamiliton one) figured in the institution of the United States' first two Banks that issued national currency under private ownership.

Later agents of the Rothschild family's (Nathaniel Biddle, August Belmont or Schoenberg, George Peabody, and Junius S. Morgan) worked to frustrate Andrew Jackson's check to any further charter for such a privately owned 'National' Bank. Denials of credit and funds to U. S. farmers and other businessmen by European bankers prompted the United States' ruinous Panics of 1837 and 1857.

Bankers' manipulations were one cause of the U. S. Civil War. Their lowering of the price of cotton pressured economies of both the South and North to desperation in the late 1850s. In 1859, too, Salomon de Rothschild, he the son of James' inheritor in Paris, Lionel, and he the great-grandson of Mayer Amschel, toured the

U. S. and defended slavery, writing that he 'would be as much a "staunch slavery man" as the oldest plantation owner in the South.' (27)

Once the Civil War began, Rothschild agent Judah Benjamin (who'd met with Salomon in New Orleans just before the war) served as a chief advisor to Confederate President Jefferson Davis while August Belmont (formerly Schoenberg) was the same to Abraham Lincoln. (28)

Another Rothschild front-man in London and New York, George Peabody, he the slave-trading founder of an iron-dealing company that became headed by this and that J. P. Morgan over the next century, supplied both Northern and Southern Armies with guns.

Peabody's and Junius S. Morgan's Company also enriched itself by wartime speculations.

'No individuals contributed so much to flooding our money markets and weakening financial confidence in our nationality than George Peabody & Company, and none made more money in the operation', the *Springfield Republic* of Illinois wrote in 1866. (29)

In 1866, too, the *New York Times* observed: 'The Bank of England with its subsidiary banks in America (under the domination of J. P. Morgan), the Bank of France, and the Reichsbank of Germany, composed an interlocking and cooperative banking system, the main objective of which was the exploitation of the people.' (30)

Then was as now, you may see, is in regard to international Banks' control for 'exploitation of the people.'

(Auld Crow: Do yah see, Sid? Facts. Facts 'und figures!

Sid the Elephant: I've pulled barges. I've crossed Oceans. I've borne rails upon my back. This is hurting my feelings ((I have soft feelings, Mr. Crow--I'm part-Black and part-Jewish and part-Mongol and not one damned bit ashamed of any of it.)) I'm getting almost angry, Mr. Crow. Yes, I am! I am Sid the Elephant!)

In 1863 the Northern States instituted another private Bank to issue U.S. currency, the National Bank. The letter that's quoted at the start of To Prevent ... , from Rothschild Brothers of London to their investment-banking associates Iklheimer, Morton and Vandergould on New York's Wall Street, is reprinted in full below. The letter, quoted in J.R. Elson's Lightning over the Treasury Building, slyly uses 'A Mr. John Sherman of Ohio' (a Congressman and later author of the Sherman Antitrust Act of 1890), as the mouthpiece for perceived advantages from this National Bank whose origins actually owed to the British Bankers Association. Always use someone else to speak for your interests as well as to fight wars for your benefit, might be said to be exploitative bankers' maxim.

'Dear Sirs: A Mr. John Sherman has written us from a town in Ohio, U.S.A., as to the profits that may be made in the National Banking business under a recent act of your Congress (National Bank Act of 1863), a copy of which act accompanied his letter. Apparently this act has been drawn upon the plan formulated here last summer by the British Bankers Association and by that Association recommended to our American friends as one that if enacted into law, would prove highly profitable to the banking fraternity throughout the world.

"Mr. Sherman declares that there has never before been such an opportunity for capitalists to accumulate money, as that presented by this act and that the old plan, of State Banks is so unpopular, that the new scheme will, by contrast, be most favorably regarded, notwithstanding the fact that it gives the National Banks an almost absolute control of the National finance. 'The few who can understand the system,' he says 'will either be so interested in its profits, or so dependent on its favors, that there will be no opposition from that class, while on the other hand, the great body of people, mentally incapable of comprehending the tremendous advantages that capital derives from the system, will bear its burdens without complaint and perhaps without even suspecting that the system is inimical (adverse) to their interests.' Please advise us fully as to this matter and also state whether or not you will be of assistance to us, if we conclude to establish a National Bank in the City of New York...Awaiting your reply, we are

     Your respectful servants.
     Rothschild Brothers.
     London, June 25, 1863' (31)

At this same time in 1863 English and French warships blockaded Northern harbors in support of the Confederacy.

When confronted with the National Bank Act and private bankers' demands for 28% interest on lending to the Northern States, President Abraham Lincoln remarked: 'I have two great enemies, the

Southern Army in front of me and the financial institutions in the rear. Of the two, the one in my rear is my greatest foe.' (32)

Lincoln resisted bankers' control by his issuance of $450 million in U. S. Constitutional Notes, currency printed by the U. S. Government itself, free of interest-bearing charges and known by the public as "greenbacks."

Lincoln's interest-free "greenbacks" moved the *London Times* to worry: 'If this mischievous financial policy, which has its origin in the North American Republic, shall become endurated down to a fixture, then that Government will furnish its own money without cost. It will pay off its debts and be without debt. It will have all the money necessary to carry on its commerce. It will become prosperous without precedent in the history of the world... That government must be destroyed or it will destroy every monarchy on the globe.' (33)

The U. S. Civil War killed 365,00 of the North, 258,000 of the South, the great majority of them soldiers, very few of them bankers before this War.

The printing of "greenbacks" was destroyed soon after Lincoln's assassination. this President killed by a secret-society conspiracy (the Knights of the Golden Circle, a Masonic offshoot), a conspiracy for which four participants other than John Wilkes Booth were convicted and hung. (34)

International banks had to wait 48 more years before they could realize another entity (the Federal Reserve System) that issued U. S. Dollars under private ownership.

During the intervening span (1863--1913) Rothschilds and their Warburg in-laws used new and plentifully funded agents and/or debtors (Jacob Schiff, John D. Rockefeller, William Harriman, the Dillon ((formely Lapowski)) family) and Corporations (the Kuhn, Loeb investment-bank of New York City; Standard Oil: U. S. Steel; the Northern Pacific and Southern Pacific Railroads) to control and fleece emergent U. S. industries and territories.

They also profited from thefts that went with Reconstruction.

They also promoted Jim Crow laws, the Ku Klux Klan and racist eugenics.

They also induced the Panics of 1873, 1893-94 and 1907 both to profit themselves and to compel re-institution of a central, 'money-lending bank for the United States that they and their allies and agents would own.

'Because of his links with the Peabody firm, Morgan [John P. Morgan, son of Junius] had intimate and highly useful connections with the London financial world, and during the 1870s he was thereby able to provide the rapidly growing industrial corporations of the United States with much-needed capital from British bankers', The New Encyclopedia Britannica relates in Jim Marrs' excellent Rule by Secrecy. And by the middle 1890s: 'Through a system of interlocking memberships on the boards of companies he had reorganized or influenced, Morgan and his banking house achieved a top-heavy control over some of the nation's leading corporations and financial institutions.' (35).

Again, then was as now.

A memo circulated among the American Bankers Association in 1891 is clear-cut as to one plot's traps and aims. "On Sept. 1st, 1894, we will not renew our loans under any consideration', this memo says. 'On Sept. 1st we will demand our money. We will foreclose and become mortgagees in possession. We can take two-thirds of the farms west of the Mississippi, and thousands of them east of the Mississippi as well, at our own price...Then the famers will become tenants as in England...' (36)

(Auld Crow: Pirates, Sid! Damned pirates behind desks!

Sid the Elephant: They rode me. They fed me. They put tassels on my tail--oh, Mr. Crow, I'm shaking now--yes, I am! I am Sid the Elephant and I know the cargo I've carried!)

The most famous J. P. Morgan was known as " 'the Corsair' ', one who concentrated wealth and power within his U. S. conquests, one who 'knew how to make governments as well as small capitalists and armies of rebellious laborers bend to his will' (Matthew Josepehson, The Robber Barons, 1934). He made competing firms merge into single Corporations (General Electric, U. S. Steel, International Harvester).

And yet the gold this " 'Corsair' " lent to the U. S. Government in 1893 came from Rothschilds of Europe (37) and at his death in 1913 only 19% of his estate of $68 million was found to be owned by his family. (38)

In December of 1913 Senator Nelson Aldrich of Rhode Island, son-in-law of John D. Rockefeller, John D. Rockefeller another Rothschild debtor via the National City Bank of Cleveland (39), sponsored the Bill that created the Federal Reserve System. Henceforth the Federal Reserve Bank of New York--owned

principally by Banks controlled by the Rothschild-funded
Rockefeller and Morgan families and their partners--determined the
money-supply and set the interest-rates for the United States. (40)
Congressman Charles A. Lindbergh, father of the aviator, declared:
'The Federal Reserve Act establishes the most giantic trust on earth ...
The worst legislative crime of the ages is perpetrated by this banking
and currency bill,' (41)

How is the Federal Reserve System unjust and dangerous for
U. S. society? Why is it an insane burden for We Masses to bear?

Through its lead Bank, the Federal Reserve Bank of New York, the
"Fed" may print more than $20 million in U. S. currency at cost to
itself of little more than $20. Further, through a marvelous invention
that's termed 'fractional reserve banking', the Fed's network of
private Banks may then value this nice profit of $20- million-from-
$20 at seven and one-half times $20 million, or $150 million, in
capital for loans.

Those who borrow from this sheer fabrication of capital--
borrowers such as home-buyers, shop-keepers, and the U. S., British,
French, German, et cetera Governments--are then charged usurious
interest-rates by private Banks.

In 1997 the 19.752.655 total shares of the Federal Reserve Bank of
New York were owned 32.35% by the Rockefeller-controlled Chase
Bank and 20.51% by the Morgan-controlled Citibank, according to
Eric Samuelson's article 'Central Banking and the Private Control of
Money' (42)

How much has the United States' debt grown since "the Fed" began
to be the nations' lender?

Sheldon Emry's very useful 'Billions for Bankers--Debts for the
People' offers a summary. In 1910 the U. S. Federal debt was $1
billion, or $12.40 per citizen. In 1920, following involvement in a
World War that financiers orchestrated, the nation's debt was $24
billion, or $228 per person, 'By 1960', Emry writes, 'the U. S.
Federal debt was $284 billion, or $1,575 per citizen, and state and
local debts were mushrooming.' (43)

Now, early in our year 2005, the U. S. Federal debt is $7.5 trillion,
individual consumers' debt is about $10 trillion, and the total debt
mounted on this nation is the barely imaginable sum of $37 trillion,
four times the U. S.'s annual gross domestic product. (44)

Jim Hoffman's and my <u>Waking</u> Up ... supposes that such debt is
setting up the U. S. public for 'Big Falls'--for a 'Crash' and

'Depression' that will exceed 1929's. The resulting ruin would let bankers again buy property for pennies on the (greatly devalued) U. S. dollar and consolidate material wealth as never before.

Based on many precedents, such a financiers-manufactured disaster will likely be accompanied by another " 'Attack on America' " to deceive the public from the economy-based disaster's real causes. And the deceiving act of terror will likely be blamed on the next target in our criminal Corporate Government's " 'War on Terror' "; Iran appears to be a prime target now.

Behind the Scenes

More than a dozen pages in the 'Lords of a Feudal 'New World Order' section of " '9/11' " <u>Facing Our Fascist State</u> survey pretexts that have been used by the United States' rulers to enter wars, invade lands and steal resources.

The survey travels from from 1898's " 'Remember the *Maine*' " to 1915's sinking of the *Lusitania* to 1941's attack on Pearl Harbor to 1964's fraudulent " 'Gulf of Tonkin incident' ".

The March 13, 1962 memorandum from the U. S. Joint Chiefs of Staff to Secretary of Defense Robert McNamara, presenting 'pretexts' which would provide justification for U. S. military intervention in Cuba', is reprinted on page 39 of ... <u>The Movement for Justice</u>.

Deceitful 'pretexts' led to our nation's terrible roll of dead soldiers in World Wars I and II, in Korea and Vietnam, and in Afghanistan and Iraq. We should also recall the many more millions of other nations' dead--56 million in World War II alone--and many more than one million in Iraq since 1991.

Behind these 'pretexts' for war and these dead in war we can see the same kind of criminal partnerships and often the same partners' surnames as we noted among the profiteering beneficiaires of the U. S. Revolutionary War and U. S. Civil War.

We can see that partnerships between financiers, nobility, and politicians form a skein or train through two and one-half centuries of bloody carnage and exploitation.

We can see partnerships between Mayer Amschel Bauer or Rothschild, William IX of Hesse, and King George III of England; between James [Jakob] de Rothschild and Napoleonic Emperors; between Lionel Rothschild, Palmerston. Disraeli and Queen Victoria; between Alfred de Rothschild and Edward VII of England; between Rockefellers, Morgans. Paul Warburg and Woodrow Wilson;

between Max Warburg, Averill Harriman, Prescott Bush and Adolf
Hitler; between Bernard Baruch and Franklin Delano Roosevelt;
between James Paul Warburg and David Ben Gurion and Dwight
David Eisenhower; between David Rockefeller (former Chairman of
both the Chase Manhattan Bank and the Council on Foreign
Relations) with heads-of-state from Richard Nixon to Lyndon
Johnson to Jimmy Carter to Anwar Sadat to Shimon Peres to George
H. W. Bush to William Jefferson Clinton to Nelson Mandela, Henry
Kissinger serving David Rockefeller since World War II; between
Guy de Rothschild and Francois Mitterand and Jacques Chirac;
between Jacob Rothschild and Warren Buffet and Margaret Thatcher
and Tony Blair and Arnold Schwarzengger.

In every one of the Wars listed above We Masses--the working-
class--have fulfilled our " 'patriotic duty' " of killing one another.

And financiers have meant every one of these Wars to leave us and
our families more fearful of chaos and more subject to their Banks
and rule. Why? They want a more complete 'novus ordo seclorum' ('a
new order for the ages'), the motto that Franklin Delano Roosevelt
directed in 1935 should be printed under a pyramid and ancients' all-
seeing eye on the U. S. $1 bill.

Their rewards are plain. 'The fact that the House of Rothschild
made its money in the great crashes of history and the great wars of
history, the very periods when others lost their money, is
beyond question', E. C. Knuth wrote in The Empire of the City. (45)

Their powers are imperial. After World War I, England's Prime
Minister, Lloyd George, spoke about the Treaties and terms that
would bring about shortages and chaos to We Masses and great
profits to leading bankers (along with fascism, the " 'Roaring 20s' ",
the " 'Great Depression' ", and World War II) in the 1920s and
1930s. Lloyd George said: 'The protocol which was signed between
the Allies and the Associated Powers and Germany is the triumph of
the international financier. Agreement would never have been
reached without the brusque and brutal intervention of the
international bankers. They swept statesman, politicians and
journalists to one side, and issed their orders with the imperiousness
of absolute monarchs, who knew there was no appeal from their
ruthless decrees.' (46)

An internal memo of August 1941 that was circulated within the
United States' Council on Foreign Relations--the CFR a private,
secretive body created in 1921 just after the Royal Institute of
International Affairs was formed in England, bankers at the head and

politicians among the body of both organizations--said as regards the
Unted States' entry into World War II on England's side: 'If war aims
are stated which seem to be concerned solely with Anglo-American
imperialism, they will offer little to the people of the world ... The
interests of other people should be stressed... This would have a
better propaganda effect.' (47)

Four months after this August 1941 memo CFR member Franklin
Delano Roosevelt oversaw with precise foreknowledge the Japanese
attack on Pearl Harbor, the pretext for U. S. entry into World War II,
another ' "Attack on America" ' that killed more than 2000
unsuspecting people. (48)

(Auld Crow: You are breathing a l'tl' hard, friend Sid.
Sid the Elephant: That is because I am stamping my foot.
Auld Crow: But, friend Sid, we s'll have to do more than snort and
whistle and stamp our feet. We s"ll have to do more than peck and
gnaw, too.)

Looking at the above, abbreviated record of cold-blooded,
calculating plans and murderous wars, We Masses, the great majority
of 'ordinary, intelligent and compassionate people' in the world, must
steel oursleves and ask: What lets the Ruling Few think and behave as
they do? What gives them their 'imperiousness'? How can they be so
cruel? What lets them plot and execute the murder of unknown
thousands and millions?

The term and concept 'New World Order' may help us to
understand the belief-system behind the Ruling Few's crimes.

We've seen that 'novus ordo seclorum' ('a new order for the
ages'), is the motto printed under a pyramid and ancient societies' all-
seeing eye on one side of the U. S. $1 bill.

'New world order' also figures in leading politicians' stated goals.

On September 11, 1990 George H. W, Bush spoke to the U. S.
Congress about 'a new world order' emerging from the " 'Gulf
War' ". 'The crisis in the Persian Gulf, as grave as it is, also offers a
rare opportunity to move toward an historic period of cooperation.
Out of these troubled times, our fifth objective--a new world order--
can emerge' George Herbert Walker Bush said. (49) <u>FOFS</u> quotes
more from this GHWB speech on its prefatory page--beneath a quote
from John D. Rockefeller Jr. in 1941 that included his belief
'love is the greatest thing in the world, ...'

11 years later, on September 14, 2001, Democrat Gary Hart,
former Senator from Colorado, spoke about the second Bush

President and " '9/11' " to a General Meeting of the Council on
Foreign Relations. Democrat Hart told his fellow CFR members:
' "There is a chance for the President of the Untied States to use this
disaster to carry out ... a phrase his father used ... and that is a New
World Order." ' (50)

66 years ago, on the eve of World War II, H. G. Wells brought out
The New World Order, a book that envisoned a body like the United
Nations as essential for governing humanity. (51) At the same time--
and there's that coincidental phrase again, *at the same time* ....--
another secret-society member and beneficiary of Western financiers,
Adolf Hitler, extolled the totalitarian homogenity of his society, a
vision whose global reach he articulated during World War II. Adolf
Hitler promised: " National Socialism will use its own revolution for
establishing a new world order." (52)

And 70 years ago *novus ordo seclorum* was first printed on the
U. S. $1 bill.

Secret Bodies for 'Population Control'

What may we gather to be general objectives of the 'New World
Order' as foreseen by the Ruling Few and those they fund?

One goal they've often stated is extermination of much of the
Earth's human population.

Literal Lords have offered their ideas about the mass killing of
homo sapiens. Prince Philip of England, husband of Queen Elizabeth
II and a White Anglo Saxon image-of-the-superior on supermarket
tabloids for decades, is also a famous opponent of 'overpopulation.'
This Prince told *People* magazine in December 1981: 'Human
population growth is probably the single most serious long-term
threat to survival.... The more people there are, the more resources
they'll consume, the more pollution they'll create, the more fighting
they will do. We have no option. If it isn't controlled voluntarily, it
will be conrtrolled involuntarily by an increase in disease, starvation
and war.' You may note that His Royal Highness, Duke of
Edinburgh, regards people as 'they'--as if 'they' were something apart
from him. Seven years later, in August 1988, Prince Philip spoke
through Germany's Deutsche Press Agentur about a hope of his. This
Prince said: ' "In the event that I am reincarnated, I would like to
return as a deadly virus, in order to contribute something to solve
overpopulation." ' (53)

In 1961 Prince Philip--himself descended from a 19th-century
King of Denmark and a British-installed King of Greece--enlisted

another European noble, Prince Bernhard of Holland, to head the British chapter of the newly formed World Wildlife Fund. The WWF has since become famous for protecting elephants and worrying about the environment.

(Sid: All this time, I thought they <u>did</u> care about me!
Auld Crow: Yes, friend--and look at what's in your feed-bag.)

Prince Bernhard had a history of serving world-changing organizations. He joined the German Nazi Party in 1934 and helped it and other interests by gathering intelligence for the I. G. Farben cartel, Standard Oil's main partner in supplying oil to the German military during World War II.

After WWII Prince Bernhard promoted the United Nations. And in 1954 he hosted a first gathering of financiers, nobility and politicians that subsequently became annual and whose membership became known as the Bilderberg Group. (54)

Princes Bernhard and Philip had much in common apart from their titles; all four of Philip's sisters married Nazis.

They also shared ties to bankers. David Rockefeller, for instance, his generation's most visible banker, has attended every meeting of the stauchly secretive Bilderberg Group.

Such meetings must be convenient and productive; European nobles such as Philip and Bernhard and Western financiers such as Rockerfellers have been concerned for more than a century with reducing the number of 'people' on Earth.

Eugenics was one effort of theirs to select populations, its so-called 'science' descended from the lies and prejudices of British East Company theorist Thomas Malthus in the early 19th cventury. Malthus wrote in *An Essay on the Principle of Population as It Affects the Future Improvement of Society*': "We are bound in justice and honour formally to disclaim the right of the poor to support'. Malthus' lies and prejudices were further popularized by Sir Francis Galton in the late 19th century.

Eugenics proposed to improve society through Governmental programs of mass sterilization for somehow handicapped or otherwise disadvantaged children, Among the Directors of the first International Congress of Eugenics in 1912 were the patricians Winston Churchill of England and U.S. Forest Service-founder W. Gifford Pinchot, both of them friends of Teddy Roosevelt's .

The movement for " 'eugenics' " attracted more Ruling Few sponsorship after World War I. Prescott Bush and W. Averill

Harriman gave Nazis passage aboard their Hamburg-Amerika Line
to 1932's Third International Congress on Eugenics in New York
City. The Third International ... unanimously chose a Rockefeller-
funded psychiatrist at Berlin's Kaiser Wilhelm Institute for Genealogy
and Demography, Dr, Ernst Rudin, to be President of the
International Federation of Eugenics Societies.

Dr. Rudin was earlier distinguished for founding the German
Society for Race Hygiene. He was later distinguished for writing the
salubrious-sounding 'Law for the Prevention of Hereditary Diseases
in Posterity' soon after Nazis assumed emergency powers due to their
burning of the Reichstag. Rudin's Law sterilized 250,000 of the
'unfit', as Webster Griffin Tarpley's and Anton Chaitkin's <u>George
Bush/ The Unauthorized Biography</u> records. (55)

After World War II, 'eugenics' persisted under different guises.

At the same time as--*a. t. s. t. a.*: that coincidence again!---the
Rothschild-funded and Warburg-led Tavistock Insitute in England
continued to design programs for mind-control, circa 1952,
Rockefeller Foundation millions begat the Population Council under
the impetus of John D. Rockefeller III and John Foster Dulles, an
attorney for Nazis who became U. S. Secretary of State in 1953.

The American Eugenics Society then moved from Yale University
(home of the Skull and Bones' "Tomb") to share a building with the
Population Council in Manhattan.

In North Carolina the slavery-enriched Gray family, owners of the
R, J, Reynolds Tobacco Company and founding donors of the
Bowman Gray Medical School, spearheaded the sterilization of
several hundred children in Winston-Salem between 1946 and 1947.
Alice Shelton Gray and James Hanes echoed Dr. Ernst Rudin's
pretensions by founding the Human Betterment League of North
Carolina. In the 1980s Alice's great-nephew, Boyden Gray (whose
father Gordon was also among the Ruling Few as National Security
Advisor in the Eisenhower Administration, he another golf-partner
of Prescott Bush's during that Administration), served as George H.
W. Bush's chief legal counsel.

In 1988, while George H. W. Bush was U.S. Vice-President,
William H. Draper III (whose father, General William H. Draper Jr.,
was yet another Nazi collaborator and also a promoter of mass
sterilization through the 1930s' Eugenics Congress and the 1960s'
U. S. Agency for International Development), became administrator
of the United Nations Development Program.

Said U. N. Program has carried out millions of sterilizations in the Southern Hemisphere at the same time as-*a. t. s. t. a.* again--the ravages known as AIDS have killed many millions more.

The Bush, Gore and Kerry families all trace lineage to European nobility. <u>FOFS</u> quotes <u>Burke's</u> <u>Peerage</u> on the supposed genealogies of George W. Bush and Al Gore respectively descending from England's Edward I and the Holy Roman Empire's Charlemagne.

(Auld Crow: Little boys! Little boys with ponies and titles and castles and costumes that make 'eem feel fit to rule the world.
Sid the Elephant: Oh, Crow, how I wish I had looked up!)

How to Become an Elitist:
Uses of Group Masturbation and Secret Societies

Along with more or less careful inbreeding (GWB and Al Gore are distant cousins; Prince Philip and his wife Queen Elizabeth II are second cousins; Rothschild-funded associates Paul and Felix Warburg married daughters of Rothschild-funded, investment-banking associates named Loeb and Schiff respectively early in the 20th century) the Ruling Few keep themselves to themselves and control to themselves with membership in secret-societies.

A self-styled " 'elite' " must naturally bond in secret societies to maintain their bigoted conspiracies. They must hold to myopia within own circles in order to deprive and kill masses of others.

Yale University's Skull and Bones Society became more known during 2004 because George W. Bush and John Kerry belong to it.

Every year 15 Junior undergradates at Yale are "tapped" for recruitment to the S and B clubhouse, "the Tomb", on campus. Their initiation is said to require each prospect to lie naked in a coffin and recite his history of sexual performance while masturbating under the watch of hooded brethren.

(Auld Crow: Imagine that, Sid. Little boys! Can yuh see where such rites of initiation will lead us?)

Skull and Bones initiates from the 20th century also include George H. W. Bush and his father Prescott, Averill and Roland Harriman, Percy Rockefeller, " 'Conservative' " commentator William Buckley and supposed anti-war leader William Sloane Coffiin, TIME/LIFE founder Henry Luce, Presidential advisers McGeorge and William Bundy, and several Whitneys, Morgans and Mellons.

The lineage of S and B members typically goes back to early families in the American Colonies who later sided with monarchy-favoring Tories during the Revolutionary War and with slavery-favoring secessionists during the Civil War. Seven Cheneys have been initiates.

In the 19th century, Skull and Bones members were founding Presidents of Cornell University (Daniel Coit Gilman) and Johns Hopkins University (Andrew D. White). The Society also supplied the United States with chairmen of the Secession Conventions of Louisiana (John Perkins, Jr.) and Mississippi (William Taylor Sullivan Barry) and the post Civil War President of the Georgia Historical Society (Henry Rootes Jackson). The Society also supplied our nation with Alphonso Taft and and Morris R. Waite, both of whom helped to dismantle African-American rights in southern States as Attorney General and Chief Justice of the Supreme Court respectively during the Rutherford Hayes Administration of 1876-80. Another S and B member, William Howard Taft, the 27th President and later Chief Justice of the United States, led the nation during invasions of the Phillilpines, Cuba and Haiti. 1888 Bonesman Henry Stimson served as Secretary of War for the Taft Administration (1911-13), Secretary of State for the Hoover Administration (1929-33) and Secretary of War for the second Roosevelt Adminstration (1940-45), Septugenarian Stimson saw and hid warnings of the Japanese attack on Pearl Harbor and then urged the dropping of atomic bombs on tens of thousands of civilians in Hiroshima and Nagasaki. (56)

Skull and Bones is just one club that selects undergraduate members at Ivy League universities who later render national and international service.

Princeton has its Ivy Club (James Baker III) and Cottage Club (Donald Rumsfeld, Frank Carlucci). Harvard its Porcelian Club (Theodore Roosevelt) and Fly Club (Franklin Delano Roosevelt).

All these clubs bond their brothers-under-the-skin to lives of privilege that owe to criminality and exploitation.

All are means of recuitment for bigoted hegemony (like the slave-owning Founding Fathers' bigoted hegemony) and for narcotics-running operations.

Trading in narcotics for purposes of profit and repression is an old story for leading families of the United States. Dope-dealing is one of the four pillars of profits for this nation's criminal Establishment: Guns, Oil, Drug and Debt (G.O.D.D.).

The Central Intelligence Agency, instituted in 1947, has regularly been headed by Ivy League graduates with connections to both investment-banking and traffic in narcotics. Some of these graduates are also S and B initiates. The 'Oil, Opium, Coca, Banks, Stocks & Power' and 'Lords of a Feudal "New World Order" ' sections of FOFS scan the CIA's involvement in opium and cocaine sales. Through research by Catherine Austin Fitts and Gary Webb FOFS shows how U. S. agents helped to flood U.S. ghettos with Crack-cocaine at the same time as (there's that *a. t. s. t. a.* again) the U. S. Department of Housing and Urban Development and private Banks foreclosed on ghetto houses.

Now, early in the 21st century, the world's leading financial insttitiuions depend on the $180 or more billion U. S. dollars a year that comes from opium grown in Afghanistan.

Such dependence on addictions is, as said, an old story.

Many of the United States' key family-fortunes owe to narcotics-traffic from the early 19th century onward.

Famous New England families (Cabot, Lowell, Higginson, Forbes, Cushing and Sturgis) shifted from trade in African slaves to trade in opium from Turkey to China *a. t. s. t. a.* our nation stole Cherokee, Seminole, and other tribal nations' land.

Connecticut's Russell and Company brought the Alsop, Coolidge, Low and Delano families into the drug-running syndicate that it had taken over from Massashusetts' Perkins-headed group. The Russell-led group partnered with the British East India Company to higher profits after captains of theirs bombarded Chinese cities during the 1839-42 Opium War. Franklin Delano Roosevelt's grandfather Warren Delano then served as chief of Russell and Company in Canton, China.

Secret societies such as the Mafia and Skull and Bones fit nicely with dope-dealing. In 1833 the head U. S. gangster in opium, William Huntington Russell, founded the Skull and Bones Society at Yale through the Russell Trust Association.

Subsequent recruits to Skull and Bones (named Taft, Stimson, Luce, Coolidge, and post-World War II U. S. officials inside and outside of the CIA such as C. Trubee Davison, Robert S. Lovett, Averill Harriman, and William and McGeorge Bundy) promoted or protected international narcotics traffic. Recently outstanding were S and B members George H. W.. and George W. Bush, as Afghanistan became the world's leading producer of opium in 1986 and resumed that supremacy after the post-" '9/11' " invasion raised the country's crop by 2000% in 2002.

Thus, 200 years of addictions to opium and heroin and all the ruined persons and homes that go with such addictions--from China to Burma to Laos to Vietnam to Colombia to Mexico to London and Paris, New York, Los Angeles, Sydney, San Diego, Capetown, Rio de Janeiro, Spokane and on--could properly be stamped with the Skull and Bones pirate insignia. (57)

Banks and other Corporations remain, however, the greatest profiteers from narcotics' traffic. Of the $180 billion minimum per year that the United Nations estimates as revenue from opium grown in Afghanistan since 2002, only $3 billion is estimated as revenue to farmers and processing plants in or nearby Afghanistan (52).

At least $177 billion thus must go elsewhere.

A much greater amount--20 times this $180-or-so billion!--or $3.6 trillion!--an amount almost double the total U. S. annual budget!-- accrues to Banks and other Corporations when illegal, secret and untaxable narcotics' profits are laundered into earnings and assets statements that then receive their 20-times multiple of speculative "Pop" on Stock Markets (53).

And the Enemy Is ... Us

And so we come back to Banks and to the few--the most decisive, secretive few of the Ruling Few--families who control the Banks that rule Governments. We come back to Lloyd George's 'international financiers', acting in concert with inbred 'nobility' to issue 'ruthless decrees.'

We see again the biggest and most hidden criminals at the core of crimes.

Finally, however, we in the West must come back to ourselves.

Without our own addiction to credit the world's most famous and prestigious Banks--all of them loan-sharking, money-laundering, 'austerity'-imposing, misery-making and Crash-bound--would fail.

Without the massively inordinate consumption of gas and oil and cars and trucks by us in the West the endless lies and wars that are necessary for Governments and Corporations (the Corporate Government) to steal more oil and gas would be unprofitable.

Without our acceptance of it repression of our freedoms and individuality couldn't continue.

Our ultimate enemy is our own behavior.

And so we must see that to help ourselves, to free ourselves, we need the courage to act concretely from our compassion and for our common interests. Always proceed with courage from compassion. One for all does one most good.

(Auld Crow: Dat-da-dot! Da-dot-da-dot-da! I wish it were so easy as our high flyer has it, Sid--changing yourself and the world!

Sid the Elephant: Now I'm settling down, Mr. Crow, I'm thinking hard. There are big chunks to chew on. The all-around-you-ness of it!

Auld Crow: So you were given your great attributes, Sid.)

RACE, ECOLOGY, AND THE NEXT "TERRORIST ATTACK"

"It's America, man. Ain't a damned thing changed."
>   Joe Rudolph, late station-manager for KPOO radio in
>   San Francisco, when asked what differences he saw from
>   the Clinton Administration, 1993

"I think I'll call it America/ I said as we hit land/ I took a deep breath/ I fell down I could not stand/ Captain Arab he started writing up some deeds/ He said let's set up a Fort/ And start buying the place with beads/ ..."
>   "Bob Dylan's 115th Dream", Bringing It All Back Home,
>   1965

'Merchant, you are a nigger; Judge, you are a nigger; General, you are a nigger; Emperor, old itch, you are a nigger: you have drunk of the untaxed liquor of Satan's still.'
>   Arthur Rimbaud, A Season in Hell, 1871

' ... and usury and mortgage and bankruptcy and measureless wealth, Chinese and African and Aryan and Jew, all breed and spawn together.'
>   William Faulkner, 'The Bear', circa 1941

'The Aquarium is gone. Everywhere/ giant finned cars nose forward like fish;/a savage servility/ slides by on grease.'
>   Robert Lowell, 'For the Union Dead', 1960

Divide and Conquer

The crimes and cover-up of " '9/11' " make clear what's always been here in the United States.

Racism has always been here, used by the Ruling Few through legislation, judiciary and media to mislead and divide We Masses.

And We Masses are always 'being attacked' and 'brought to do the bidding of the leaders' (Hermann Goering) because we fail to rid ourselves of the real 'terrorists who seek to do us harm' (George W. Bush).

And we're always led to blame the Other: the "sneaky" and "savage" Indians, the "lazy" and "opportunistic" "niggers", the "greedy" Hun, the "treacherous" Viet Cong, the "fanatical" and "cowardly" al Queda.

And cloaks of official Religion have always helped to hide the crimes that we of privilege in the U. S. ourselves commit and abet. God has always been on our side in our Wars, we've heard and we've said and we've sung.

Blinding us, too, are false differences and allegiances in regard to ethnicity.

Thus titled criminals named Rothschild can further creation of the State of Israel to further their control of Middle East oil at the same time as (*a. t. s. t. a.*) they and the media they control with Warburgs, Ochs, Hearsts et cetera (Reuters, the *New York Times*, et cetera) can facilitate or allow the extermination of hundreds of thousands and then millions of Jews in the Nazi Germany that Rothschilds and Warburgs, Bushes and Harrimans also financed.(54)

Thus the nominally Baptist Rockefellers can fund evangelical Churches in Latin America with tens of <u>millions</u> of dollars *a. t. s. t. a.* Banks or other Corporations that Rockefellers control (United Fruit, International Telephone and Telegraph, Anaconda mining, Pfizer pharmaceuticuals) take tens of <u>billions</u> of dollars from Latin American nations and impoverish unto death tens of millions of Christian people. (55)

Their system is one I first summed up under the acronym G. O. D. D. in <u>Waking</u> <u>Up</u> <u>from</u> <u>Our</u> <u>Nightmare</u>: it functions through Guns, Oil, Drugs and Debt. The supreme, abiding belief of secret-society financiers/gangsters is belief in their system of G. O. D. D. .

What's new post-" '9/11' " is the extremity of perils that we face in combination with the powers of repression that the Ruling Few hold.

Our Boiling Pot

Let's briefly survey some perils to our whole Earth.

Climate-change is obvious in both statistics and everyday experience. The ten hottest years of global mean temperature have come since 1991. Heat killed thousands in Europe during Summer 2003. 20% of the Earth's coral reefs and the food that they provide have been lost in the past 30 years. Both North and South Poles show accelerated warming. An ice-shelf 1/5 of the mass of Antarctica has broken off. The Arctic and its tundra are thawing and releasing clathrates of methane, a greenhouse gas 20 times more potent than CO2 in terms of trapping heat. An estimated 400 billion tons of methane is held in the Arctic. The last time such an amount of methane entered the Earth's atmosphere, 251 million years ago, closing the Permian Age, 94% of marine life died. (58)

While ecological devastations and perils are real, We Masses should also note (as I failed to note in <u>FOFS</u>) that the Ruling Few control leading bodies in the " 'environmental movement.' "

The World Wildlife Fund, the World Bank, and That Old N. W. O.

The World Wildlife Fund whose study <u>FOFS</u> quotes ('Between 1970 and 2002 the Earth's forest cover has shrunk by about 12%, ...') was founded by the same Prince Philip of England who wishes to be re-incarnated as a virus so that he can do his perceived part against "overpopulation".

Philip chose his fellow Prince, Bernhard, whom we've also gotten to know, first as a young Nazi and then as the initial host of the Bilderberg Group, to head the British office of the WWF.

The Club of Rome's 1972 best-selling <u>The Limits to Growth</u> accompanied early years of 'Earth Day'. This Club was begat at the Rockefeller family's villa in Bellagio, Italy and annnounced by the former President of the Fiat Motor Company, Aurelio Peccei. (59)

Both Cyrus Vance (Jimmy Carter's Secretary of State and a shaper of the 1980 *Global Future: A Time to Act* report) and Lester Brown, Director of the Rockefeller-funded Worldwatch Institute, have called for 'a new world order' as an environmental solution.

Brown wrote in the Worldwatch Institute's post-Iron Curtain <u>State of the World 1991</u> that 'the battle to save the planet will replace the battle over ideology as the organizing theme of the new world order'; Brown also wrote that with 'the end of the ideological conflict that dominated a generation of international affairs, a new world order, shaped by a new agenda, will emerge'. (60)

Lester Brown thus echoed George W. Bush's speech to Congress on September 11, 1990: 'Out of these troubled times, our fifth objective--a new world order--can emerge'

Lester Brown, George H. W. Bush and Cyrus Vance all belonged to the Council on Foreign Relations when they said the 'new world order' statements that are quoted above.

What would a 'New World Order', run by the partnership of financiers and nobies we know now, mean for We Masses?

Based on precedents and on their own statements and formulas, such a 'New World Order' would NOT bring liberating transfers and ownership of technological and industrial capacities to the world's underdeveloped nations.

Instead, such an NWO would increase Corporations' control of those capacities at the same time as (*a. t. s. t. a.*) it brought more billions of U. S. dollars in debt-payments to Banks in the Northern Hemisphere. (61)

Financiers' NWO would NOT change instruments such as the World Bank, the International Monetary Fund (the IMF), the General Agreement on Tariffs and Trade (the GATT), and the World Trade Organization (the WTO) except to increase these loan-sharkings instruments' lethal powers and to further oil-fueled programs and projects of theirs that worsen climate-change.

Here in our 'America' we can see from the increasing gap between the very rich and the working-class and/or poor that the NWO ' "free market forces" ' of David Rockefeller's 1973 Trilateral Commission in practice intend 'a feudal order that will be extended across continents' (FOFS).

Clubs Wielding Clubs

Perils from our genuine ecological crisis and from global capitalism's increasing liabilities--both of which come from a self-styled elite's drives and prejudices--are reason for the Ruling Few to expand repression of We Masses in the 21st century.

'Out of chaos, order' is among their mottos.

Out of more more bloody chaos in the 21st century can come more of the Ruling Few's 'New World Order'.

Laws passed since " '9/11' " allow unprecedented control of 'people' in the United States by our Government.

One such law allows forced vaccination of anyone in this nation.

Section 304 of the Homeland Security Bill, passed by Congress in November 2002, lets the U. S. Secretary of Health and Human Services declare 'that an actual or potential bioterrorist incident or other actual or potential public health emergency makes advisable the administration of a covered countermeausre to a category or categories of individuals.'

According to Jennfier van Bergen's 1/14/03 article 'Smallpox in America', the National Vaccination Information Center maintains that Section 304 is the 'fulfillment of a federal plan in development for several years to allow public health officials to force vaccination and medical treatment on Americans without their informed consent while removing all accountability from drug companies and those who participate in enforcement of the policy.' (62)

Regarding 'drug companies', my October 24, 2001 column for the *San Francisco Bay View* relates information about Bayer and BioPort, the exclusive suppliers of vaccines against anthrax within the U. S.

An earlier *Bay View* column (10/10/01) supposed that the 'Next Wave of '"Terror" ' to strike us might be the "bio-chemical warfare" that Dick Cheney had named in December 2000 as the last of three threats confronting the new Bush Administration. A recession and an attack by terrorists on domestic U. S. targets were the first two threats that Cheney somehow foresaw then,

Another law passed immediately after " '9/11' ", PATRIOT Act 1 from October 2001, says in its Section 802 (a) (5) that 'domestic terrorism' is defined as 'activities that that 'appear to be intended ... to intimidate or coerce a civilian population' or 'to influence the policy of a government by intimidation or coercion'. (63)

Thus, protests such as won the vote for women in the U. S.-- protests such as led to passage of the 1964 Civil Rights Bill--and protests such as helped to end the U. S. occupation of Vietnam-- may now be judged a form of 'coercion' meant 'to influence the policy of a government'.

Thus, those who engage in 'domestic terrorism' may be considered 'enemy combatants'--like Jose Padilla--and arrested and detained without charges, counsel or trial for indefinite lengths of time.

The Next Terrorist Attack Is "Virtually a Certainty"

Leaders in the Bush Administration, in media, and in high finance continue to anticipate that another, even more deadly "terrorist attack" will soon strike within the United States.

In January 2004 Vice-President Dick Cheney, he the former Draft-dodger and Secretary of Defense, he the descendant of five prior members of Yale's Skull and Bones Society, told the World Affairs Council in Los Angeles that the next 'terrorist attack' in the U. S. might cost ' "tens of thousands or even hundreds of thousands of lives" ', according to the *Los Angeles Times*. (64)

The night after Cheney's forewarning, on 1/15/04, the then Secretary of Homeland Security, Tom Ridge, met with the heads of the News Departments of the ABC, CBS, CNN and FOX Networks along with Network anchors Aaron Brown, Tom Brokaw and Peter Jennings at Steven Brill's home in Manhattan. According to the *New York Post*, Ridge and the Network heads and anchors met 'to discuss how they'll cover the next terrrorist attack'. (65)

In December 2004, following the obvious vote-fraud and theft of another Presidential election, huge majorities in the U. S. Senate and House of Representatives passed the Intelligence Reform and Terrorism Prevention Act of 2004, the Act that's cited at start of this Introduction, an Act that requires domestic passports and checkpoints for all within the U. S., an Act that was supported by Skull and Bones brothers John Kerry and George W. Bush

What and who would profit from a "terrorist attack" that used "bio-chemical warfare" within the U. S.?

Part of a four-page tabloid that I wrote in February 2003 and published with the help of Betsy Culp of sfcall, the *Fight Back Bugle*, relates the partnerships between Western pharmaceutical Corporations for exclusive control of vaccines against anthrax and smallpox in the United States. (66)

Three of these partner Corporations, BASF, Bayer, and Hoechst, emerged from Nazi Germany's central cartel, I. G. Farben, the Standard Oil and General Electric partner whose Zyklon B gas accelerated Nazi concentration-camps' mass murder of Jews, Roma, Leftists and others, with U.S. approval after World War II. BASF, Bayer, and Hoechst belong to the Pharmaceutical Research and Manufacturers of America (PhRMA) along with these colleague Corporations: American Home Products, Eli Lilly, G. D. Searle, and

GlaxoSmithKline. Donald Rumsfeld, the current and former U. S. Secretary of Defense, was the CEO of G. D. Searle & Co from 1977 to 1985, a span in which Searle brought poisonous aspartame to the public via NutraSweet and Equal.

In November 200, two months after " '9/11' ", the Pharmaceutical Research and Manufacturers of America formed a task-force 'to deal with the health consequences of terrorist activities.' The PhRMA task-force, headed by Richard Markham, CEO of Hoechst subsidiary Aventis, the licensee for smallpox and anthrax vaccines in the U.S., subsequently met with U. S. Government officials.

For ostensible reasons of national security, these meetings were private. (67)

Since September 2001 more than 30 of the world's leading microbiologists--researchers whose knowledge might combat or refute supposed sources of a new " 'plague' from a viral or other bacteriophage--voices who might point to the real sources of "bio-chemical warfare" in a '"terrorist attack'--have died due to causes termed 'suicide' or 'accident.' (68)

The next "terrorist attack" might alternatively use nuclear weaponry, a 'dirty bomb' such as brown-skinned Jose Padilla is supposed to have intended for a target within the U. S.

In May 2002 another financier linked to major events of the 9/11/01 day, Warren Buffet, spoke to shareholders of the Berkshire Hathaway company that he heads. On the morning of 9/11/01, Buffet, ranked by AOLTimeWarner's *FORTUNE* magazine as the 'second richest man in the world', coincidentally hosted a breakfast party for fellow CEOs at Offutt Air Force Base nearby Omaha, Nebraska. Offutt Air Force Base is home to the U. S. Strategic Air Command Center. It was also the refuge for George W. Bush on the 9/11/01 afternoon. On May 5, 2002 Warren Buffet told media after a meeting with Berkshire Hathaway shareholders that a nuclear attack by terrorists in the Uhnited States was ' "virtually a certainty." '

Four months later (September 16, 2002) Warren Buffet was photographed with Arnold Schwarzenegger and Lord Jacob Rothschild at a meeting on Rothschild's English estate of investors in Buffet's NextJet company. Buffett has since called the threat of a nuclear attack in the U. S. "the number-one problem of our time." (70)

Berkshire Hathaway was a big financial winner after 9/11/01.

In 2002 Berkshire Hathaway's insurance holdings saw revenue from their post-" 9/11' " premiums rise by more than $6 billion and thus more than triple from 2001's revenue.

It joined other giant Corporations such as the American Insurance Group or AIG (headed by Maurice Greenberg, the former Chairman of the Federal Reserve Bank of New York) and Marsh and McClennan (then headed by Maurice's son Jeffrey and the corporate home to 295 fatalities from the South Tower's devastation) in enormous profits from insurance-premiums post " '9/11' ". (71)

Executives Jump to Opportunities

To better understand minds of the Ruling Few, we should look here at how 'opportunties' for 'price increases' concerned high-level executives immediately after human disasters. On the night of the day that their firm had 295 deaths, 9/11/01, Marsh & McClennan Vice-President Charles A. Davis sent a FAX to his President, Jeffrey Greenberg, which 'suggested the formation of a new subsidiary that would underwrite corporate policies', according to the *Wall Street Journal* of November 15, 2001. The *Journal* quoted Davis: ' "We were absolutely thinking about the impact of the attacks and what the opportunties were in front of us." '

Nine years earlier Jeffrey Greenberg, then a Vice-President in his father's AIG, was thinking similarly. In the wake of Hurricane Andrew's devastations to Florida, the younger Greenberg wrote in an inter-company memo that the disaster offered AIG 'an opportunity to get price increases now.' The *Wall Street Journal* wrote two months after " '9/11' ": 'Insurance stocks have jumped 7% since the attacks, outpacing the broader market, and the atmosphere in the industry is one of eager anticipation.' (72)

SEEING THROUGH OUR CAPTORS' EYES

'Our--
Bodies undergoing   Fast mutation   Spread in lines
Compact with dispossession   From the U. S. casting

Into ev'ry heart   Ev'ry mind   And ev'ry eye--eye-I-I-I-eye
    With the spurious perk of a Pop jingle
    A-mer-i-Modern! It does things for you--
          America'
               '<u>AmeriModern</u>', 1977-1982

By now you may be thinking about the Ruling Few: what monsters!

You may be thinking: What totalitarian realties already surround us in the U. S.!

You may be thinking: What a Corporate State already watches and enfolds us!

You may be thinking: What a future of disasters, repression and regimentation appears to be plotted for us!

You may also be pausing with wonder at the reasons why.

Why is so much devastation, pain, loss and trouble evidently ahead for 'people' in the world? How does any of this make sense?

We must learn to see, I think, from the Ruling Few's points of view.

What reasons might these Few have for the obviously foreseeable bog of bloodshed that this Bush Administration has made in Iraq? Why might financiers whose institutions remain European at their bases want the George W. Bush Administration to extend the already struggling U. S. Military into more war in the Middle East? Why would an already strapped military invade Iran or Syria?

Why are We Masses here in the U. S. still being offered lines of credit to pile on our mountains of debt when the amount owed on home-buyers' mortgages here has risen by $3 trillion since 1999?

The answer may be that the Ruling Few intend to gut the last remnants of the public's power in the U. S.

The answer may be that the United States which many of We Masses have always hoped would be--the 'America' of democracy, freedom, choice and opportunity, the home to working-people's hopes that wave like grass throughout Walt Whitman's multiracial cosmos, the American 'Eagle' of William Blake's whose revolutionary Demon was to leave Europe's 'Guardian overthrown' (<u>AmeriModern</u>) --that ideal of 'America' which has never been realized during our actual history of mass murder, slavery, theft and exclusion under an eternal oligarchy of successive gentry and gangsters ... the answer may be that such a hoped-for ideal of a truly 'New World ... America' is meant by largely hidden forces to be finally undermined and wrecked.

European financiers have always coveted the wealth of natural resources in 'America'.

These families of financiers, based primarily in Europe, have always feared natives' genuine self-determination anywhere.

European financiers have three times used agents to impose control of United States currency by private Banks. 'Is there no danger to our liberty and independence in a bank that in its nature has so little to bind it to our country?" Andrew Jackson said in vetoing a second charter to the Bank of the United States in 1832 (73). And we know that share-holding control of the key, interest-setting Bank in the Federal Reserve System, the Federal Reserve Bank of New York, extends from JP Morgan Chase and Citibank back to institutions in the City of London and elsewhere in Europe.

The present burden of debts on the United States and its people may make perverse sense to you if seen as the grounds for two objectives.

First is maintenance of the supranational systems of credit that lets the West's major private Banks and other financial pillars stand despite trillions of U. S. dollars in liabilities (liabilities noted with some detail in FOFS and Waking Up ...).

Second is the ruin of the general, mortgage-holding public of the U. S. when Banks again--as in 1857, 1894, 1929 and other years-- refuse more credit, demand payments, and then balance their own liabilities by sweeping up debtors' properties for nothing or next-to-nothing.

Financiers who have long proved their allegiance to no nation-- their State may be said to be of Profits-And-Power-Alone (PAPA), just as their system is of Guns-Oil-Drugs-Debt (GODD)--may also devalue the U. S. dollar for their ends.

Since 1971 the U. S. dollar has been cut from the gold-standard or any other solid, material basis. Despite rising U. S. deficits and debts the value of the U. S. dollar has been kept up because U. S. military might and other economies' co-dependence on illusions compels the world's most traded commodity, oil, to be purchased in U. S. dollars. Massive influxes of U. S. dollar-buying capital from the Far East have also sustained our credit-economy. Within the past six months, of 2004-2005, however, the Eurodollar has risen about 30% in value against the U. S. dollar.

Sooner or later--and probably soon--nations and Banks outside the

the U. S. will declare that buying and selling oil in dollars that are actually worth 70 cents is not sound fiscal policy

Then will come a 'Crash' such as not seen before, a Crash anticipated even by Establishment economists Stephen Lynch and Paul Volcker. When supports to the U. S. dollar are pulled away-- when one major supplier or buyer of oil (such as Russia or China or even Norway) declines to use the U. S. dollar as its means of exchange and to rather, say, trade in Eurodollars on Iran's prospective Bourse, nothing solid will be there to stop U. S. currency's fall. The heaps of paper wealth housed on suburban Hills of the U. S. will be subject to disappearance like homes in fire and flood.

In this scenario, too, the supranational Corporate Government's intention of reducing an already traumatized U. S. populace (recall the Rothschild Brothers' letter of 1863: ' ... the great body of people, mentally incapable ...') to credit-enslaved servitude can be more fully realized.

With the crash of the U. S. dollar and that crash's accompanying wreckage, possibilities for natives' resistance to bankers' control could finally be disarmed. The U. S. could be made <u>more</u> like Third World societies of a managerial Few above laboring Masses.

Recall also the American Bankers Association memo of 1891 and its intentions: 'We will foreclose and become mortgagees in possession. We can take two-thirds of the farms west of the Mississippi, and thousands of them east of the Mississippi as well, ... Then the famers will become tenants as in England...'

If such ruin and re-ordering (the New World Order is 'both fascist and feudal at its roots', <u>FOFS</u> observed) is the Ruling Few's objective, the permitted vote-fraud of 11/2/04 and the past four U. S. Presidencies' especially destructive and thieving policies make sense for the Ruling Few.

If such ruinous objectives are among the Ruling Few's goals, the bloody bog in Iraq and a further miring of the U. S. in the Middle East make sense for them. 'The New World Order will have to paid for in blood as well as diplomacy and economic policy,' Harvard Professor of History Arthur S, Schlesinger, adviser and biographer of John F, Kennedy and member of the Council on Foreign Relations, said in 1995. (74)

If such final pillage of the public's posterity is the Ruling Few's objective, the Clinton and two Bush Administrations' looting of social services ($1.9 trillion taken away during the Clinton Administration's eight years, $1.5 trillion taken away during the first GWB term as U. S. President) makes similar sense. (75)

If a Crash and a Draft and other violent assaults on personal well-being are intended for the U. S., the police-state powers of the Homeland Security Bill, PATRIOT Act I, and the Intelligence Reform and Terrorism Prevention Act of 2004 make sense.

And if such further ruin and definitive repression are intended, nothing makes better sense for the Ruling Few than the execution of another " 'Attack on America' ", another 'terrorist attack' that could fulfill Dick Cheney's prediction of the loss of ' "tens of thousands or even hundreds of thousands of lives" ', in order to blind We Masses as to the real causes of the devastations we're to suffer.

Such are the prospects we must act to prevent.

(Auld Crow: Well. Sid. Friend. How are yuh feelin' down there?

Sid the Elepehant: I feel cold and hollow and angry at the same time, Mr. Crow. I feel betrayed as if my master stole my children. I am seeing with straight eyes. I am ready to charge, Auld Crow.)

RENEWABLE ENERGIES AND RIGHTEOUS MOVEMENTS

'We are all responsible. You, reader, are responsible. If you are a Republican, your party has made this action part of its national policy. If you are a Democrat, your party, by its vote in the House of Representatives, made the war possible ...'

The *San Francisco Argonaut* editorializes in 1902 on its readers' complicity with the United States' war to make the Phillipines our colony instead of Spain's; this little-know U. S. war killed more than a million Filipinos

Willie: What is it with you, Freeman? What do you want out of this? Power? Money?

Freeman: I want to be free.

      from "The Spook Who Sat by the Door", 1971 movie written by Sam Greenlee and Mel Clay and directed by Ivan Dixon.

'I do believe, from the experiences that I have had with them, that the whites of the younger generation, in the colleges and universities,

will see the handwriting on the wall and many of them will turn to
the *spiritual* path of truth--the *only* way left to America to ward off
the disaster that racism inevitably must lead to.'
Malcolm X in his 1965 <u>Autobiography</u>

'In no way can we get such an overwhelming idea of the grandeur
of Nature, as when we consider, that in accordance with the law of
the conservation of energy, throughout the infinite, the
forces are in a perfect balance, and hence the energy of a single
thought may determine the motion of a Universe.'
Nikolas Tesla, 'On Light and Other High-Frequency
Phenomena', talk in Philadelphia and St. Louis, 1893

Abolish the Federal Reserve System!
Our Own Banks. Our Own Currencies.

There are peaceful ways out of our predicament in the U. S.

Each will require radical changes and collective action by We
Masses if they're to succeed. Each will require us to refuse denial,
abandon illusions, shake off the traumas that have been visited on us,
throw off repression, and pursue remedial justice that includes
everyone in our society.

Each will require people's righteous movements across lines of race
and class--movements such as HAVE succeeded here and elsewhere
in the world.

In the United States the first, fundamental task of realizing a
Government by, for and of the people and not a Government by, for
and of Corporations is, I think, abolition of the Federal Reserve
System and its currency-issuing, interest-setting, debt-holding Banks.

As I hope is now clear, the primary motive for the criminal
monsters who orchestrated " '9/11' ", the latest of their families'
centuries-long 'pretexts' for U. S. wars, is their desperation to sustain
a system so irrational, so decrepit, and so *contra natura* that its most
exploitative parts, the most major private Banks (JP Morgan Chase,
Citibank, Bank of America, et cetera), are themselves most
overloaded and vulnerable due to the debts that they too have
assumed to keep going.

We must step out and away from their holds, their death-grips
(*mortgages*), and their lying and bigoted rationales for insanity.

We must remove our resources from a system which criminalizes and endangers us before another " 'Crash' " of that system crushes us.

A Government that prints its own money is free of the insanity of letting private institutions--controlled by a relatively few Banks that are themselves owned by a relatively few families--create the Government's money at no cost to themselves except that of printing bills.

Such an insanity is literally compounded when private, for-profit, national Banks lend money and charge interest to their supposed Governments from the very money that said Governments let said Banks print.

If, however, we abolished the "Fed" and had a Government that printed its own money--a Government such as was briefly present during the Presidencies of Abraham Lincoln and John F. Kennedy--we in the U. S. might achieve that independent State which was dreaded by the financiers-owned *London Times* in 1863: 'that Government will furnish its own money without cost. It will pay off its debts and be without debt. It will have all the money necessary to carry on its commerce. It will become prosperous without precedent in the history of the world.'

We can also can make changes on our own at local levels.

Credit unions are one way to step away from Banks.

Credit unions can arise from the pooled resources of any community, whether the community is from a neighborhood or from a grouping of working-people or from a combinations of groupings from neighborhodds and working-people.

Community currencies are an even bigger step for groups to achieve financial independence.

Community currencies substitute local means of exchange for State money. During the 1930s Depression more than 1900 local currencies arose in the U. S. Now--after the so-called " 'dot.com' " Bust of 1999-2001--more than 1900 local currencies are being exchanged in different places around the world.

Ithaca's 'Hours' are exchanged within a 50-mile radius of this town in upstate New York. Alain Pilote writes: 'Over 1,000 goods and services are available for purchase with Ithaca Hours, and they are accepted in some 250 businesses throughout the area. Since 1991, over $60,000 of local paper money has been issued, causing 2,000,000 of local trading to be added to the "Grassroots National Product".' (76)

In Minneapolis, Minnesota 'Community Hero Cards' have been exchanged instead of U. S. dollars since 1998. In Austin, Texas 'Liberty Dollars' have begun to circulate.

In Japan, following a 1999 TV documentary about the Swiss writer Michael Ende, more than 100 communities have begun to use each's own form of debt-free money; more than 500,000 Earthday bills have changed hands in Tokyo's Shibuya district alone.

Barter is spreading via the Internet. *Barter News* estimated 1997's trade in barter to be $650 billion. Websites engaging in trade without the use of commercial Banks' money are proliferating.

Our Own Power. Our Own Food
Community-based production of electricity and food is likewise increasing.

By 1995 19 German cities with a total population of 5 million were offering rate-based incentives for the installation of photo-voltaic cells to provide solar power. (77)

In Denmark agricultural cooperatives and individual farmers have combined to produce 1000 megawatts of wind-power annually since 1981. The Global Wind-Power Conference in Chicago in March 2004 found that: 'Wind power has expanded at an average of 28% annually over the past five years. The United States added 1,687 megawatts of clean, renewable wind energy capacity; Europe added 5,467 megawatts during the same time period.' (78)

Wind-power is already most inexpensive. The European Wind Energy Association's current measurement of 3.79 European cents cost per kilowatt-hour of wind-power compares with the U. S. national average cost for electricity in April 2004 of 7.56 U. S. cents per kilowatt-hour. European wind-power's cost to consumers is thus about half the cost of electricity to consumers in the U. S.

The above alternatives are referenced in the 'Cooperative Solutions' section of <u>Waking Up from Our Nightmare</u>.

James Richards of New York City recently sent out an e-mail compilation of additional alternatives to oil and gas.

Brasil now uses ethanol from sugar beets, sugar cane, corn and potatoes (www.newstarget.com/001494.html), Manufacturers in Sweden are turning to methanol (www.iags.org/n54404t3.htm). Roy McAlister continues to explain and promote fuel cells and hydrogen generators (www.knowledgepublications.com/page2.htm.) Yokayo Biofuels reminds us that the diesel engine was originally designed to run on peanut oil (www.ybiofuels.org/bio_fuels/history_diesel.html).

Organic farming can also reduce our dependence on fossil fuels.

Cuba's change to organic farming after its loss of Soviet Bloc oil in 1989-90 is the largest such conversion in world history, according to the U.S.-based organization Food First. More than 8000 community-gardens now grow food in Havana. In 2003 *The New Farm* magazine stated that: 'No chemicals are used in 68% of Cuban corn, 96% of cassava, 72% of coffee, and 40% of corn.' (79)

We can make mass changes here to community currencies, renewable energy and organic farming.

We don't need our dependence on petroleum for food and electricity.

We can begin to make changes tomorrow that would free us from usury-based banking.

Two Trains Running

We should also, I think, acknowledge the debts our national history owes. The 'America' of the United States and in fact all the 'America' of the Western Hemisphere owes people of color.

"The first thing America needs to do is get right with the Red man," Bob Dylan once remarked. We of White America need also to "get right" with Black, Brown, and Yellow men and women. For riches past and riches present White America owes people of color on this continent and around the world.

Reparations are a step toward balancing material accounts (80), but current racism can be combated only by equal inclusion in opportunity and rewards. That is, current racism--shown in the growth by 100,000s of Black, Brown and 'narcotics'-related inmates to perform super-exploted labor in U. S. prisons over the past 35 years--can be combated only by an exact reversal of the this nation's norms, its continuing history of exclusion, repression, and theft, crimes against our own residents that have been heightened by the Ruling Few since " '9/11' ".

That is, we here in the U. S. can achieve material remedies only through a new, moral and spiritual commitment to benefit every one of us, the whole of We Masses.

Unity among We Masses is the change the Ruling Few fear most. "They don't want to see us unite/ ... All they want to do is/ Keep us killing one another', ," Bob Marley sang in "Top Rankin' ". The Ruling Few fear us mixing in community such as <u>FOFS</u> found in the multiracial Rogers Park neighborhood of north Chicago on the eve of the 4th of July in 2002.

Please glance back at pages late in <u>FOFS</u> and reflect on the murals and slogans that are represented in Rogers Park, eight or so miles north of Chicago's Gold Coast along Lake Michigan. You may see and feel---again--how invigorating youthful hope and determination can be.

Every day, still, here and now, we have <u>more</u> of the mix potential for a 'new America'. We have still and again the potential for a liberating 'America', the 'America' of immigrants' desires for freedom and prosperity, the 'America' that brought my mother across the border from Canada in 1956.

Our mix, our range and density of races and ethnicities in this country, is <u>greater</u> than ever. We may now know more musics-- taste more foods--combine more dances--and enjoy more differences in our companionship than ever before.

We also have through the Internet <u>more</u> of instant access to distant worlds.

And the Ruling Few fear the creation of more freedom and more life from and among We Masses.

As D. H. Lawrence and others have observed, these Few depend on eating death that produces profits. They eat death from their system of G. O. D.--from Guns, Oil, Drugs and Debt.

And we here and now on Buckminster Fuller's 'Spaceship Earth' are inextricably aboard <u>both</u> of two, opposed trains, trains that run side by side like Einsteinean reality-and-shadow.

At the same time as (there's that *a. t. s. t. a.* again--opposing forces forever together--like " 'God' " and " 'the Devil' ") we can see possibilities for shared awareness and unprecedented general prosperity and freedom through our technological capacities ... at this same 21st-century time, everyday Corporate commerce turns us ever more to debilitating, deathly channels,

Now even the affluent among us must work more than 60 hours per week for ends that are rapidly <u>destroying</u> our posterity.

('Shaped bodies! Used buyers!/ Split as schedules rife!/ Consuming and of course consumed!/ ...' the title poem of <u>AmeriModern</u> exclaimed about 25 years ago.)

Now all of us who depend on Corporate gas are inextricably involved in the U.S./British invasions of Afghanistan and Iraq.

The good news is that we're waking up.

<u>To</u> <u>Prevent</u> ... has surveyed the growing recognitions among us
about " '9/11' " and our subsequent Homeland Security State.

More and more of us are noticing the All-Seeing Eye that sits in
uncounted Corporate and Government logos.

More and more of us feel and see the 'Matrix' that encloses us.

We have yet, however, to act effectively. We have yet to undertake
the alternatives that may save us and our children.

We have yet to realize who and what we can be.

We, the people, remain the determinative power in the world.

The Ruling Few of financiers, so-called nobles, and politicians have
never invented or accomplished anything of societal significance
without employing our collective energy and/or our individual
genius.

They're nothing without us and without our submission to their
systems. They depend on our being 'incapable of comprehending'
their advantages. They depend on us being dupes addicted to
comforts and illusions. They depend, in truth, on our lacking clarity
and courage.

What Genuine Revolutions Have Done and May Do

We have only to remember what people's righteous movements
have achieved over the past two centuries.

We have only to look at the unprecedented gains in societal well-
being that came through collective action soon after the Russian,
Chinese, Cuban Revolutions and--yes, more than two centuries
ago--'American' Revolutions.

To counter a strictly conspiratorial view of history, one which may
itself be debilitating through attribution of much too much
to the secret powers of a Ruling Few, we have only to look at how
dynamic, productive and ultimately fulfilled people were and are in
societies changing toward true representation of their rights.

We have only to look at the human energies that are building
together in Venezuela and elsewhere now.

We have only to remember our own United States of America and
its artisans' guilds. farmers' cooperatives, multiracial Unions, protest
movements and Rogers Park-like and Ithaca-like communities.

We have only to remember, too, the cultural advances in music and
painting and cinema that have always sprung from the mix in
revolutionary societies.

So we can still change, combine, and advance now.

We can enjoy <u>our</u> <u>own</u> kind of simultaneous activity.

Look at the mix in our music alone.

At the same time as (*a. t. s. t. a.*!--a positive instance of our modern capacities for *a. t. s. t. a.*!) Dolly Parton sings from the Scottish Highlands and her guitarist plays chords from Mali and Billie Holliday owes to Tin Pan Alley and Charlie Parker owes to Jewish show-tunes at taxi-dances, so do all American musical idioms owe to the Blues.

And the Blues owes to Roma and their flamenco *duende* in suffering migration from India. And Camaron in his turn owes to Charley Patton. And the Allman Brothers owe to Muddy Waters. And Caetano Veloso owes to Billie Holliday and to Judy Holliday. And Bob Marley owes to his " 'Black' " mother and " 'White' " father and numberless ancestors and influences for the glorious admixture of his genius that also went from backwoods and ghetto to its truly uplifting, global reach.

So too would reach We Masses' global 'America'--the America of visionaries' hopes and no boundaries--if we chose to so make it.

So the cultural America of the United States began to be and to reach in the two decades when our races most mixed and fed each other here.

In the 1930s and the 1960s we in the United States most mixed-- mixed in music, in politics and in struggle. Those decades of our past included the Lindy and jitterbug, --Hullaballoo-- and --Shindig--, Woody Guthrie and at least the promise of the Grand Coulee Dam, dancing in Brandon, Manitoba to Count Basies's band on the radio from Chicago and dancing on the sands of Venice, California and Venice, Italy to Delta fishfries' backbeat, Django Reinhardt and Benny Goodman both drawing from Bartok's Night Music *at the same time as* Picasso represented and portended fascism's slaughters and malevolence. Then New Men and Women in Free Jazz found the right way to advance their lines, Sinatra sang Jobin and Jamal, Carlos Kleiber took off from Ellington and vice-versa, *Led Zeppelin* learned from Blind Willie Johnson, Laura Nyro learned from Nelson Riddle and the *Shirelles*--<u>and</u> inventors and Home Brew Computer Clubs pushed up from the grassroots of societies their intention of enlarging the capacities of each and every person in the planet.

Now, this 21st-century, post-9/11 present of ours, we ride on ever more powerful and opposed trains or waves.

At the same time as We Masses are carried toward ecological and financial disaster--carried toward bogs of war, disease and famine--carried toward an era like decades of War in Europe and decades of the Plague--carried by traumas toward that era of "endless war" foreseen by Dick Cheney, an era to be entirely overseen by the Ruling Few and their frightened, enslaving drives ... *at this same time* we have MORE THAN EVER the capacities to change our whole world to one of fairness, opportunity, sustainability and even prosperity for everyone.

And: There is no Other.

They of the Ruling Few and We of the Masses are one.

We are they and they are us.

We all are both our enemy and our salvation in our predicaments on this planet.

We are the problem. We are the solution. We are all in this together.

Everything backward, fearful and brutal can be reversed by changes of consciousness, the true illumination of our mutual interest, leading to universal empathy.

Always proceed with courage from compassion.

One for all does one most good.

And progress belongs to all 'people'. Science's benefits belong to all people. Never have we 'poor Preterite' (Thomas Pynchon, Gravity's Rainbow) had more potential at our command. The wealth of all the great Valleys and their learned Cities can be spread faster and wider than ever.

And so the morning gospels of Fortaleze can join the drums and rainsticks of Pelourhino and the masks of Barranquilla, And so Charlie Chaplin and Johnny Depp can do soft-shoes with potatoes as Om Khalsoun sings across mosques and synagoges. And so Dostoyevsky's Zossima can talk with Li Po and Tu Fu and this trio can accompany musicians of Ghana, Jajouka, the West Counties, and the Gamelan. And so Rosalyn Franklin and James Watson and Marie and Pierre Curie and Tesla, Einstein and Goethe can inquire together. And so Audrey Hepburn and Lena Horne and Kate Smith and Julie Andrews and Etta James (for a quintet, the *Jolly Quintet*, you may want to pause and imagine) can be as radiant as the sunlight on leaves that's also part of our collective energy.

And so all the unknown of the past and unknown of the present and the unborn of the future can emerge in each's own possible energies and genius.

There is no Other. We are all each other's benefit and salvation.

We need only to realize what our compassion, our inclination to cooperation, and shared desire for freedom, tell us. We need only the courage and will to act from what we know to be true.

Our choices--for giving or taking, for compassion or brutality, for an era of endless war or an era of unprecedented creation and general prosperity--will make the whole of our fate.

We are the one God and Gods watch.

Sid the Elephant: I can dance. You've seen me, Mr. Crow. I'm a little slow, but my rhythm is not bad. You have seen me and a considerable number of my family dance to Count Basie's Band.

My wife remembers all the steps.

I can think and I can dance and I can tell the difference between water and sand. I have quite a lot of love inside me, Auld Crow. That's something endless it itself, wouldn't you say? We still have endless possibilities, Auld Crow, and I feel there is much still to be seen and much in us that we don't yet know.

Auld Crow: Aye, Sid. You have said it, friend. We have only to act on what we know, and there's more in us than we know now. Let me now tap a little two-step on your broad head,my good friend, and let us see if we can both dance around like some still do, and then we we can look with thanks to the earth and sky.

ENDNOTES

1. 'What is Fascism?' at www.fordham.edu/halsall/mod/mussolini-fascims.html from entry in 1932 <u>Italian</u> <u>Encyclopedia</u> by Benito Mussolini and Gemmi Gentile.

2. 'Central Banking and the Private Control of Money', Eric Samuelson, *Nexus,* December 1998--January 1999, pg. 12

3. <u>The</u> <u>Secrets</u> <u>of</u> <u>the</u> <u>Federal</u> <u>Reserve</u>, Eustace Mullins, Bankers Research Institute, 1984, pg 3

4. <u>The</u> <u>Control</u> <u>of</u> <u>Oil</u>, John M. Blair, Pantheon Books, 1976, pp. 144-46, 149; <u>Power, Inc.</u>, Morton Mintz and Jerry Cohen, The Viking Press, 1976, pp. 297-303

5. <u>Waking</u> <u>Up</u> <u>from</u> <u>Our</u> <u>Nightmare</u>, Don Paul and Jim Hoffman, Irresistible/Revolutionary, 2004, pg. 62, endnote 11, quoting the *New York Times* of 10/28/93 and the *Washington Post* of 10/29/03 as well as 'Troubling Questions in Troubling Times' by James S. Adam at http://www.serendipity.li/wot/adam.htm .

6 .<u>The</u> <u>9/11</u> <u>Commission</u> <u>Report</u>, the National Commission on Terrorist Attacks Upon the United States, W. W. Norton & Company, 2004, pg. 72

7. Alan Waldman, 'How the Grinch Stole the White House ... Again', *Online Journal* 11/20/04, archived with additional footnotes by Dave Ratcliffe at http://www/ratical.org/ratville/2004Waldman.html .

8. http://www.betterworldlinks.org/book109h.htm .

9. htto://www.buzzflash,com/alerts.04/11/The_unexplained_exitpoll-discrepancy_v00k.pdf .

10. http://66.102.7.104/search?q=cache:FITtOTCZVzYJ:www.uscountvotes.org/ucvAnalysis/US/USCountVotes_Re_Mitofsky-Edison.pdf+uscountvotes+edison+mitofsky&hl=en .

11 'Voting Machine Controversy' Jule Carr Smyth. *Cleveland Plain Dealer,* August 28, 2003, reprinted at http://www.onlisareinsradar.com/archives/001684.php12 .

12, http://www.betterworldlinks.org/book109h.htm .

13.http://911research.wtc7.net/papers/dustvolume/volume.html

16. *Atlanta Journal-Constitution*

17. *George* magazine November 1996, cited in <u>Everything</u> <u>Is</u> <u>under</u> <u>Control</u>, Robert Anton Wilson with Miriam Joan Hill, HarperCollins, 1998, pg. 1

18. http://www.prouty.org; <u>Understanding</u> <u>Special</u> <u>Operations</u> ... interview with L. Fletcher Prouty by David T. Ratcliffe, rat haus reality press, 1989; 'The JFK Assassination', David Giacometi at http://www.abovetopsecret.com/forum/thread2065/pg1 .

19, http://www.questionsquestions.net/docs04/0526_donpaul.html

20. ... and the truth shall set you free, David Icke, Bridge of Love, 1998, pp. 81-83, quoting from the Congressional Record of the 76thU. S. Congress and from Carroll Quigley, The Anglo-American Establishment, pg. 169.

21. www.leftgatekeepers.com; Conspirators' Hierarchy: The Story of the Committee of 300, Dr. John Coleman, America West, 1992, pp. 235-36.

23. http://teacher.scholastic.com/researchtools/researchstarters/women; http://www.bessel.org/foundmas.htm

24, http://www.constitution.org/cs_found.htm; 'The Evolution of Suffrage Institutions in the New World', Stanley L. Engerman and Kenneth L. Sokoloff, 2005

25. http://www.sptimes.com/2005/01/19/Columns/Debt_games_could_sink.shtmlhttp://www.forbes.com/home/strategies/2005/01/07/cx_da_0107topnews.html

26. http://www.prudentbear.com/archive_comm_article.asp?category=Guest+Commentary&content_idx=40498

27. http://www.jewish-history.com/Salomon/salo01.html, excerpt from 'A Casual View of America: The Home Letters of Salomon de Rothschild, 1859-1861'

28. Judah P. Benjamin: The Jewish Confederate, Eli N. Evans, The Free Press, 1988, pg. 237

29. 'The House of Rothschild', Chapter 5, pg. 53, in Secrets of the Federal Reserve, Eustace Mullins, published online at http://www.federal-reserve.net/secrets.htm .

30. 'Reconstruction Carpetbaggers Money Fund', *New York Times*, 10/31/1866, quoted in Lightning over the Treasury Building, John Elson, Meador Publishing Company, 1941, pg. 53

31. http://americaondebt.com/quotes.htmlson, pg.

32. On "greenbacks" and Lincoln quote, see The American Heritage Picture History of the Civil War, Bruce Catton narrative,1960, pg. 395; The Creature from Jeykll Island, G. Edward Griffin, American Media, 1994, pg. 384; and http://www.perfecteconomy.com/principal---historic-parable-of-perfect-economy.html

33. 'Abraham Lincoln and the "Greenback" ' in Chapter 2.1 ('National Bank of the United States') of the Modern History Project up at http://www.modernhistoryproject.org/mhp/ArticleDisplay.php?Article=FinalWarn02-1#Greenback

34. Rule by Secrecy, Jim Marrs, HarperCollins, 2000, pg. 213

35. The New Encyclopedia Brittannica, Volume 8, pg. 320.

36. Memo printed in the U. S. Congrressional Record of 4/29/1913, quoted in The Money Masters, 1995 and 1998, Bill Still and Patrick S. J. Carmack (an overview of how 'International Bankers Gained

Control of America'), video script posted by Peter Myers at http://users.cyberone.com.au/myers/money-masters.html .37. <u>Rule</u> <u>by</u> <u>Secrecy</u>, pg. 57

38. <u>The</u> <u>Money Masters</u>, video-script, pg. 46

39. <u>Rule</u> <u>by</u> <u>Secrecy</u>, pg. 45

40. <u>The</u> <u>Secrets</u> <u>of</u> <u>the</u> <u>Federal</u> <u>Reserve</u>. pg. 3

41. <u>Waking</u> <u>Up</u> <u>from</u> <u>Our</u> <u>Nightmare</u>, pg. 40, quoting from http://www.documentationexpress.com/article7-a<u>bout-money.html</u> .

42. *Nexus,* December 1998--January 1999, pg. 12

43. At this and many sites on the Web; http://centre.telemanage.ca/links.nsf/articles/668DD4CD677629EF85256FA500663E9A49.

44. U. S. Federal and total debt in 'The U. S. Economy/ The Other Side of Prosperity', Marshall Auerback, *San Francisco Chronicle*, 2/20/2005 at http://www.sfgate.com/cgi-bin/article.cgi?file=/chronicle/archive/2005/02/20/INGG9BBCVK1.DTL&type=printable; U. S. consumers' debt as of January 2004, according to Federal Reserve Board, at http://www.wsws.org/articles/2004/jan2004/debt-j15.shtml

45. <u>The</u> <u>Empire</u> <u>of</u> <u>the</u> <u>City</u>, E. C. Knuth, 1944, available at www.themoneymasters.com, pg. 71

46. Lloyd George to the *New York Journal American*, 6/24/1924, quoted in <u>...</u> <u>and</u> <u>the</u> <u>truth</u> <u>shall</u> <u>set</u> <u>you</u> <u>free</u>, pg. 96

47. <u>When</u> <u>Corporations</u> <u>Ruled</u> <u>the</u> <u>World</u>, David R. Korten, Kumarian Press, 1995, excerpt at http://thirdworldtraveler.com/Korten/BuildEliteConsens_WCRW.html .

48. Army Review Board report 10/20/1944, quoted in <u>Pearl</u> <u>Harbor:</u> <u>Mother</u> <u>of</u> <u>All</u> <u>Conspiracies</u>, Mark Emerson Willey, X Libris, 2001, report transcribed by Larry Jewell and up at http://www.geoc ities.com/Pentagon/6315/pearl.html . See also <u>Infamy</u> by John Toland
and <u>Day</u> <u>of</u> <u>Deceit:</u> <u>The</u> <u>Truth</u> <u>about</u> <u>FDR</u> <u>and</u> <u>Pearl</u> <u>Harbor</u> by Robert B. Stinnett.

49. http://www.usembassy.de/usa/etexts/speeches/rhetoric/gbaggres.htm .

50. http://tinyurl.com/5hja5 .

51. http://www.theforbiddenknowledge.com/hardtruth/new_world_order_hgwells.htm .

52. http://illuminati-news.com/worldleaders-quote-nwo.htm Skull and Bones 19th- to 20th-century

53. http://www.aboutsudan.com/dossiers/british_monarchy/prince_philip_reich.htm .

54. http://www.bilderberg.org/bernhard.htm#Hand. This site links to several worthwhile books, among them Antony G. Sutton's <u>Wall</u> <u>Street</u> <u>and the</u> <u>Rise</u> <u>of</u> <u>Hitler</u>, Raymond Bonner's <u>At the</u> <u>Hand</u> <u>of Man</u>

Peril and Hope for Africa's Wildlife, Charles Higham's Trading with the Enemy: An Expose of the Nazi-American Money Plot 1933-49, and Christopher Simpson's Blowback.

55. George Bush/ The Unauthorized Biography, pp. 45-62

56. George Bush/ The Unauthorized Biography, pp. 115-37.

57. Ibid 119-27 and 460-68; Defrauding America, Rodney Stich former Federal Aviation Administration investigator), Diablo Western, 1998, pp. 295. 312-14. See also Dark Alliance by Gary Webb and Whiteout by Alexander Cockburn and Jeffrey St. Clair (review by Scott Loughrey at http://66.102.7.104/search?q=cache:ZpfUGAJNx14Jwww.mediacriticism.com/)CIA_Whiteout_1999.html+whiteout+cockburn&hl=en .

58. http://www.newmediaexplorer.org/sepp/2005/02/01/global_warming_methane_could_be_far_worse_than_carbon_dioxide.htm

59. The Rockefeller File, Gary Allen, '76 Press, 1976, pg. 152

60. State of the World 1991: A Worldwatch Institute Report on Progress toward a Sustainable World, Lester R. Brown, W. W. Norton, 1991, pg. 3

61. 'How the IMF Props Up the Bankrupt Dollar System'. William Engdahl, http://www.serendipity.li/hr/imf_and_dollarf_system.htm .opium revenue

62/ http://www.scoop.co.nz/stories/HL0301/S00061.htm .

63. http://www.ratical.org/ratville/CAH/Section802.html .

64. 'Cheney's Grim Vision: Decades of War ...', http://sfgate.com/cgi-bin/article.cgi?f=/c/a/2004/01/15/MNGK14AC301.DTL65.

65. http://www.notinourname.net/media/brill-15jan04.htm . See also Brill with PBS interviewer Charlie Rose on his new company's Verfied Identity Card and Larry Silverstein's insurance claims at http://www.charlierose.com/archives/archive3.shtm .

66. http://66.102.7.104/search?q=cache:kexodoQVZo8J:www.911truthla.orgresources.html+fight+back+bugle+part+3&hl=en .

67, http://www.healingcelebrations.com/smallpoxandanthrax.htm .

68, Paul Thompson's timeline at http://www.cooperativeresearch.org.timeline.jsptimeline=complete_911_timeline&theme=anthrax, referring often to *Toronto Globe and Mail* article 'Strange Cluster of Microbiolgists' Deaths under the Microscope' by Alanna Mitchell, Simon Cooper and Caroyln Abraham, 5/4/2003. Later timeline by Steve Quayle at http://freepress2005.blogspot.com/2005/01/author-theorizes-40-microbiologists.html .

69. http://research.lifeboat.com/cnn.htm and http://slate.msn.com/id/2067112/ .See also http://www.cfr.org/pub7410/robert_l_gallucci_graham_t_allison/nuclear_terrorism_the_ultimate_preventable_catastrophe.php ,

70. http://surviveanukeattack.com/2008/01/21/warren-buffet-on-nuclear-bombs/

71. http://www.insurancejournal.com/magazines/southcentral/2003/12/15/coverstory/35033.htm .

71. 'Insurance Industry Stands to Profit from Changes Wrought by Sept. 11', Christopher Oster, *Wall Street Journal*, 11/15.2001, among articles assembled by Al Martin at http://www.the-catbird-seat.net/AlliedWorldAssurance.htm .

72. Christopher Story's Winter 2004-05 *International Currency Review*, pg. 82, quoted at Henry Makow's http://www.savethemales.ca/000834.html .

73. "The Money Masters" video script, pg. 19, at http://users.cyberone.com.au/myers/money-masters.html .

74. *Foreign Affairs* (published by the Council on Foreign Relations) July-August 1995, quoted at http://www.pushhamburger.com/nov_pearl.htm .

75. http://www.ironwoodpublications.com/pages/856709/, interview with Allen W. Smith, author of The Looting of Social Security: How the Government Is Draining America's Retirement Account, Carroll & Graf, 2003.

76. 'Over 50 Towns in North America Now Have Their Own Currencies', Alain Pilote, at http://www.cyberclass.net/towns.htm .

77. Who Owns the Sun, Daniel Berman and John T, O'Conner, Chelsea Green Press, 1995, pp. 231-33.

78. 'Wind Force 12 Study', EWEA, p. 74, http://www.ewea.org/03publications/WindForce12.htm, See www.ewea.org and www.awea.org on the growth of power-generation by wind. See http://store.sundancesolar.com/rearerepecrr.html on renewables altogether.

79.

80. See http://www.house.gov/conyers/news_reparations.htm
http://www.swagga.com/obadele.htm
http://www.commondreams.org/headlines01/0830-05.htm

"I think three kinds of explosives were used to bring down the Twin Towers. I think that RDX-shaped charges, more conventional explosives, were used to cut some beams due to the predictable precision of these charges. I think that more powerful, thermite-laced charges were used to cut through each Tower's 47 central steel columns at crucial junctures--Steven Jones' has an excellent lecture about this likelihood in print, online and on DVD. I think that by far the greatest destruction of each Tower was accomplished through thermobaric weapons placed in the buildings' freight-elevator shafts. A thermobaric weapon shoots an aerosol spray that's then ignited by a charge so its explosiveness is multiplied in outward waves--a lot more powerful than conventional, commercial explosives."

Interview by investigative author Bob Feldman published online October 18, 2006 at www.towardfreedom.com

(While visiting Boston to be part of a panel with students at the University of Massachusetts who had volunteered from Common Ground Relief in New Orleans, I sat down at an outdoor table nearby Copley Plaza one Sunday evening for another interview with Bob Feldman.
The interview here is edited to take out some repetitions of material that's printed earlier in this book and it also is somewhat altered to increase accuracy and fluency.)

Toward Freedom interviewed author and activist Don Paul about the DVD he recently co-produced, <u>9/11 Guilt: The Proof Is In Your Hands</u>.

TOWARD FREEDOM [TF]: Five years after the September 11, 2001 collapse of the World Trade Center buildings, there have been a lot of DVDs and movies about the 9/11 events produced. How is the DVD that you and Jim Hoffman produced similar to or different from the other 9/11-related DVDs and movies?

DON PAUL [DP]: Well, the only DVDs that I've seen are the second edition of <u>Loose Change</u>, one of David Ray Griffin's talks, and one of Steven Jones' and Kevin Ryan's recent talks about some of the physical evidence which shows that three World Trade Center buildings were brought down by controlled demolition. I've seen only those three DVDs about 9/11.
 I would say that Jim's and my DVD, <u>9/11 Guilt: The Proof Is In Your Hands</u>, is distinguished by the concision of the physical

evidence that Jim presents. His part of the DVD is titled 'Proving
Controlled Demolition of World Trade Center Building 7 and the
Twin Towers.' In the last ten or so minutes of his presentation Jim
offers more than five "features" and then five "proofs" of
demolition--along with some very pointed graphics. He shows
beyond question, I think, that all three Buildings were taken down by
different methods of controlled demolition. The Twin Towers were
exploded as no buildings have been before or since and about seven
hours later World Trade Center Building 7 was imploded in a classic,
conventional demolition.

Another distinction of our DVD, I think, is that we get into the who
and why of the crimes.

Both our presentations were recorded to be played at the second
convening of the Los Angeles Citizens' Grand Jury on the Crimes of
September 11, 2001. My presentation is called "Indicting the
Financiers Behind the Crimes of September 11, 2001." I name five
individuals as deserving of further investigation by a Grand Jury:
Larry Silverstein, Peter G. Peterson, David Rockefeller, Dick Cheney
and George W. Bush.

Larry Silverstein is the developer of World Trade Center Building
7, completed in 1986, and the head of a group that took over the
lease to the Twin Towers and much other World Trade Center
property from the New York Port Authority just seven weeks before
September 11, 2001.

Why should a Grand Jury indict Larry Silverstein? One reason,
Bob, would be to find out exactly why Larry Silverstein said on PBS,
on national TV, in September of 2002 that he and a New York City
Fire Department Chief had decided in the late afternoon of 9/11/01
about WTC 7 that they should "pull it"--"pull it" meaning that this 47-
story skyscraper should be demolished--though WTC had not been
hit by either aircraft or much debris and showed only small fires in
that late afternoon, seven hours after the second Twin Tower went
down.

Then WTC 7, 570 feet tall, fell is less than seven seconds,
imploding straight-down into its own footprint. Jim's website,
www.wtc.net, has excellent footage of this implosion.

In February 2002 Silverstein and WTC 7's lease-holders (the
Blackstone Group, Banc of America Securities, and the General
Motors Acceptance Corporation) were awarded an insurance pay-out
of $861 million, about $475 million more than the total investment
in WTC 7 before the building's demolition.

My presentation reports from the website of Controlled Demolition,
Inc. about the amount of time that preparations for implosion of a .

building the size of WTC 7 would require. It took 24 days to simply place the charges that took down the 35-story JL. Hudson building in Detroit in 1998. So weeks of planning and placement must have preceded the obvious demolition of WTC 7 on September 11, 2001.

On 9/11 Peter G. Peterson was Chairman of the Blackstone Group, an investment-banking firm that was one of WTC 7's leaseholders along with Banc of American Securities and the General Motors Acceptance Corporation. I say in 9/11 Guilt that Peter G.Peterson should be indicted because leaseholders of a property as valuable of WTC 7 should be responsible for foreknowledge of the lengthy preparations to demolish it.

I say also that Peterson and David Rockefeller should be investigated for their larger roles in a financial establishment whose irrational, destructive, debt-driven needs make crimes such as 9/11 inevitable. On September 11, 2001 Peter G. Peterson was also Chairman of the Council on Foreign Relations and Chairman of the Federal Reserve Bank of New York.

Toward Freedom's readers should check out, if they haven't already, what the CFR and the Federal Reserve System are truly doing to the possibilities for liberty in our country and the world. David Rockefeller, a former Chairman of the Chase Bank and the Chairman for 15 years of the C F R, was the individual most responsible for construction of the World Trade Center and especially the Twin Towers. He and his brother controlled the Port Authority of New York and New Jersey in the 1960s and 1970s and allies of the Rockefeller family controlled the Port Authority at the time in 2001 of the Port Authority's transfer to Larry Silverstein and his partners of a 99-year-lease for the Twin Towers and other WTC properties.

9/11 Guilt also notes that the Twin Towers were obsolescent "white elephants", laden with asbestos and needing hundreds of millions of dollars in modernization; they were worth more in insurance pay-outs if demolished than if they'd stood.

So, in sum, I think it would be very healthy and useful for our society if David Rockefeller and Peter G. Peterson were questioned about 9/11 by a Grand Jury. Dick Cheney and George W. Bush, whose roles in our economy and society are perhaps less consequential, already are subject to some scrutiny by the public in this society.

Another part of 9/11 Guilt examines how much the U.S./British invasion of Afghanistan that followed the crimes of September 11, 2001 increased the opium crop there--a 2000% increase in 2002-- and how much this Afghan opium crop means to the world's illegal economy (about $180 billion when 3500 metric tons of opium are turned into street-corner heroin) and the world's legal economy (about $3.6 trillion when that $180 billion is laundered into Stock Markets and processed through institutions such as the Chase Bank). The DVD's other main creator, Celestine Star, did an excellent job with graphics in this part.

These are some of the elements in "9/11 Guilt" that I think may be special to it.

TF: Now, if there was an economic motivation on the part of Silverstein and Rockefeller to bring down the "white elephants", why didn't they just bring it down at night, when there weren't any people involved? Why turn it into a mass-casualty thing?

DP: Because--I think--another large part of the intention behind the horrors committed in Lower Manhattan on 9/11/01 was to traumatize the world's populace and especially the U. S. public. The public was meant to receive a series of shocks and that delivery of psychological trauma couldn't have been accomplished if the crashes and Twin Tower demolitions happened at night.

If you look at the amount of casualties from the Twin Towers, it's remarkably low, given what they might have been. I know when I watched the collapses, I was thinking that thirty thousand--fifty thousand--people must have been killed. Because TV commentary was saying over and over that fifty thousand was the normal workday population of the Twin Towers.

Fatalities were minimized not for any humane reason, I think, but to reduce the number of victims' relatives and friends who might be suspicious afterward.

At the same time, the suddenness and violence and scale of the Twin Towers' collapses (more explosions and disintegrations, really, than collapses) had to be overwhelming so that we, the public, would be more incapable of considering what we were seeing. I think, as others have observed, that 9/11 was meant to be the biggest psychological operation, or "psy-op", in history.

Two other, related points. The number of deaths in New York City on 9/11/01 is close to the number of deaths at Pearl Harbor in December 1941, another instance of a U. S. Administration facilitating an attack that killed thousands. It's seemed to me for five years that the spectacular attack on "9/11" was the 'new Pearl Harbor' wanted by Zbignew Brzezinski in The Grand Chessboard, 1997, and by the "neo-cons" of the Project for a New American Century in their year 2000 paper--it was meant to move the U. S. public into backing invasions of Central Asia and the Middle East.

TF: Now, could you recap what your current explanation is for the collapse of the World Trade Center buildings on 9/11/01? The Federal Emergency Management Agency, the National Institute of Standards and Technology, the 9/11 Commission Report, and the

U. S. State Department have all issued explanations that say the Twin
Towers came down due to airliners' impacts and the subsequent fires
(though they say little or nothing about WTC 7).
DP: I think three kinds of explosives were used to bring down the
Twin Towers. I think that RDX-shaped charges, more conventional
explosives, were used to cut some beams due to the predictable
precision of these charges. I think that more powerful, thermite-laced
charges were used to cut through each Tower's 47 central steel
columns at crucial junctures--Steven Jones' has an excellent lecture
about this likelihood in print, online and on DVD. I think that by far
the greatest destruction of each Tower was accomplished through
thermobaric weapons placed in the buildings' freight-elevator shafts.
A thermobaric weapon shoots an aerosol spray that's then ignited by
a charge so its explosiveness is multiplied in outward waves--a lot
more powerful than conventional, commercial explosives.

If you look at footage of the fall of each Tower--footage that's
available on many sites online-you can see several phenomena that
can't be explained by the building's potential gravitational energy.

For me, the acronym of E. P. V. S. S. helps to break down what
you can see. E for Explosiveness--the instantaneous, violent thrust of
matter horizontally at the start of each Tower's destruction. P for
Pulverization--90,000 tons of concrete slabs in each Tower blown to
100-micron particles instantaneously. V for Velocity--steel beams
shot sideways as far as 500 feet at 100-feet-per-second early in each
Tower's fall. Then one S for Speed--the rate at which the Towers fell,
a rate close to free-fall, a rate identical for both matter falling through
the footprint area of those 47 central steel columns and falling
through the air outside each Tower's footprint area. And the last S for
Symmetry--each Tower plummeting straight-down like a
disintegrating elevator, instead of toppling as dozens of other
skyscrapers have in earthquakes.

These obvious phenomena--and several more that Jim details in his
presentation--are there for anyone to see who cares to look
objectively. The Towers were demolished. Mass murder was
committed in a series of psychological shocks on 9/11/01. The
demolition of WTC 7 is even more obvious, I think, for anyone who
cares to study footage of that building's inward collapse.
TF: O.K. Now what about the Pentagon? Based on your
investigation, what caused that destruction of that side of the
Pentagon?
DP: Well, Bob, I think it was certainly not an aircraft that could have
been flown by the Official Story's purported pilot of it, Hani
Hanjour. Also, I'm still sure that whatever aircraft struck the
Pentagon's west wedge <u>could</u> <u>not</u> have been flown by any human

pilot aboard it, based on what I hear from commercial airline pilots and former military pilots, given this aircraft's maneuvers of descending 7,000 feet in two-and-a-half minutes and executing a 270-degree turn in that span of space and time.

You and I know that there's a lot of dispute and furor over whether or not a Boeing 757-200--that is American Airlines Flight 77--was the aircraft that hit the Pentagon. To me, this uncertainty--an uncertainty that's been enhanced by more or less self-incriminating evidence released by the U. S. Government from its load of confiscated video-tape--doesn't matter. It doesn't matter as to who must have executed and orchestrated this part of the crimes of 9/11/01.

We know from other indisputable facts there that there had to be a U. S. military stand-down which allowed the Pentagon to be struck by an aircraft 34 minutes after the second Tower was hit and that this aircraft must had computerized and/or remote piloting in order to execute the maneuvers to brought it to impact with the Pentagon.

Neither the stand-down nor the computerized and/or remote piloting could have been done by Al Queda. So the deliberately unsettled question as to what kind of aircraft struck the Pentagon doesn't matter as to who must have party and guilty in the crimes of 9/11/01.

TF: What about the fourth plane that went down in Pennsylvania--or it disappeared in western Pennsylvania? What happened there? What's your sense of what happened?

DP: My view is that this aircraft was United Airlines Flight 93 and that it was shot down by U.S. military, most likely shot down because passengers aboard it were in fact on the verge of gaining control of the aircraft. The aircraft left an 8-mile range of debris and a one-ton piece of one engine was found 2000 yards away from the aircraft's main impact-zone--signs that it was shot apart in mid-air. Jim's 911research.wtc7.net site has an excellent summary and good aerial photos of the sites in western Pennsylvania.

TF: Why do you think the Kean Commission's official story of what happened on September 11, 2001 is not accepted by most people in the United States and around the globe these days?

DP: Well, because people still can see straight.

No, really, the public's more and more widespread and pronounced disbelief of the official story is a very good sign.

It shows that we haven't yet ben overwhelmed by the Big Lie--that we can still tell a violent explosion from a " 'pancake collapse,' "

To me The 9/11 Commission Report is another elaborate construct of complex but ill-fitting lies, and more and more people are seeing through it. By "most people" I think you mean the polls last Spring

which reported, you know, that 83% of us believe along with Charlie
Sheen that there has been a cover-up of thecrimes of 9/11/01. And
another poll, run by the *Washington Post* just after it published a
lengthy piece by Michael Powell around September 8 of this year.
That poll asked: 'Do you believe any of the conspiracy theories
suggesting the U. S. government was somehow involved in 9/11?'
Out of 64,000-some respondents, 59% answered: 'Yes. The
government has left many questions unanswered about that day.'

The public's avowed doubts are proof that the Corporate
Government's "psy-op" is not working, five years on....

TF: Who are the individuals who should be held accountable for the
collapse of the World Trade Center?

DP: Well, I've named the five for whom indictments are sought in the
<u>9/11 Guilt</u> presentation--Rockefeller, Peterson, Silverstein, Cheney
and Bush. Indubitable criminals all, acting against our society's well-
being long before 9/11/01, I think. In the past year more has come to
light about individuals who might be questioned on the operational
level about the World Trade Center demolitions--individuals who
were far inside planning of mock terrorist incidents or far inside
'security' for the WTC and for crucial Airports. Readers of *Toward
Freedom* might want to do Internet seaches on L. Paul Bremer,
Jerome Hauer, Marvin Bush, Wirt Walker and Michael Cherkasky.

But to me the real culprit behind the crimes of 9/11 and the pretexts
provided by these terrible crimes is the economic system that holds us
in thrall and that makes such crimes inevitable. After " '9/11' " came
the bomb-blasts in Madrid on 2/11/04, in London on 7/7/05, in Bali
on 10/1/05. All of these further acts of mass murder show heavy
signs that <u>Western</u> agents carried them out, not al Queda, and all of
them have been used to perpetuate the " 'War on Terrorism' " and
increase State repression

In Jim's and my 2004 book <u>Waking</u> <u>Up</u> <u>from</u> <u>Our</u> <u>Nightmare</u> I use
another acronym, G. O. D. D., to sum up the four main working-
parts of this system that holds us in thrall. G for Guns--armaments
and all the business of wars. O for Oil--obvious in Central Asia and
the Middle East. D for Drugs--also obvious, once you know about
the billions unto trillions of dollars that are reaped annually from
Afghan opium and Andean coca. And D for Debt--the greatest
instrument, I think, that Banks and other financial institutions wield
to maintain their amazing global empire over us of bondage through
money-from-nothing, death-grips and fears.

And it's Banks' own colossal debts that most endanger us. Their
machinery is getting more and more abstract and desperate. They're
<u>combining</u> 'derivatives' now into 'Collective Debt Obligations'.

And I have to say that we ourselves are accomplices as well as
victims of this G. O. D. D. system. It's up to us to show what we
know and up to us to force a turn from this system ...

TF: Some people might say "Well, just like after WWII, you had the
Nuremburg Trials. Put the officials of the U.S. government in the
docket for 9/11." It sounds like you're saying it's deeper than that:
"It's the System." And you wouldn't necessarily think it would be a
valid option to go after the individual officeholders?

DP: Well, Nuremburg itself was a show trial because it didn't reveal
the thoroughgoing involvement of U.S. and British corporations in
Nazi Germany and Fascist Italy.

You know there could not have been a rise of Adolf Hitler without
the support of George W. Bush's grandfather, Prescott Bush, a
Republican who later became a U. S. Senator from Connecticut, and
Prescott Bush's partner in the Brown Brothers Harriman investment-
banking firm, W. Averell Harriman, a Democrat who later became
Governor of New York.

These bankers, brothers in Yale University's secret-society of Skull
and Bones (George W. Bush and John Kerry are brothers in the same
secret-society) co-owned a mine in Poland that employed labor from
Auschwitz into 1942.

Nazi Germany's Wehrmacht could not have fought into 1944
without parts from Ford, General Motors and I.T.T. and oil from
Standard Oil....

So I think that putting Dick Cheney on trial won't really get us out
of the deeper crises we're in....

The last little book I did, <u>To</u> <u>Prevent</u> <u>the</u> <u>Next</u> <u>" '9/11' "</u> /
<u>Abandoning</u> <u>the</u> <u>'New</u> <u>World</u> <u>Order'</u> <u>of</u> <u>Financiers'</u> <u>Corporate</u> <u>State</u>,
notes some of the repressive legislation that has passed in the U. S.
since 9/11--particulars in the Homeland Security Bill and the Patriot
Act of 2001 and the Intelligence Reform and Terrorism Prevention
Act of late 2004.

Now, this Fall of 2006, a few factors point to much broader
U. S./British/Canadian war in the Middle East and further State
repression. The Military Commissions Act of 2006 recently sailed
through the House and Senate of the U. S. This Act lets the U. S.
President declare anyone an 'unlawful enemy combatant' and
imprison that person--perhaps imprison him or her in one of the
huge detention-centers that Halliburton subsidiary Kellogg, Brown
and Root is building with the $385 million awarded it last January.
Readers can check out Marjorie Cohn's recent article for more
information.

Now, too, naval and land forces are massing near the borders of
Syria and Iran. A pretty detailed overview of this build-up is up on
the www.globalresearch.ca site that Michel Chossudovsky edits. The

2006 *Toward Freedom* interview

globalresearch site also shows that the 2006 Afghan opium crop has increased about 50% above recent years' crops--and about 3000% above the last year, 2001, that the Taliban governed Afghanistan.

So: more signs of "broadening the War on Terrorism" coincident with passage of more means of State repression to terrorize the public <u>and</u> increased business-as-usual from narcotics traffic.

The long-story-short to me, Bob, is that we, the majority of the U.S. and Western world who now suspect that the crimes of 9/11/01 were an inside-job, ... need to make our knowledge ever more visible. We need to choose a day for a mass demonstration and nationwide teach-ins.

Basically we need to show the mass-murderers that their standard-operating-procedure of false-flag terror won't work anymore.

We've gained a lot in terms of a skeptical, aware public in the past three years, but we have a lot more to win.

TF: How can people obtain a copy of your new DVD?

DP: Well, the easiest way for most Internet-empowered folks is through **www.wireonfire.com/donpaul** . Jim's www.wtc7.net also offers <u>9/11 Guilt</u> and other material.

SAN DIEGO CITIZENS' GRAND JURY
ON
THE 9/11/01 CRIMES IN NEW YORK CITY

WHY DID THE WORLD-TRADE CENTER TWIN TOWERS EXPLODE INTO DUST?

CHIEF PROSECUTOR　　　**CHIEF INVESTIGATOR**

DON PAUL　　　**JIM HOFFMAN**

EXPERT WITNESSES

RICHARD GAGE　　　**STEVEN E. JONES**　　　**KEVIN RYAN**
Architect, AIA　　　Physicist　　　UL whistleblower

SAN DIEGO STATE UNIVERSITY　AZTEC CENTER
SATURDAY, APRIL 14　12:00 PM – 8:00 PM
SDG911.org　　Sponsored by San Diegans for 9/11 Truth

CHIEF PROSECUTOR'S RECORD OF FINDINGS, CHARGES, INDICTMENTS AND PRESENTMENTS FROM THE
SAN DIEGO CITIZENS' GRAND JURY ON THE CRIMES OF SEPTEMBER 11, 2001 IN NEW YORK CITY

(*The* San Diego Citizens' Grand Jury on the Crimes of September 11, 2001 in New York City *originated after a talk I gave at the Otto Center in Balboa Park in May of 2006 that was sponsored by the group* San Diegans for 9/11 Truth. *That meeting led Nelisse and Ted Muga, Mike Copass, April, Tom, Rob Leslie, several others of the group and I to plan an event for the following Spring, an event that would expand on efforts pushed by Lynn Pentz, Kathleen Ferrick-Rosenblatt and Chris Condon with two Citizesn' Grand Juries in Los Angeles (October 2004 and August 2005).*

The San Diego event took place on Saturday April 14, 2007 from 12:00 noon till about 8:30 that night in a large meeting-room in the Aztec Center on the San Diego State University campus, a space that had been secured for us by the SDSU chapter of Amnesty International and Professor Jesus Nieto. Considerably more than 100 people attended the proceedings as spectators.

In the weeks after the Grand Jury reached its conclusions there was controversy over wishes by some Jurors to augment or amend those conclusions.

What's printed below is a true 'Record' of decisions reached at the end of the April 14 in a final deliberative session among Jurors, Chief Investigagtor Jim Hoffman and myself. Much of the 'Record' can be corroborated by DVD or audio tape. Contrary to the subsequent controversy, Jurors chose to conclude their deliberations on April 14 and insisted on the "stronger" charge of Conspiracy to Commit Mass Murder. You can hear the entire public proceedings, recorded and Webcast by "Al uh Looyah", at http://www.911blogger.com/node/7886,

I remain entirely positive about the results that we achieved and entirely positive about the great value of Citizens' Grand Juries as a means for empowerment of the public.

The closing paragraphs of a note I sent to Nelisse and Jurors in late April of 2007 may convey the uplifted sense I had at the end of our proceedings on April 14. (I agree with criticism of my misses as Chief Prosecutor and the rushed, unrehearsed quality of the event.)

'Why, if many were dissatisfied with the evidence that was
presented and the conclusions that were reached, was everyone I
remember at the end of our private session smiling, congratulatory
and rather jubilant? Why so many hearty hugs and handshakes
around the room then?

I think one source of the general good feeling then was that we'd
publicly declared ourselves in pursuit of justice for crimes and lies
that still hold the United States in a kind of prison. You yourselves
had done a lot more than I'd asked for in terms of stepping up with
Charges. We'd gotten deeper into the criminal heart of " '9/11' " than
any public body so far, I think. And maybe it's not too much to say
that we'd taken a fairly big step toward freedom.'

*A discussion of the controversy, presenting letters from Jim Hoffman
and Victoria Ashley, is posted via the very active 911blogger.com
site--http://www.911blogger.com/node/8593 ,*

*The 'Wanted Poster' that was created by SDCGJ organizer Rob
Leslie is posted at http://stj911.org/paul/SDGJWantedPoster.pdf as a
PDF for anyone to print.*

*The San Diego Citizen Grand Jury's brave conclusions helped, I
think, to prompt questioning of Rudolph Giuliani and David
Rockefeller by members of We Are Change groups. These revealing
interactions can be seen at http://www.wearechange.org/2007/05/
change-confronts-david-rockefeller.html .*

*The 'Record' that follows is also posted at the Scholars for 9/11
Truth and Justice site (thanks again to Jim and Victoria)--
http://stj911.org/paul/CPFindings_SDCGJCharges.html . For those
with Internet access, reading this 'Record' online and clicking on
urls about each suspected criminal may be a handier medium
for gaining or reviewing information. The whole study, ingesting
one source after another through the 78 ((by my count)) urls,
might require several hours, or even a few days, but would, I
think, form for the investigator a fairly complete picture.*

*Lastly, let me thank everyone who made the SDCGJ happen
and to especially thank its several organizers, mentioned above, and
Expert Witnesses Richard Gage, Ted Muga, and (on tape) Steven
Jones and Kevin Ryan. The process of assembling evidence by phone
and Internet here in New Orleans, before and after the SDCGJ day,
led me to learn and tie together a lot more than I'd known before.)*

INTRODUCTION

The *San Diego Citizen's Grand Jury on the Crimes of September 11, 2001 in New York City* was convened in the Student Council Chambers of the Aztec Center at San Diego State University on 12:00 noon Saturday, April 14, 2007. Twenty-three primary Jurors and more than a dozen alternate Jurors were present. Proceedings concluded that evening by majority-vote of Jurors.

The **Findings** that follow from our proceedings are the Chief Prosecutor's. The **Charges**, **Presentments** and **Indictments** in regard to acts that constituted or enabled crimes that were committed in New York City on September 11, 2001, and/or in regard to crimes that ensued from acts of September 11, 2001 in New York City, such as have attached to the United States' invasions of Afghanistan and Iraq, were reached by majority-vote of the Grand Jury at the conclusion of our proceedings on April 14, 2007.

The **Findings, Charges, Presentments** and **Indictments** that follow are based on evidence presented by Expert Witnesses Richard Gage, Ted Muga, Steven Jones, and Kevin Ryan; by Chief Investigator Jim Hoffman; by myself; and based on knowledge and/or beliefs held by a majority of the Grand Jury independent of the said evidence that was presented on April 14, 2007, particularly regarding the grounds for the **Presentments** issued by the Grand Jury.

Submitted on August 18, 2007, with much respect for the Grand Jury majority's conclusions,

Don Paul, Chief Prosecutor,
San Diego Citizen's Grand Jury on the Crimes of September 11, 2001 in New York City

CHIEF PROSECUTOR'S FINDINGS

The Chief Prosecutor submits under **Findings** that the following acts enabled or constituted crimes that occurred in New York City on September 11, 2001 (9/11/01):

1. That American Airlines Flight 11, a Boeing 767-200 bearing eighty-one passengers, two pilots and nine flight-attendants, struck World Trade Center Building 1, the North Tower, at 8:46 a.m. Eastern Daylight Time on September 11, 2001, and that all persons on board this airliner died due to its crash.

2. That United Airlines Flight 175, a Boeing 767-200 bearing fifty-six passengers, two pilots and seven flight-attendants, struck World Trade Center Building 2, the South Tower, at 9:03 a.m. on September 11, 2001, and that all persons on board this airliner died due to its crash.

3. That procedures for interception of off-course commercial aircraft were fatally violated by parties responsible for them in the **Federal Aviation Agency (the F.A.A.)**, the **North American Aerospace Command (NORAD)**, and the United States' Executive and Military chains-of-command.

4. That World Trade Center Buildings 1 and 2 (the Twin Towers), two 110-story structures that were home to many companies' offices and that were supported by 400 million pounds of steel, and World Trade Center Building 7, a 47-story structure that was home to several companies' offices and 2,000,000 square feet of floor-space, were demolished by internal explosives on September 11, 2001.

5. That the multiple failures to properly investigate attacks on buildings that foretokened the crimes of September 11, 2001 in New York City (such as the February 20, 1993 bombing of the Twin Towers and the April 19, 1995 bombing of the Murrah Federal Building in Oklahoma City, Oklahoma), promoted oversights and misdirection that furthered attacks on the World Trade Center complex of September 11, 2001.

The Chief Prosecutor further submits the following acts ensued from crimes in New York City on 9/11/01:

6. That evidence of the above-named airliners' crashes and World Trade Center Buildings' demolitions was either removed from the crime-scenes and destroyed, and/or misrepresented, and/or hidden, and/or denied, and/or ignored, by parties responsible for investigation of crimes in New York City and the State of New York and within the United States, such as persons in offices of the **Mayor of New York City**, the **Port Authority of New York and New Jersey**, the **Federal Bureau of Investigation (the F.B.I.)**, and by **executives, lease-holders and insurers of the destroyed properties**, and by parties responsible for investigation of the destruction of buildings that impact the public's safety, such the **Federal Energency Management Agency (F.E.M.A.)** and the **National Institute for Standards and Technology (N.I.S.T.)**.

7. That the multiple failures to properly investigate crimes of September 11, 2001 in New York City have resulted in widely publicized misattributions of guilt--deceptions--that produced public support for the United States' invasions of Afghanistan in 2001 and Iraq in 2003 and for the Patriot Act and the Homeland Security Bill of 2001 and the National Identity Card Act of 2005--for international war and domestic repression--at the same time as these failures and deceptions have produced enormous profits by the Corporations and individuals responsible for them.

GRAND JURY'S CHARGES, INDICTMENTS
AND PRESENTMENTS

The following **Charges, Indictments** and **Presentments** were reached by majority-vote of the San Diego Citizens' Grand Jury in the final stage of our proceedings on April 14, 2007. An **Indictment** is delivered by the Grand Jury against a person introduced to them by the Chief Prosecutor. A **Presentment** is delivered against a person by the Grand Jury's initiative. That is, a **Presentment** 'is an accusation issued by the grand jury on its own knowledge, without any bill of indictment having been previously drawn up by the prosecutor'-- Columbia University Press Encyclopedia.

Our **Charges** are hybrids, drawn from popular, centuries-old concerns of Common Law and from language embodied in many State and Federal statutes.

Each of the **Charges** below bear on the perpetration of Capital Crimes:

1. *Destruction of Evidence*
2. *Obstruction of Justice*
3. *Negligence Resulting in Wrongful Death*
4. *Conspiracy to Defraud Private Individuals and the Public Interest through Acts of Terror that Furthered Legal and Illegal Profits*
5. *Conspiracy to Commit Mass Murder*.

URLs to articles about the individuals whom the Grand Jury wished to further investigate are listed underneath brief biographies of each said individual. The articles may help others to research details of definite connections and possible conspiracies among suspected persons. To help with connecting them to each other, the name of any such individual is capitalized and bold-faced in all of the **Charges** and brief biographies below.

FOR THE CHARGES OF (1) *DESTRUCTION OF EVIDENCE* AND (2) *OBSTRUCTION OF JUSTICE*

INDICTMENTS

RUDOLPH GIULIANI: Mayor of New York City between 1994-12/31/2001, collaborating with **JEROME HAUER** as his Director of Emergency Management between 1996-2000; Assistant U. S. District Attorney in the Southern District of New York 1970-1975, collaborating with Jules Kroll; Associate Attorney

General of the United States 1981-83; U.S. Attorney for the Southern District of New York 1983-89, collaborating with Michael Chertoff, **MICHAEL CHERKASKY** and **ELIOT SPITZER**.

Useful articles about **RUDOLPH GIULIANI,** Mayor of New York City on 9/11/01:
http://www.boston.com/news/daily/26/photo_ban.htm
http://www.usatoday.com/news/nphoto.htm
http://www.china.org.cn/english/2002/Jan/25776.htm
http://www.fireengineering.com/login/index.htm

THOMAS VON ESSEN: Fire Commissioner of New York City 1996-12/31/2001.

Useful articles about firefighters' complaints on lack of investigation into the crimes and crime-scenes of 9/11/01:
http://stj911.org/evidence/wtc.html
http://911review.com/articles/griffin/nyc1.html

JAMES KALLSTROM: Federal Bureau of Investigation (**F.B.I.**) Agent in New York City between 1971-1997. Senior Advisor for Counter-Terrorism to the Governor of the State of New York from 2002 to present. Member of Board of Directors of the **Lower Manhattan Development Corporation** from 2002 to present. (According to its Website: 'The Lower Manhattan Development Corporation was created in the aftermath of September 11, 2001 by then-Governor Pataki and then-Mayor Giuliani to help plan and coordinate the rebuilding and revitalization of Lower Manhattan, defined as everything south of Houston Street. The LMDC is a joint State-City corporation governed by a 16-member Board of Directors, half appointed by the Governor of New York and half by the Mayor of New York.')

Useful article about F.B.I. involvement in the 1993 bombing of the **Twin Towers** and the F.B.I.'s subsequent cover-up of said involvement, and useful biographies of multiply connected Board of Directors of the Lower Manhattan Development Corporation:
http:www.serendipity.li/wot/adam.htm
http://www.renewnyc.com/AboutUs/board.asp

THOMAS PICKARD: Acting Director of the **F.B.I.** between June 25, 2001-September 4, 2001. Special Agent in the F.B.I.'s New York City office 1975-1979. Supervisor and Assistant Special Agent for

White-Collar Crime in N.Y.C. 1984-1989. Special Agent in Charge of the National Security Division in N.Y.C., supervising trials of defendants in the first **Twin Towers'** bombing (collaborating with **MICHAEL CHERKASKY, ELIOT SPITZER** and **JAMES KALLSTROM**), and of the Manila Air conviction of Ramzi Youssef, and of the TWA Flight 800 explosion, between 1993-1996.

Useful articles:
http://www.time.com/time/covers/1101020603/memo.html
www.projectcensored.org/newsflash/unanswered_questions_911.html
http://www.democraticunderground.com/articles/
02/09/26_failed.html

ROBERT MUELLER: Director of the **F.B.I**. from September 4, 2001 to present.

Useful articles about F.B.I. involvement in the production or confiscation of evidence that bears on the 9/11/01 attacks in the United States:
http://www.democraticunderground.com/articles/
02/09/26_failed.html
http://www.fbi.gov/pressrel/speeches/speech041902.htm
http://web.archive.org/web/20041030023935/http:/www.philly.com/
mld/dailynews/news/local/10033802.htm

JANET RENO: Attorney General of the United States between 1993-2000.

Useful records about U. S. Government's misrepresentation or confiscation of evidence that bears on the 1993 bombing of the **Twin Towers** and the 1995 bombing of Oklahoma City's Murrah Federal Building.
http:www.serendipity.li/wot/adam.htm
http://www.all-natural.com/oklahoma.html
"Cover-Up in Oklahoma City" video by Jerry Longspagh

MICHAEL CHERKASKY: Various jobs in the **Manhattan District Attorney's Office** between 1978-94 (Chief of Investigations into crimes of the **Bank of Credit and Commerce International** and into the 1993 bombing of the **World Trade Center Twin Towers**). Various jobs at **Kroll and Associates** security-firm (contracted to improve security at the **World Trade Center** after the 1993 bombing there). Chief Executive Officer of **Kroll, Incorporated** between May 2001 and October 2004. CEO and President of **Marsh & McClennan** insurance-firm from October 2004 to present.

Useful links about the career and connections of **Michael Cherkasky**, about oversight of security at the **Twin Towers** from August 2001 to September 11, 2001, and about apparent suppression of evidence after recovery of hard-drives from wreckage of the **Twin Towers**:

http://www.usatoday.com/educate/college/careers/profile40.htm
http://www.pbs.org/wsw/tvprogram/20030912.html
http://www.ratical.org/ratville/CAH/VonBuelow.html
http://globalresearch.ca/articles/KUP311A.html
http://demopedia.democraticunderground.com/index.php/Kroll

JEROME HAUER: Director of Mayor **RUDOLPH GIULIANI**'s Office of Emergency Management between February 1996 and March 2000 (where he was primary in building the City's Emergency Command Center on the 23rd floor of the **World Trade Center Building 7** and in warning about emergence of the West Nile Virus one year before it appeared in New York City); Managing Director of **Kroll, Inc.** on 9/11/01 (when he advised Dan Rather of **CBS** that demolition had not brought down a **Twin Tower** and that the day's attacks bore "the fingerprints of Osama bin Laden"; **Senior Adviser to U. S. Secretary of Health and Human Services for National Security and Emergency Management** between June 2001 and November 2003; coordinator of the **National Institute of Health's** investigation of anthrax deaths in Fall of 2001, deaths that came from the Ames strain of anthrax thought to be available only at the U. S. Army Medical Research Institute of Infectious Diseases at Fort Detrick, Maryland, the N.I.H. investigation producing no suspects named by Jerome Hauer except Osama bin Laden and al Queda; current Director on the Boards of the companies **Emergent Biosolutions** and San Diego-based **Hollis Eden Pharmaceuticals.**

Useful articles about the career and connections of **Jerome Hauer**, about warnings of attacks on the Twin Towers, and about selective warnings against exposure to anthrax from September 11, 2001 onward:
http://www.saic.com/news/nov99/news11-30a-99.html
http://www.fromthewilderness.com/free
ww3/121505_jerome_hauer.shtml

post911timeline.org/article006.html
http://911research.wtc7.net/cache/wtc/analysis/wtc7/
nty_burningdiesel.html
http://911research.etc7.net/wtc/background/wtc7/html

FOR THE <u>CHARGES</u> OF (1) *DESTRUCTION OF EVIDENCE* AND (2) *OBSTRUCTION OF JUSTICE*

<u>PRESENTMENTS</u>

GEORGE W. BUSH: President of the United States 2001 to present.

Useful articles about U. S. Government agencies' confiscation of evidence about the crimes of 9/11/01 and to Presidential resistance toward independent investigation of said crimes:
http://911independentcommission.org/questions.html
http://tvnewslies.org/html/covering_up.html

JOHN ASHCROFT: Attorney General of the United States between 2001-2005.

Useful articles about aforesaid confiscation of evidence:
http://911independentcommission.org/questions.html
http://tvnewslies.org/html/covering_up.html

LOUIS FREEH: Director of the **F.B.I.** 1993-2001; F. B. I. Special Agent in New York City and Washington DC offices 1975-1981; Assistant U..S. Attorney for the Southern District of New York 1981-1990; U.S. District Court Judge for the Southern District of New York, appointed by President George H. W. Bush, 1991-93.

Useful articles:
www.gnn.tv/threads/11866/
http://physics911.ca/pdf/2005/briley_batf_blocked.pdf
http:www.serendipity.li/wot/adam.htm

LARRY SILVERSTEIN: Primary lease-holder of the **Twin Towers** and World Trade Center Buildings 4, 5, and 6 on 9/11/01, as the group he led took official possession of the properties from the **Port Authority of New York and New Jersey** seven weeks earlier; developer and primary owner of **World Trade Center Building 7** on

9/11/01; recipient of insurance-awards worth hundreds of millions of dollars (**WTC 7**) or $4.55 billion dollars (the **Twin Towers**) since 9/11/01; interviewee who told the Public Broadcasting System documentary 'America Rebuilds' of September 2002 that he and a New York Fire Department Commander had jointly decided about WTC 7 on 9/11/01 to "pull it."

Useful articles:
http://www.wanttoknow.info/070320worldtradecenter7wtc7collapse
http://www.panynj.gov/pr/pressrelease.php3?id=80
http://www.fema.gov/pdf/library/fema403_ch5.pdf
http://physics911.net/stevenjones

ELIOT SPITZER: Attorney General for the State of New York between 1999-2006; disregarded a 'Petition' by more than 14,000 signatories, including dozens of 9/11/01 victims' family-members, accompanied by a Citizens' Complaint, to investigate unanswered questions about that day's crimes; Assistant District Attorney in Manhattan 1986-92, working with **MICHAEL CHERKASKY,** at the same time as the current Secretary of Homeland Security, Michael Chertoff, worked with **RUDOLPH GIULIANI** in the Manhattan U. S. Attorney's office; current Governor of the State of New York.

Useful article:
http://www.911truth.org/article.php?story=20041026093059633

PHILLIP ZELIKOW: Executive Director of the **National Commission on Terrorist Attacks Upon the United States (the 9/11 Commission or the Kean/Hamilton Commission)** between 2002-2004; various jobs with U. S. State Department during the Reagan Administration; member of the **National Security Council** with Condoleeza Rice in the George H. W. Bush Administration; co-author with Ashton Carter and John Deutsch of the 1998 article 'Catastrophic Terrorism: Tackling the New Danger' in the **Council on Foreign Relations'** quarterly, Foreign Affairs ('Like Pearl Harbor, the event would divide our past and future into a before and after. The United States might respond with draconian measures, ...'); selected by Condoleeza Rice to author paper on U. S. 'national security strategy' in September 2002.

Useful links to pieces about misinformation and oversights in the

9/11 Commission Report and within the National Commission on
Terrorist Attacks Upon the United States:
http://911research.wtc7.net/post911/commission/report.html
http://www.911inquiry.org/Presentations/JoyceLynn.htm
http://911research.wtc7.net/post911/commission/report.html
http://www.911inquiry.org/Presentations/JoyceLynn.htm

FOR THE CHARGE OF (3) *CRIMINAL NEGLIGENCE RESULTING IN WRONGFUL DEATH*

INDICTMENTS

GEORGE W. BUSH: President of the United States 2001 to present.

Useful articles about warnings prior to 9/11/01 of attacks on major
targets in the United States:
http://www.infoimagination.org/ps/911/index.html
http://www.buzzflash.com/perspectives/911bush.html
http://www.villagevoice.com/news/0648,lombardi,75156,2.html

RICHARD CHENEY: Vice-President of the United States 2001 to
present; C.E.O. of the **Halliburton Corporation** between 1995- 2000
(a period in which Halliburton's off-shore tax havens increased from
9 to 44); member of the **Project for a New American Century**
(PNAC) with Donald Rumsfeld, James Woolsey and several others; U.
S. Secretary of Defense 1989-93.

Useful articles about changes to command of U. S. Military in 2001
prior to 9/11/01 and about behavior of the U. S. Vice-President on
and after 9/11/01:
http://www.mikehersh.com
Bush_and_Cheney_Block_911_Investigation_.shtml
http://www.thememoryhole.org/911/911-preventable.htm
http://www.geocities.com/kidhistory/bcr911.htm

DONALD RUMSFELD: Secretary of Defense of the United States
2001-2006; member of the Board of Directors of Zurich-based **ABB
Corporation** during time (1999) that ABB sold two nuclear reactors
to North Korea; C. E. O. of **General Instrument Corporation**
1990-1993; C. E. O. of **G. D. Searle & Company** during the time
(1985) that Searle won approval from the U. S. Food and Drug
Administration for aspartame.

Useful articles about changes to command of U. S. Air Defense in
2001 prior to 9/11/01 and about behavior of the U. S. Secretary of
Defense on and after 9/11/01:
http://www.geocities.com/kidhistory/bcr911.htm
http://911research.com/sept11/trillions.html
http://portland.indymedia.org/en/2004/03/284651.shtml

MARVIN BUSH: Member of the Board of Directors of **Securacom**,
another firm entrusted with security for the Twin Towers as of
9/11/01 (also entrusted with security for United Airlines and
Washington D.C.'s Dulles Airport as of 9/11/01) between
1996-2000.

Useful articles:
http://www.commondreams.org/views03/0204-06.htm
http://www.informationclearinghouse.info/article3336.htm
http://www.sourcewatch.org/index.php?title=Marvin_Bush

WIRT WALKER: C.E.O. of **Securacom** (later **Stratasec**) between
1999-2003

Useful articles:
http://www.informationclearinghouse.info/article3336.htm
http://www.margieburns.com/blog/_archives/
2006/2/26/1784217.html

RICHARD MYERS: Acting Chairman of the U. S. Joint Chiefs of
Staff on 9/11/011; disregarded first airliner crash into a Twin Tower
that morning to instead attend meeting with Senator Max Cleland;
confirmed as Chairman of the Joint Chiefs of Staff by U. S. Senate on
9/30/01; served as such till 2005; Commander of North American
Aerospace Command (**NORAD**) between August 1998-February
2000

Useful articles:
http://www.911independentcommission.org/questions.html
http://www.benfrank.net/nuke/modules.php?
name=News&file=article&sid=245

RALPH EBERHART: Commander of somehow ineffectual **NORAD**
on 9/11/01 ('NORAD uses a network of ground-based radars, sensors

and fighter jets to detect, intercept and, if necessary, engage any threats to the continent'---Canadian Defense website); Commander of **Northern Command** at Peterson Air Force Base in Colorado, directing U.S, Canadian and Mexican military from October 2002 to January 2005; Commander of **Air Combat Command at Langley Air Force Base in Virginia** between June 1998-February 2000.

Useful articles:
http://www.911independentcommission.org/questions.html
http://www.benfrank.net/nuke/modules.php?
name=News&file=article&sid=245

FOR THE <u>CHARGE</u> OF (3) *CRIMINAL NEGLIGENCE RESULTING IN WRONGFUL DEATH*

PRESENTMENT

JOHN ASHCROFT

FOR THE <u>CHARGE</u> OF (4) *CONSPIRACY TO DEFRAUD PRIVATE INDIVIDUALS AND THE PUBLIC INTEREST THROUGH ACTS OF TERROR THAT FURTHERED ILLEGAL AND LEGAL PROFITS*

INDICTMENTS

L. PAUL BREMER: Executive with the **Marsh & McClennan** insurance-firm (two-hundred ninety-five deaths in the South Tower) on 9/11/01; C.E.O. of **M & M's post 9/11/01 'Marsh Crisis Consultancy'** offshoot between October 2002-May 2003; Presidential Envoy to Iraq and Administrator of the **Coalition Provisional Authority** May 2003-December 2004 (where he promoted civil war by antagonizing Shia and then Sunni Muslims and by issuing '100 Orders', among which 'Orders' were 40-year, tax-free ownership of Iraqi business by non-Iraqi Corporations and 'full immunity' from Iraqi laws for non-Iraqi contractors; Chairman of the U. S. Congress' **National Commission on Terrorism** between 1999-2000, a period in which he too warned of 'catastrophic terrorism' that could cause 'tens of thousands of casualties' and cause 'the American people' to be 'screaming for a response, ... the example we use is Pearl Harbor'; Managing Director of **Kissinger Associates**

between 1989-2000; **U. S. Ambassador-at-Large for Counterterrorism** between 1986-1989.

Useful articles about the career and connections of L. Paul Bremer and about **Marsh & McClennan** profits from 9/11/01 and the " 'War on Terror' ":
http://www.inthenationalinterest.com/Articles/Vol1issue5/
Vol1issue5Bremer.html
http://rightweb.irc-online.org/profile/1053
http://transcripts.cnn.com/TRANSCRIPTS/0403/05/ltm.02.html
http://findarticles.com/p/articles/mi_m0JQP/is_360/ai_108648125
http://www.fas.org/irp/congress/2004_cr/s091004.html
http://demopedia.democraticunderground.com/index.php/
Paul_Bremer

PETER G. PETERSON: C.E.O. of the **Blackstone Group**, one of three lease-holders (along with **Banc of America Securities** and the **General Motors Acceptance Corporation**) of **World Trade Center Building 7** on 9/11/01, thus sharing in unquestioning receipt of $861 million in insurance payments for the demolished **WTC 7** (February 2002); also Chairman of the **Federal Reserve Bank of New York** and the **Council on Foreign Relations** on 9/11/01; the Blackstone Group an investor in **Kroll, Inc.** (1993) and an investment of the **American International Group** insurance-firm ($150 million, or a 7% stake, from **A.I.G.** in 1998), A.I.G. then headed by **MAURICE GREENBERG**, a former Chairman of the Federal Reserve Bank of New York, and the Blackstone Group a partner with **Kissinger Associates** and **A.I.G.** from February 2000 onward. (At the time the latter 'venture' was announced Peter G. Peterson spoke in a press-release thus: "In this new global economy, with its requirements ... for cross-border mergers and acquisitions, for government privatizations of major industries and for restructuring of industries battered by the recent global financial crisis, we believe each of these entities bring some special knowledge and expertise to the table. We at Blackstone very much look forward to working with AIG and Kissinger Associates and capitalizing on these opportunities.").

Useful articles about the career and connections of Peter G. Peterson:
http://globalresearch.ca/articles/CHO403B.html
http://demopedia.democraticunderground.com/index.php/
Peter_J._Peterson
http://bookstore.petersoninstitute.org/book-store/3837.html
http://justanotherblowback.blogspot.com/2006/10/911-revolution-in-
military-affairs.html

DAVID ROCKEFELLER: Principal in creating the **World Trade Center** and in building the **Twin Towers** as Chairman of the **Downtown-Lower Manhattan Association** between 1958-1975; beneficiary of more than $1 billion in public funds for said construction; beneficiary of his brother, the Governor of the State of New York, Nelson Rockefeller, installing more than 20,000 State employees into **WTC 2**, the South Tower, in the 1970s; potential loser of billions of dollars from renovations necessary to the **Twin Towers** by the year 2000; President of the **Chase Manhattan Bank** 1961-69; C.E.O. of the Chase Manhattan Bank 1969-1981; Chairman of the **Council on Foreign Relations** 1970-1985; co-founder with Zbigniew Brzezinski and George Franklin of the **Trilateral Commission** in 1973.

Useful articles about construction and tenancy of the **World Trade Center**, about financiers' use of public funds, and about Banks' money-laundering of narcotics-traffic profits:
http://people.howstuffworks.com/wtc.htm
http://www.ericdarton.net/html/tallstories.html
http://www.city-journal.org/html/11_4_the_twin_towers.html
http://www.amazon.com/exec/obidos/tg/detail/-/B00005VW2O/lewrockwell/
http://911research.wtc7.net/wtc/evidence/asbestos.html
http://www.garlicandgrass.org/issue8/Don_Paul.cfm

PRESENTMENTS

MAURICE GREENBERG: C.E.O. of **A.I.G.**--'the leading U.S.-based international insurance organization and the largest underwriter of commercial and industrial insurance in the United States' according to its Website in February 2000--between 1968-2005.; **A.I.G.** a major share-holder in **Marsh & McClennan** (headed by Maurice Greenberg's son Jeffrey on 9/11/01), in **ACE International** (another insurance-firm, headed by Maurice Greenberg's son Evan on 9/11/01), and in **Kroll & Associates / Kroll, Inc.**; **A. I. G.** connected to narcotics traffic and money-laundering by its **C.I.A.**-funded predecessor the **Starr Corporation** and by reporters Jonathan Kwitny, Sally Denton and Roger Morris; **A.I.G.** a beneficiary of the increase in insurance premiums post-9/11/01, its sales increasing by more than 35% between 2001-2003 and its profits more than doubling between 2000 and 2005, exceeding $11 billion in the latter year; Maurice Greenberg a former Chairman of the **Federal Reserve**

Bank of New York (1994-1995) and Honorary Vice-Chairman of the **Council on Foreign Relations**.

Useful articles:
http://www.sourcewatch.org/index.php?title=Maurice_R._Greenberg
http://www.csmonitor.com/2005/0401/p03s01-usju.html
http://www.onlinejournal.com/artman/publish/article_1261.shtml
http://onlinejournal.com/artman/publish/article_1291.shtml
http://www.fromthewilderness.com/free/ciadrugs/part_2.html

LARRY SILVERSTEIN

FOR THE <u>CHARGE</u> OF
(5) *CONSPIRACY TO COMMIT MASS MURDER*

<u>INDICTMENTS</u>

RUDOLPH GIULIANI

JEROME HAUER

<u>PRESENTMENTS</u>

THOMAS PICKARD

MICHAEL CHERKASKY

GEORGE W. BUSH

LARRY SILVERSTEIN

RICHARD CHENEY

DONALD RUMSFELD

MARVIN BUSH

WIRT WALKER

RICHARD MYERS

RALPH EBERHART

L. PAUL BREMER

PETER G. PETERSON

DAVID ROCKEFELLER

MAURICE GREENBERG

(My only regret from our procedures on April 14, 2007 is that the Jurors did not receive from me information which might have moved them to call for the further investigation of at least two other individuals, **MICHAEL CHERTOFF** and **BERNARD KERIK,** on one or more **Charges**.

Let me now, again, offer congratulations to the Jurors for their splendid courage, deep backgrounds of knowledge, acute questions, and thoroughgoing determination.

Congratulations to them for taking a brave step toward truly countering terrorism.

May their courageous step further Citizens' Grand Juries and even more concrete steps by concerned citizens around the world. May it further an unstoppable movement to reach answers about the crimes of 9/11/01 that prevent more of such crimes--more of such atrocities against civilian populations--in our futures, from this day forward, August 18, 2007

You can download the poster at http://stj911.org/paul/ SDGJWantedPoster.pdf if you want to use it to convey information, provoke discussion, and advance efforts for justice and freedom.)

WANTED

INDICTMENTS

RUDOLPH WILLIAM LOUIS GIULIANI III

JEROME HAUER

PRESENTMENTS

 THOMAS J. PICKARD
 MICHAEL CHERKASKY
 GEORGE WALKER BUSH
 LARRY A. SILVERSTEIN
 RICHARD BRUCE CHENEY

 DONALD HENRY RUMSFELD
 MARVIN PIERCE BUSH
 WIRT D. WALKER III
 RICHARD BOWMAN MYERS
 RALPH E. "ED" EBERHART

 LEWIS PAUL BREMER III
 PETER GEORGE PETERSON
 DAVID ROCKEFELLER, SR.
 MAURICE R. "HANK" GREENBERG

IT'S THEIR GAME

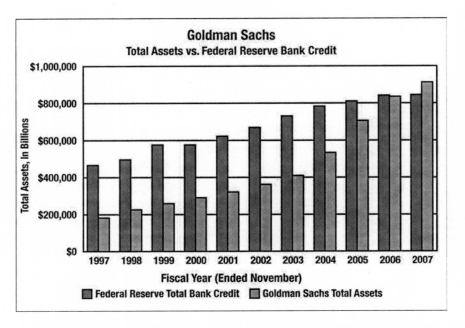

In 2001 the largest U. S. investment-banking firm, **Goldman Sachs,** held assets worth about twice as much as the amount of credit extended to it by the **Federal Reserve System consortium**.

By 2007 **Goldman, Sachs** owed more to the **FRS consortium** than it altogether owned. A typical **Goldman, Sachs** executive's bonus in the 21st century was $5 million per year.

Who or what should pay to sustain **Goldman, Sachs** and its like now?

Should we, the laboring people of the world, the people whose work produces the world's food and tools and vital goods, not OWN the results of our labor, the homes our years of work have enabled, rather than suffer disasters and ruin from the murderous empire of money-lenders that has exploited us for centuries?

Should we not justly repudiate such " 'debts' "--" 'debts' " our sweat and blood have paid for many times over?

(In March 2008 the **FRS consortium** gave the United States' most indebted financial institution, **J.P. Morgan Chase**, $30 billion to buy the **Bear, Stearns** investment-bank at $2 per share. U.S. Treasury Secretary at the time, Henry M. Paulson, headed **Goldman, Sachs** from 2004 till May of 2006. Paulson made $37 million as CEO at **Goldman, Sachs** in 2005, according to *Forbes Magazine*.)

PRECURSORS OF A U.S. POLICE STATE
THAT'S PRECIPITATED BY ANOTHER TERRORIST ATTACK

In late 2006 and in 2007 acts of Federal legislation and Presidential Directives and Executive Orders combined with both utterances from high Government officials--in particular Homeland Security Director Michael Chertoff--and reports from mass-media to further prepare the United States for martial law in response to another " 'terror attack.' "

At the same time as (there's that darn a.t.s.t.a again!) these Directives, Orders and alarms were happening, U/S. home-buyers' woes increased and the Federal Reserve System and other nations' central Banks printed hundreds of billions of dollars to support big businesses.

In September 2007 I participated in events with 9/11 Truth groups in Sacramento, California and Houston, Texas. The events were accompanied by hand-outs of the informational timelines for 'Precursors of ... Another Terrorist Attack' that are printed below.

Let us <u>immediately</u> proceed with courage and compassion.

Michael Chertoff, Director of U. S.
Department of Homeland Security

•October 17, 2006: Two new measures, Public Law 109-364 and the Military Commissions Act, are signed by President George W. Bush. The former 'allows the President to declare a "public emergency" and station troops anywhere in America and take control of state-based National Guard units without the consent of the governor or local authorities, in order to "suppress public disorder." http://www.towardfreedom.com/home/content/ view/911/"

•May 9, 2007: George W. Bush signs National Security Presidential Directive NSPD 51 and Homeland Security Presidential Directive HSPD 20. The *Washington Post* writes: "The prospect of a nuclear bomb being detonated in Washington without warning, whether smuggled in by terrorists or a foreign government, has been cited by many security analysts as a rising concern since the Sept. 11, 2001, attacks... The new directive gives the job of coordinating policy to the president's assistant for homeland security and counterterrorism -- Frances Fragos Townsend, ..."

•May 11, 2007: Coincidentally, the *San Francisco Chronicle* reports on a conference co-sponsored by Stanford and Harvard Universities three weeks earlier. The conference was titled "The Day After" and its subject was responses to a domestic nuclear attack on the U. S.

•May 11, 2007: Coincidentally, the Council on Foreign Relations website features an article on "The Next Attack".

•July 10, 2007: Homeland Security Director Michael Chertoff tells editors of the *Chicago Tribune* that he has a "gut feeling" that al-Qaeda will attack on U. S. soil by the end of Summer 2007.

•July 10, 2007: Coincidentally, *USA Today* features an *Associated Press* piece that begins: "U.S. counterterror officials are warning of an increased risk of an attack this summer, given al-Qaeda's apparent interest in summertime strikes ..."

•July 11, 2007: Coincidentally, *ABC News* reports: "Senior law enforcement officials said today that growing signs of a "Summer of '07" terror attack on the U. S. have led the FBI to dispatch dozens of agents ..."

•July 16, 2007: Paul Craig Roberts, Assistant Secretary of the U. S. Treasury in the Reagan Administration, writes in a column that's titled *The End of Constitutional Democracy*: 'Bush has put in place all the necessary measures for dictatorship in the form of "executive orders" that are triggered whenever Bush declares a national emergency. Recent statements by Homeland Security Chief Michael Chertoff, former Republican senator Rick Santorum and others suggest that Americans might expect a series of staged, or false flag, "terrorist" events in the near future.'

• July 17, 2007 and August 1, 2007: George W. Bush signs Executive Orders that empower seizure of assets of anyone who opposes U. S. efforts in Iraq ("Blocking Property of Certain Persons Who Threaten Stabilization Efforts in Iraq" - July 17, 2007) or who acts to destabilize the government of Lebanon.

PRECURSORS OF A FINANCIAL MELTDOWN WHOSE TRUE CAUSES MAY BE HIDDEN FROM THE PUBLIC BY ANOTHER TERRORIST ATTACK

• MARCH 23, 2006: The Federal Reserve System, the private, un-audited banking business that determines interest-rates and money-supply to the U. S. public, ceases to publish its M3 index, thereby hiding the amounts it itself is purchasing in bonds or printing in fiat currency to postpone failures from mounting U. S. debts. These debts include Federal, State and local Governments', individual consumers', and (by far the biggest debtors) major financial institutions' such as Jp Morgan Chase. The U. S. Federal debt, risen from $0.9 trillion in 1980 to $5.9 trillion in 2004, has grown by more than 20% each of the past two years, while major Banks' liabilities due to derivatives has grown to exceed $300 trillion by the end of 2005.

• DECEMBER 31, 2006: U. S. trade-deficit is $860 billion for the past year.

• FEBRUARY 2007: The *New York Times* writes: 'The slump in home prices from the end of 2005 to the end of 2006 was the biggest year over year drop since the National Association of Realtors started keeping track in 1982.'

• MAY 2007: U. S. consumers' credit-card debt rises 9.2% during this one month.

• JUNE 2. 2007: Widespread reports of United Nations' prediction that U. S. dollar must suffer devaluation due to the nation's ' "unsustainable" ' debt.

• AUGUST 10 and AUGUST 11. 2007: Responding to a " 'liquidity crisis' , the Federal Reserve System and other nations' central Banks pump more than $300 billion of fiat currency into faltering businesses. The *Wall Street Journal* reports that the FRS has created $62 billion for ailing lenders/debtors in these past two days, that the the European Central Bank has added $213.56 billion (166 billion Euros), the Bank of Japan $8.3 billion (1 trillion yen), the Reserve Bank of Australia $4.18 billion, and so forth. Martin Weiss in the online *Market Oracle* notes that the Bank of International Settlements 'calculates that the total "notional" value of all derivatives outstanding in the world is a mind-boggling $415 trillion.' Or: 'Over eight times the GDP of the entire world economy ... twenty times the total value of all U.S. stocks ... and fifty times all the Treasury debts of the U.S. Government.' He also notes that the U.S. Officer of the Comptroller of the Currency finds that 'Just FIVE Banks control 97.1% of the derivatives in the entire U. S. banking system', led by JPMorgan Chase, the Hongkong and Shanghai Banking Corporation, Citibank, and Bank of America.

* THE FORESEEABLE PRESENT: The U. S. public stands liable to lose homes and savings due to a ' "Crash" ' that owes directly to major money-lenders' schemes and failings.
   The U. S. military stands bogged in Afghanistan and iraq in occupations that owe directly to the pretext of " '9/11' ".
   The Bush Administration is sinking under low-approval ratings, much like it and Stock Markets (Big Oil, Big Arms, Big Drugs, and above all Big Banks) were sinking in August 2001.
   The situation of both the U. S. public (we, the people, the masses) and our elitist rulers is very like our/their situation immediately before the " 'Great Depression' " and " '9/11' ".
   Therefore we must act to remedy our situation.
   The need for clear sight of our realities and for radical, compassionate change is more urgent than ever.

A Brief Guide to Proofs
that the World Trade Center Twin Towers
Fell due to Controlled Demolition /

Explosiveness: Pulverization: Speed:
Symmetry: Molten Metal

THE TOWERS' STRUCTURES AND MASSES

Let's consider, first, the sheer size of the Twin Towers and the strength of their structures.

The North Tower (World Trade Center Building 1) and the South Tower (WTC Building 2) were 1362 feet and 1368 feet tall respectively. Each Tower weighed about one billion pounds (485,000 to 500,000 tons). Over 200,000 tons of each Tower's weight was made up of steel columns, I-beams, H-beams, trusses and pans. Over 100,000 tons of each 110-story Tower was made up of concrete floor slabs.

Each Tower had four outer walls 209 feet wide. Each had core structures that measured 87 feet by 135 feet. Within each's Tower's core structure were 47 central columns of structural steel. The radial dimensions of these core columns ranged from 52" by 22" (more than four feet wide) to 36" by 22". The core columns' steel was 5"-thick at their base and tapered to 1/4" when they transitioned into H-beams about 1000 feet (the 92nd floor) above street-level in Lower Manhattan. Each Tower also had 236 perimeter columns, measuring 13.5" by 14", for additional support.

The floors of each Tower's 87' by 135' core-structure were framed by structural steel I-beams two to three feet high (or "deep"). Extending outward from the core-structure to each Tower's four 209' exterior walls were corrugated steel pans, supported by primary double trusses and secondary transverse trusses. The primary trusses were about three feet (900 millimeters) high or deep. Each floor was overlain by about four

inches (10 centimeters) of concrete slab in at least its diaphragm
The concrete, decking and trusses were integrated structures,
more than three feet thick for each floor.

Virtually all of the above-specified mass in each Tower somehow
blew into clouds of gritty dust, or became huge horizontal
projectiles, or dropped straight to ground in less than 15 seconds,
on September 11, 2001.

The Internet pages below offer visual and analytic information
about the Towers' structures.
http://911research.com/wtc/evidence/plans/index.html
http://911research.com/wtc/arch/core.html
http://www.ae911truth.org/twintowers.php

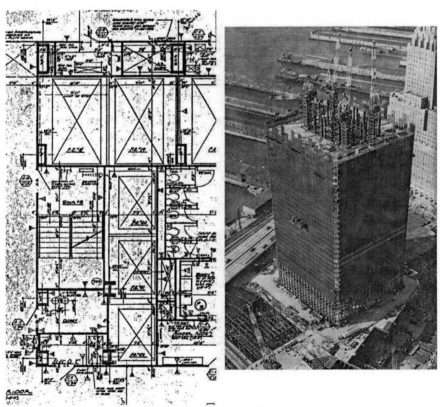

Blueprint of the North Tower's 50th floor shows the continuing
strength of its 47 central steel columns, as does the photo.

EXPLOSIVENESS

Destruction of each Tower began suddenly in and above the impact-zones of American Airlines 11 (which struck the North Tower, WTC Building 1, between floors 94 and 98 at 8:46 a.m) and United Airlines 175 (which struck the South Tower between floors 78 and 84 at 9:03 a.m.)

Horizontal ejections of concrete and steel threw thousands of tons of matter sideways within the first five seconds of each Tower's fall.

Rippling downward from floor to floor as if rent by belts of charges and yet spewing upward like a volcanic eruption, each Tower's collapse threw out clouds of smoky matter more than five times times the radius of each Tower's 836-foot diameter.

None of the above phenomena of explosiveness can be explained by jet fuel's or office equipment's fire, the airliners' impacts, or each Tower's potential gravitational energy.

The Internet pages below offer visual and analytic information that pertains to explosiveness of the Towers' destruction.

http://911research.com/wtc/analysis/collapses/shattering.html

Left--The South Tower about four seconds into collapse. *Right*--Damage to the World Financial Center's 16th to 24th floors due to projectile steel thrown from the North Tower about 400 feet away.

PULVERIZATION

Videos show that massive ejections of fine particulates follow glimpses of boiling-red matter inside each Tower at the onset of each Tower's destruction. Ever-increasing clouds of dust then roll outward (steel columns somehow disappearing) and mushroom into pyroclastic forms several times wider than each Tower's diameter.

How could slabs of concrete be instantly blown into dust?

Jeff King, an electrical engineer and a graduate of the Massachusetts Institute of Technology, stated in 2002: 'Remember that dust begins to appear in quantity in the very earliest stages of the collapses, when nothing is moving very fast relative to anything else in the structure. How then is reinforced concrete turned into dust and ejected laterally from the building at high speed?'

King and Jim Hoffman have also noted that one source of energy can't account for two simultaneous effects. U. S. Government explanations (FEMA, NIST) hold that the Towers' potential gravitational energy produced both the thorough pulverization of concrete and the near free-fall descent of the 110-story buildings. The truth, however, is that potential gravitational energy doesn't suffice to explain either one of these effects, much less both.

Only internal explosives can explain 4"-thick slabs of concrete blowing into 25-micron bits early in each Tower's collapse.

Left--The North Tower exploding just below UA 175's impact-zone and just above the 78th-floor Sky Lobby.
Right--Later spew of this Tower.

SPEED

Speed here refers to the rate of the Towers' descents.

A baseball--or an acre of concrete, the size of each floor of the Twin Towers--would have fallen from the top of each 110-story Tower to plaza-level of the World Trade Center in approximately 9.2 seconds if either object had dropped through nothing but air.

Each Tower's actual collapse on 9/11/01 was completed in a little less than 15 seconds, a speed close to free-fall.

Also, video footage shows each Tower's inward structure collapsing on itself and through itself as fast as rubble falls through the air by the 70th floor of each Tower's descent.

We know about the 3-foot high I-beams that horizontally supported every floor of the Towers' core-structure. We know about the 47 central columns and 235 perimeter columns of structural steel that were each Tower's main vertical supports.

We know that this huge lattice-work of steel supports should have drastically impeded the Towers' fall.

The North Tower, destruction descending, within and without.

SYMMETRY

'Oh, they fell so fast, they fell straight down
...
Fell like elevators erupting to the ground....'

Almost all of the steel masses of the South Tower and the North Tower fell about their vertical axes with near-perfect symmetry.

Their supports gave way with a synchrony that kept them from toppling and causing much less predictable destruction.

Jim Hoffman elaborates: 'Getting buildings to fall vertically (i.e.: symmetrically about their vertical axes) is what the art and science of controlled demolition are all about.' He points out how such demolition is made to happen: the careful placement and timing of explosives 'cause the simultaneous and symmetric failures of all the main structural supports.' Regarding the Twin Towers in particular, he writes: 'It is inconceivable that any random event or combination of events, such as aircraft collisions, fires, or fuel tank explosions, could cause the simultaneous failure of all the support columns in a building--especially a tall steel-framed building-- needed to cause it to collapse vertically.'

http://911research.wtc7.net/wtc/analysis/collapses/symmetry.html
http://911research.wtc7.net/wtc/analysis/collapses/steel.html

Symmetry of the South Tower's destruction, two southern views.

MOLTEN METAL

Molten iron, iron so hot that it was liquid, burning at
temperatures far higher than uncontrolled fire can produce,
persisted at Ground Zero of the World Trade Center for months
after 9/11/01, according to many officials and scientists who
worked at the site. Such long-lasting molten iron can be
explained by thermite or thermate explosives as its source.

Government Computer News of September 2002 reported:
'For six months after Sept. 11, the ground temperature varied
between 600 degrees Fahrenheit and 1,500 degrees, sometimes
higher.' G C N quoted Greg Fuchek, Vice-President of Sales for
LinksPoint Inc. of Norwalk, Connecticut: ' "In the first few weeks,
sometimes when a worker would pull a steel beam from the
wreckage, the end of the beam would be dripping molten steel,"
Fuchek said.'

Alison Geyh, Ph.D, was quoted in the *Johns Hopkins Public
Health Magazine* as to work at Ground Zero in late October
2001: ' "Fires are still actively burning and the smoke is very
intense. In some pockets now being uncovered, they are finding
molten steel." '

In 2005 Steven Jones, then Professor of Physics at Brigham
Young University in Utah, began to publish papers that
posited thermite as a plausible source of Ground Zero's molten
iron.

Professor Jones wrote in 'Why Indeed Did the WTC Builidngs
Completely Collapse?' of 2006: ... thermite reactions may well
have resulted in substantial quantities (observed in pools) of
molten iron at very high temperatures – initially above 2,000 °C
(3,632 °F). At these temperatures, various materials entrained in
the molten metal pools will continue to undergo exothermic
reactions which would tend to keep the pools hot for weeks
despite radiative and conductive losses.... Thus, molten metal was
repeatedly observed and formally reported in the rubble piles of
the WTC Towers and WTC 7, metal that looked like molten
steel or perhaps iron. We maintain that these observations
are consistent with the use of high-temperature cutter-charges
such as thermite, HMX or RDX or some combination thereof,
routinely used to melt/cut/demolish steel.'

Both Professor Jones and the National Institute of Standards and Technology's <u>Report</u> note that strange flows and glows of evidently molten metal in the northeast corner of the South Tower's 80th floor immediately precede that Tower's destruction. Jones writes: 'An intriguing photograph found as Figure 9-44 in the NIST report provides evidence for a highly exothermic reaction at the corner of the South Tower just minutes before its collapse.' He quotes the NIST <u>Report</u>: ' "An **unusual flame** is visible within this fire. In the upper photograph {Fig 9-44} **a very bright flame, as opposed to the typical yellow or orange surrounding flames**, which is **generating a plume of white smoke**, stands out.' Jones proceeds with his quoting of the National Institute's findings: ' "NIST reported (NCSTAR 1-5A) that just before 9:52 a.m., **a bright spot appeared** at the top of a window on the 80th floor of WTC 2, four windows removed from the east edge on the north face, **followed by the flow of a glowing liquid**. This flow lasted approximately four seconds before subsiding. **Many such liquid flows were observed from near this location in the seven minutes leading up to the collapse of this tower."** Source: http://wtc.nist.gov/pubs/factsheets/faqs_8_2006.htm (August 2006) '.

The evidently exothermic flows and glow can be been in this horrific video from the Camera Planet Archive, titled 'Molten Metal WTC Thermite': http://video.google.com/ videoplay?docid=545886459853896774&q=cameraplanet %209/11&hl=en '

One explanation for the extraordinary explosiveness seen throughout each Tower's destruction may be found in an article by John Gartner in *Technology Review* of January 21, 2005, its title 'Military Reloads with Nanotech', that Steven Jones' paper also quotes.

Gartner's piece highlights 'superthermites'. Gartner writes: 'Researchers can **greatly increase the power of weapons by adding materials known as *superthermites* that combine nanometals such as nanoaluminum with metal oxides such as iron oxide**, according to Steven Son, a project leader in the Explosives Science and Technology group at Los Alamos. "The advantage (of using nanometals) is in how fast you can get their energy out," Son says.... Son, who has been working on nanoenergetics for more than three years, says that scientists can engineer nanoaluminum powders with **different particle sizes to**

vary the energy release rates. This enables the material to be used in many applications, including underwater **explosive devices**... However, **researchers aren't permitted to discuss what practical military applications may come from this research." '**

(We may here remember that the Manhattan Project which produced the world's first atomic bombs was kept secret despite involving more than 130,000 participants over several years, just as the U. S. Government's 'Operation Northwoods' ((intending to blame Cuba for destruction of a commercial airliner and to thus provoke war)) remained hidden for 39 years.)

Steven Jones' 'Why Indeed Did the WTC Buildings Collapse' led to an upsurge in public interest in physical evidence for the crimes of 9/11/0. He was the keynote speaker for Project Censored's dinner to spotlight under-reported journalism of 2006. Negatively, however, he was put on paid leave by BYU in September 2006; he's now a retired Professor there. See http://deseretnews.com/dn/view/0,1249,645200098,00.html .

His 'Why Indeed ...' paper is one of many worthwhile investigations (46 articles) available at the website that's edited by him, Dr. Kevin Ryan and Dr. Frank Legge: http://www.journalof911studies.com/

The most succinct and comprehensive Internet article I know about official explanations' failings and real phenomena's meanings in regard to World Trade Center Buildings' demolition is Jim Hoffman's 'Building a Better Mirage ...', available at http://911research.wtc7.net/essays/nist/ .

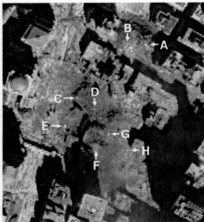

Left--The 'bright' orange 'flame' or 'liquid flow' noted by Professor
Steven Jones and NIST is presented and explained in color at
http://911research.wtc7.net/wtc/analysis/theories/thermite.html .
'These frames show the northeast corner of the South Tower
seconds before its precipitous fall. The spout of orange molten metal
and rising white smoke has the appearance of a thermite reaction.'
Right--The U. S. Geological Survey interpreted NASA aerial
photographs of 9/16/01 as showing that temperatures within the
footprints of the Twin Towers and WTC 7 were still 1376 degrees
Fahrenheit on that date. http://pubs.usgs.gov/of/2001/ofr-01-0429/
thermal.r09.html
How did these places get so hot? Why did they stay so hot?

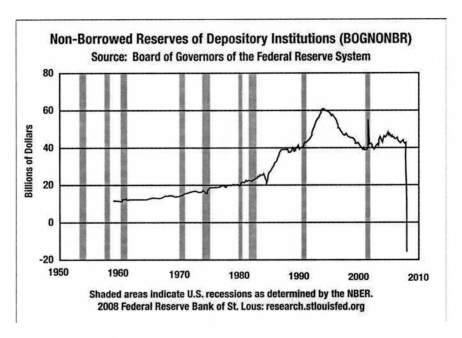

Non-Borrowed Reserves of Depository Institutions (BOGNONBR)
Source: Board of Governors of the Federal Reserve System

Shaded areas indicate U.S. recessions as determined by the NBER.
2008 Federal Reserve Bank of St. Lous: research.stlouisfed.org

By March of 2008, two years after the **FRS consortium** ceased to publish its M3 Index as to how much fiat currency it itself was generating, the borrowings of Banks in the U.S. plummeted far beneath their assets, according to the Federated Reserve Bank of St. Louis. Suddenly there was much less than no 'money' in these Banks.

Given this very graphic fact (see above), we should remember the advice of two U. S. Presidents and act on it.

We need to take power away from the supranational money-lenders.

President Thomas Jefferson wrote to U.S. Secretary of the Treasury Albert Gallatin in 1802: 'If the American people ever allow private banks to control the issue of currency, first by inflation, then by delation, the banks and corporations that will grow up around them will deprive the people of all property until their children will wake up homeless on the continent their fathers conquered. The issuing power should be taken from the banks and restored to the people, to whom it properly belongs.' .

President Abraham Lincoln said upon issuing interest-free "greenbacks" in 1862: 'The privilege of creating and issuing money is not only the supreme prerogative of Government, but it is the Government's greatest creative opportunity ... By the adoption of these principles, the ... taxpayers will be saved immense sums of interest. The financing of all public enterprises, and the conduct of the Treasury will become matters of practical administration. Money will cease to be master and become the servant of humanity," .

"9/11 IS A BIG LIE"

A)
9/11   is a Big Lie (Nine----Eee-lev-on ...)
9/11   is a Big Lie
9/11   is a Big Lie
And we're gonna shout-shout-shout it
Loud and high
...

B)
Airliners off-course across hours of sky
34 minutes between two planes' hits
Towers exploding into bits
Hundreds thousands tons of concrete
           Blown to dust
And tens thousands tons of steel
           Brought straight down

C)
Oh, they fell so fast, fell straight down,
Fell through beams and columns as much as four feet thick
Fell through their cores of steel as fast as dust
Fell with oceans' roar and volcanoes' rush
Fell like elevators erupting to the ground
As their victims screamed and we hugged ourselves

D)
Oh what'a--what'a--what'a are we to make of this
Blows that struck--struck--struck us like a fist
Blows whose shock hid their source
Blows that hammered past our eyes
Blows meant to inflame and galvanize
Blows meant to numb and paralyze
Blows meant to send us into the 'Endless War'
That is a Ruling Few's 'New World Order'

A)
9/11   is a Big Lie
...
And we're gonna shout-shout-shout it

Loud and high
And we're gonna shout-shout-shout it
To the skies

B)
Giuliani knew the South Tower would "collapse"
He fled his post as firefighters died
Jerry Hauer told Dan Rather on CBS
The planes did it under bin Laden's hands
Cherkasky and Bremer chimed right in,
Sitting on evidence that would indict them,
While Larry and Pete, GMAC and GE,
Raked in profits from insurance plans,
From weapons, oil, and Afghan opium
Like Maurice Greenberg and his sons
They all got richer, oh yes indeed
Like Rockefellers and Rothschilds over hundreds years,
They all got richer amid our tears
Like so many killers over hundreds years
They all got richer amid our tears
From blasted Buildings, molten earth,
Victims' screams and broken dreams
They all got richer amid our tears

D)
Oh what'a--what'a--what'a are we to make of this
Blows that struck us--struck us--struck us like a fist
Blows whose shock hid their source
Blows that hammered past our eyes
Meant to make us fear, obey, and stand in lines
Under Universal Debt to One Big Bank,
Meant to send us into the 'Endless War'
That is a Ruling Few's 'New World Order'

A)
9/11   is a Big Lie
...
And we're gonna shout-shout-shout it
Loud and high
And we're gonna shout-shout-shout it
To the skies

B)
Six years now the Official Story has spun
Like the Sun around Earth. not the reverse
A Dark Age indeed, one of Kings and serfs
And trusty hacks that are sure to hide facts--
On FEMA, on NIST, on *Times* and on *Post*!--
In the mighty Wurlitzer's universe,
Pods and flashes highlit to matter more
Than mass murder from skyscrapers
                              Brought straight down--
Than Endless War bound to concrete
                              Blown to dust--
Than a past and future Terror
                              None can trust

D)
And yet--yet--yet we people of the round,
Truths are there for us to take up
Truths simple but supple like a circle's hands
Truths that can span all seas and lands

A)
9/11   is a Big Lie
...
And we're gonna shout-shout-shout
What we see!
And we're gonna shout-shout-shout
The truth free!

F)
We'll throw back the Cards dealt to us
We'll refuse to die under torn-out skies
We'll fight--fight--fight with our tools
We're gonna fight--fight--fight for this century
Now we have the tools for all to be free
We're gonna fight--fight--fight for this century
Now we have the tools for all to be free
                    earlier version October 16. 2007
                    current, more *Beatles*-anthemic version February 8, 2008

INDEX

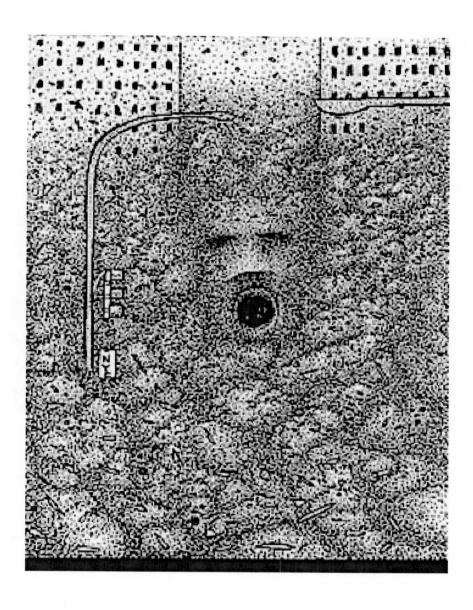

The people united ...

March on the Golden Gate Bridge, May 31, 2008, by parents and children for non-toxic alternatives to the spraying of pesticides. An account of how the efforts of thousands won a partial victory against spraying to 'eradicate' the Light Brown Apple Moth in California is up on the Organic Consumers' Association website-- organicconsumers.org/organic/organicsolutions.pdf.

A great deal more about this issue and related issues can be found at the websites of organizers who have worked phenomenally hard: LBAMspray.com, stopthespray.org, cassonline.org, stopthespraymarin.com, pesticidewatch.org, ...

Through work with Stop the Spray Marin I learned about existing strengths of organic growers and consumers and about the public's vulnerabilities to Genetically Modified seeds and food. This learning led to the 4-pager that's partially reprinted on the next several pages.

LOCAL CONTROL and ORGANIC SOLUTIONS
Choices for a Sustainable Future
(July 2008)

People in California Already Have the Power to Decide the Quality of their Food, Air and Water

The number of people now belonging to **Organic Consumers Assocations** in California exceeds 90,000, a membership nearly three times larger than that of one of California's most influential lobbyists, the California Correctional Peace Officers Association.

There are more than 2000 **Certified Organic Farmers** in California. There are 524 officially recognized **Farmers' Markets** in the State.

Across the United States the amount of acreage that's devoted to organic food has grown from 935,450 in 1992 to 4,003,973 in 2005. During the same span organic livestock has increased almost 2000% --from 11,647 to 229,788. Organic poultry has increased more than 22,000%--from 61,363 to 14,193,270!

In California the consumption of organic food has increased hugely, too. Between 2000 and 2005 the total sales of organic bee, dairy, livestock, poultry products in the State grew more than 600%--from $12,121,323 to $82,767,951

The people of California and the U. S. clearly recognize that organic food is the way to go for a sustainable future.

All that's lacking for our choices to have broad effect are comparable increases in our economic and political organization and influence.

The 21st Century Is an Age of Crises That Requires Cooperative Partnerships

Every day, the combination of a severely changing climate and a deepening shortage of resources causes crises in California, crises that can only be answered by local, cooperative control of matters basic to 21st-century life.

2008's headlines tell a story of weather extremes across the U. S. Floods drown crops in the Midwest. Droughts parch the Southwest. On June 25, 2008, wildfires in California were the unprecedented total of 1001. Tornadoes multiply in number year by year.

At the same time, one gallon of Regular gas costs over $4.50 and is predicted to cost over $7 by 2010. Prices of food rise correspondently. Wages and salaries for California's middle-class, however, are falling further against inflation, and the U. S. dollar has never been valued less outside this nation.

We need basic solutions. We need local control of our economies and environment.

We need food that's grown close to its markets. We need to minimize costs for oil and gas, fertilizers and pesticides.We need work that involves production of goods rather than speculation on debts. We need to be sure of the contents in sprays (see '**The LBAM Example**' on page 2) and to rid our air of its poisonous haze. We need to know for sure, through local examination and regulation, that what we eat and drink is safe and nutritious (see page 3 on '**Global Monopolies Reach across All Fields**).

The surest way to meet these needs and accomplish these goals is to further organize ourselves (as the many '**Organic Victories**' on the back page here show).

Food as Fuel: Local Organic or Global GMO?
Global Monopolies Reach across All Fields

Big Oil is as Big Ag as is Big Chem as is Big Media: the concentration of power among global producers and distributors of pesticides, fertilizers, and food rivals the consolidations among oil-and-gas and mass-media corporations over the past 25 years.

A handful of multinational corporations (MNCs) hold dominant power.

According to Malaysian journalist Anil Netto, 'Syngenta, Bayer, Monsanto, BASF, Dow and Dupont together control 85%' of the annual pesticide market valued at $30 billion US dollars.'

Netto's piece from December 2007, 'MNCs Gaining Total Control over Farming', also states: 'Three companies--Cargill, Archer Daniels, Bunge--control nearly 90 per cent of global grain trade while Dupont and Monsanto dominate the global seed market. Eleven firms account for about half the world sales of seeds, of which about a quarter are genetically engineered seeds.'

Such dominant power can make tyrannical decisions. In 2003 *ABC News* reported that 92% of the more than 1000 people in its national poll wanted identifying labels on food that was grown with GMOs. All nations of the European Union require such labeling. None of such labeling has so far come from producers and sellers who use GMOs in the U.S.

Such interlocking power also allows contamination that profits the contaminator. Between 1996 and 2006 the amount of acres planted with GMO-infused crops grew 60-fold worldwide, to 1. 4 billion acres. This increase made 'biotech crops ... the fastest adopted crop technology in recent history', wrote the *International Service for the Acquisition of Agri-Biotech Applications*. The United States accounts for more than 65% of the world's GMO croplands. According to the *Non-GMO Project*, 'It is currently estimated that in the U. S., 61% of corn, 89% of soybeans, 83% of cotton and 75% of canola grown are genetically modified.'

The "drift" of seeds and pesticides for GMO crops affects neighboring and distant areas. Also, the simple presence of GMO crops invades the DNA of subsequent seeds that are supposed to be 'traditional' and not 'biotech'. The *Union of Concerned Scientists* analyzed two laboratories' results from testing in 2004: 'The most conservative expression of the combined results is that transgenically derived DNA was detected in 50% of the corn, 50% of the soybean, and 83% of the canola varieties tested.'

In short, the 'traditional' became artificial by association, and then went into people's stomachs.

Double-Good for Monsanto, Not So Good for Us

Like CheckMate's sprays for the Light Brown Apple Moth (LBAM), Big Ag's GMO crops are proving to be not so good in their delivery of performance.

The Center for Food Safety and *Friends of the Earth* brought out a study in February 2008 that's titled 'Who Benefits from GM Crops?: The Rise in Pesticide Use.'

This study points out: 'Roundup Ready soybeams, the world's most widely planted GM crop, have 6% lower yield than conventional soy, according to University of Nebraska researchers.' These soybeans are, however, specifically 'Ready' for pesticides made by Monsanto. The study notes: 'Four of every five acres of GM crops worldwide are Monsanto's Roundup Ready varieties, designed specifically for use with glyphosphate, the weed-killing chemical that Monsanto sells under the name of Roundup.'

The multiplying use of Roundup's glyphosphate, a use corresponding with that 60-fold increase in GMO croplands, has produced new mutations: weeds resistant to Roundup and dosed now with increasing amounts of another toxic chemical, 2.4-D, which was a part of the Vietnam War's killing, deforming and deranging defoliant, Agent Orange, when produced by Dow Chemical, the corporation that Monsanto ingested in -----.

In 2007 Monsanto's profits from the Roundup pesticide alone were about $1 billion, the *New York Times* reported. Cargill's 2007 profits were up 36% to $2,340,000 and Archer Daniel Midland's 2007 profits were up 67% to $2,200,000 billion.

And Triple-Bad for an Organic Food-Supply

The triple whammy that Big Ag and Big Chem hold over the world's public in the 21 century (controlling seeds, crops and pesticides) especially slams growers and consumers of organic food.

While the U.S. people steadily increase their choice of organic food, the number of wholesale distributors of such food has fallen from 28 in 1982 to 3 in 2005. Dozens of organic producers have been bought by major food-processing corporations.

And the "drift" goes on.

In 2004 the *Uniion of Concerned Scientists* wrote: 'Transgenic contamination of traditional seed varieties poses a special threat to the future of organic agriculture, an increasing important sector of U. S. agriculture.... Organic farmers strive to produce crops that are free of transgenically derived DNA. If, through no fault of their own, they are unable to supply such products, they face eroding markets. The ease with which the traditional seed supply can be contaminated with transgenically derived DNA unfairly frustrates organic farmers seeking to deliver high-quality products.'

And yet—as our closing page shows—a countervailing force of success-stories among growers and consumers of organic food is also rising: networks that are like oases and lifelines in a landscape both homogenized and apocalyptic.

By combining our powers we can win a sustainable future.

Organic Victories

1997--2006 'In just one decade, from 1997 to 2006, sales of organic food have grown by nearly 80 percent to $17.7 billion' in the U.S.'
Raleigh News and Observer (North Carolina)

1998-2007 The **Organic Valley** group of cooperative organic farmers, begun by seven Wisconsin farms in 1988, grows its sales from $15 million in 1998 to $432.5 million in 2007—and grows to more than 1200 farms across the U.S.

2000-2001 The **Sacramento Natural Foods Cooperative**, begun in 1972, adopts through input from more than 2000 owner-members and ultimate consensus a strategic plan 'for the future of the business they own together.' The Sac. Coop now has more than 9000 members and a 'community-run' farmer's market in low-income Del Paseo Heights.

2003 'In a nationwide 2003 survey, 69% of the consumers responded that they were more likely to purchase food produced by a farmer-owned cooperative, and 64% agreed that food produced by a farmer-owned coooperative was of better quality that food produced by other types of companies.'
Shermain Hardesty, Univ. of California at Davis

2004 Mendocino County in northern California passes Measure H, becoming the first county in the United States to render it "unlawful for any person, firm, or corporation to propagate, cultivate, raise, or grow genetically modified organisms." Trinity, Marin, and Santa Cruz Counties follow with similar anti-GMO measures in California.

2004-2005 Bio-diesel use across the U.S. increases from 250 to 750 million gallons.

2005-2006 Local and national resistance defeats a California legislative measure (Senate Bill 1056) that would have removed Counties' ability to prohibit GMO crops. "The further you get away from the local level, the more trouble it will cause," says Karen Keene, an advocate for the **League of Calfornia Cities**.

2006 The Black-owned **Federation of Southern Cooperatives** records 73,516 loans for $211.4 million by its credit-unions over 40 years.

2007 The **Organic Consumers Association** and allies win an abandonment by Monsanto of its GE RoundUp Ready wheat and an abandonment by Starbuck's of any milk adulterated by recombinant Bovine Growth Hormone.

2007 **Co-op America's** '1% in Community Campaign' moves 'nearly $1 billion into low-income communities – creating jobs, affordable housing and locally owned businesses.'

2007-2008 'April 2007-2008 dry grocery dollar sales growth in organics was 10 times greater than non-organics, by a 28.8% to 2.8% comparison.'
              Flex News, July 14, 2008
2008 Farmers dispossessed of their 14 acres in South Central Los Angeles begin planting and harvesting nearby Bakersfield, CA.

2008 The **Davis Co-op** (8000 members in a city of 65,000) maintains sponsorship of an instructional Farmers Market on the UC-Davis campus.

Resources: Organizations

Consumers
Organic Consumers Association (U.S.), 6771 S. Silver Hill Dr., Finland, Minnesota 55603 : www.organicconsumers.org, : 218-226-4164
International Federation of Organic Agricultural Movements (IFOAM) Bonn, Germany : www.ifoam.org : 49-228-92650-10.
Co-op America 1612 K Street NW, Suite 600, Washington DC 20006 : www.coopamerica.org : 800-584-7336
Non-GMO Project 2599 Huntington Dr., Upland, CA 91786 : www.nongmoproject.org : 909-626-0809

Farmers and Grocers
Organic Trade Association POB 547, Greenfield, MA 01302 : www.howtogoorganic : 413-774-7511

National Cooperative Grocers Association 389 E. College St., Iowa City, IA 52240 : www.ncga.coop :319-466-9029

California Certified Organic Farmers 2155 Delaware Avenue, Suite 150, Santa Cruz, CA 95060 : www.ccof.org : 831-423-2263

South Central Farmers 1702 E. 41st St., Los Angeles 90058 : www.southcentralfarmers.com : 800-249-5240

Federation of Southern Cooperatives 2769 Church St., East Point, GA 30344 : www.federation.coop : 404-765-0991

Alternatives to Pesticides

Pesticide Action Network, North America 49 Powell St., Ste. 500, San Francsico, CA 94102 : www.panna.org : 415-981-1771

Pesticide Watch 1107 9th St., Ste. 601, Sacramento, CA 95814 : pesticidewatch.org : 916-551-1883

California Alliance to Stop the Spray and many allied organizations and websites (**cassonline.org, LBAMSpray.com, stopthespray.org, 1hope.org, stopthespraymarin.org, playnotspray.org,** ... Be sure to watch the excellent videos, including "It'll Stay" and "Into the Sky") : 200 Washington St., Ste 170, Santa Cruz, CA 95060 : 831-464-1777

(Thanks in particular to the cooperative that funded the writing, printing and distribution of 'Local Control and Organic Solutions', the Organic Valley Family of Farms, *CEO George Siemon, and to the two friends who helped with lay-out, Henry Dakin and Terbo Ted. Ted is also known as Theodore Terbolizard and was a 2008 Republican Candidate for the U. S. Congress in the 49th District, California's Gold Country.)*

Again, the full 4-pager and its account of of how thousands of activists won in their opposition to LBAM spraying can be seen online at the Organic Consumers Association website-- http://www.organicconsumers.org/organicsolutions.pdf .)

Next, the problem of our money-supply. In my view, the reality as to who controls our money-supply is as vital as the reality as to who controls our food-supply in the 21st century.

IN AND FROM THE TEMPLE

Henry Paulson, Ben Bernanke, and Securities and Exchange
Commissioner Christopher Cox at close of Oct. 2008 "bail-out" deal

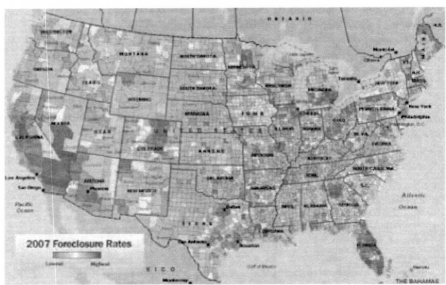

Foreclosures against would-be U.S. home-owners rose more than
200% in the first nine months of 2008

GETTING RID OF THE "FED",
STANDING UP ON OUR OWN
(September 25, 2008)

Making Good News from Bad:
For Public Ownership of the United States' Money-Supply

In 2005 the amount paid by in individual income-tax to the Internal
Revenue Service was $927 billion, or about 36% of the U.S. Federal
Budget of $2.5 trillion for that year.

Please note that all of 2005's wide-ranging Federal expenditures
(Defense, Education, Medicaid and Medicare, Social Security, ...)
were in that year's $2.5 trillion Budget.

Now, September into October of 2008, we face a Bail-out Bill and
other U. S. Government funding of speculator Corporations' bad debts
that already totals more than $1 trillion.

That is, what's commonly known as 2008's ongoing "bail-out of Wall
Street" (the Bear, Stearns and J.P.Morgan Chase investment-banks last
March, the Fannie Mae and Freddie Mae mortgage-guarantors earlier
this month, the American International Group or A.I.G. conglomerate
last month, and an unknown number of exposed lending institutions in
the future) is to cost about $200 billion more than individuals paid in
U.S. income-tax to support our Government's entire operations three
years ago, and to COST ABOUT HALF THE AMOUNT allocated in
the NATION'S WHOLE BUDGET for the fiscal year 2005.

These numbers are presented to give a sense of the "bail-out" that's
underway.

It's colossal; it's unprecedented in this nation before 2008; it
demands 'unreviewable' powers; and it's doomed to fail due to the
irredemably more colossal amounts of debt in 'derivatives' that are
owed by its principal U. S.-based and Europe-based beneficiaries.

It throws bundles of money onto sinking ships.

No School, no Road, no wind-farm will come from it.

And the instrument that the U. S. Government has used for funding
of the $1 trillion-and-counting to the bettor/debtor Corporations is one
that requires interest be paid to it for any funding it provides: the
Federal Reserve System, that unaccountable intermediary that has
plagued the United States for almost one century.

We can turn the enormity of this year's bad economic news into salvational transformation if we use it to get rid of the Federal Reserve System.

What is the Fed?--
"The Worse Legislative Crime of the Ages is Perpetrated by This Banking and Currency Bill"

The Federal Reserve System, or Fed, is a unique, privately owned and finally unaccountable part of the U.S. Government.

Created in 1913 by bankers and legislators representing the Rothschild and Rockefeller families to govern the United States' money-supply, the Federal Reserve System is controlled by a consortium of Banks, most of them based in Europe. It has never been audited by the U. S. Congress. Upon passage of the Act that established the FRS just before World War I, Congressman Charles A. Lindbergh said: "When the President [Woodrow Wilson} signs this bill, the invisible government of the monetary power will be legalized.... The worst legislative crime of the ages is perpetrated by this banking and currency bill."

The primary of the FRS' 12 regional Banks, the Federal Reserve Bank of New York, sets daily interest-rates for the System's 8.437 (or less, now) Member Banks. The Federal Reserve Bank of New York is thus the most central controller of capital's daily flow in the U. S. The former Chairman of A.I.G., fortunate recipient of $85 billion in U.S. Government funding this month, Maurice Greenberg, is a former Chairman of the Federal Reserve Bank of New York.

Like its nominal parent, the Federal Reserve Bank of New York is owned by a consortium of Banks independent of the U. S. Government. In 1997 the Chase Manhattan Bank owned 32.35% and Citibank owned 20.51% of the total 19.752,655 shares of the Federal Reserve Bank of New York, according to a study by Eric Samuelson.

By 2002 the Chase Manhattan Bank was merged into J.P. Morgan Chase and Citibank was named Citigroup. During that year, six years before the current "bail-out" to prevent a supposed "melt-down" on Wall Street, my book " ' 9/11' " / Facing Our Fascist State noted that J.P. Morgan Chase was at risk for $23.5 trillion in "derivatives" (debt derived from revenue-producing assumption of responsibility for others' investments), Citigroup was at risk for $9 trillion in derivatives, and Bank of America for $10 trillion. The mind-boggling magnitude of the three top U. S. Banks' total liability from derivatives, $42.5 trillion, was more than $40 trillion more than their assets then.

In short, the current "crisis" has had a very long foreground, one that's been calculated daily by experts who continued to make billions of dollars per year through issuing credit and printing and lending money. In 2005 the current U.S. Treasury Secretary, Henry Paulson, he and Ben Bernanke of the FRS the main pitch-men for the proposed "bail-out", made $37 million as Chief Executive Officer of the Goldman, Sachs investment-bank, according to *Forbes Magazine*. (See the chart on page 271 and page 325 for Goldman, Sachs' borrowing from the FRS between 2000-2007.)

All of this unchecked progress toward crisis, a crisis now most felt by would-be home-owners or those already homeless across the U. S., came under the watch of the Fed, the entity somehow in place to lend funds at interest to the most richly endowed nation on Earth.

Now the game that the Fed has led appears to be foundering.

Speculator Corporations lurch like dinosaurs bloated and diseased. Then they topple. Then they are eaten by even more bloated bettor/debtor Banks, producing even greater and more toxic monsters. And we the public are forced to live with them and to absorb their losses.

Centuries ago, U. S. Presidents warned us about our current predicament and also pointed the way toward prosperity.

Jackson, Jefferson and Lincoln all rejected the nonsense of a private, central Bank or System that issues or controls the nation's money-supply.

The basic changes and choices we need to make for remedy to our predicament are simple as a hand-clap. We need to be rid of the Fed, to throw out distant middle-men, and to take control of our nation's money-supply and hence our destiny.

'The Government's Greatest Creative Opportunity'

Andrew Jackson successfully fought renewal of the charter for the United States' second privately owned, money-issuing central Bank, the so-called Bank of the United States. Asked on his death-bed what he judged to be his Presidency's most important accomplishment, Jackson said: "I killed the Bank."

Battling against the United States first such Bank, an institution especially championed by Alexander Hamilton, U. S. President Thomas Jefferson wrote the U.S. Treasury Secretary, Albert Gallatin, in 1802: 'If the American people ever allow private banks to control the issue of currency, first by inflation, then by deflation, the banks and corporations that will grow up around them will deprive the people of all property until their children will wake up homeless on the continent their fathers conquered. The issuing power should be taken from the banks and restored to the people, to whom it properly belongs.'

Upon taking the step of issuing interest-free "greenbacks" as the U. S. currency during the Civil War, a war promoted by European financiers, Abraham Lincoln wrote in 1862: 'The privilege of creating and issuing money is not only the supreme prerogative of Government, but it is the Government's greatest creative opportunity ... By the adoption of these principles, the ... taxpayers will be saved immense sums of interest. The financing of all public enterprises, and the conduct of the Treasury, will become matters of practical administration. Money will cease to be the master and become the servant of humanity.'

Big Bankers' Worries, Plots and Admissions

The year after Abraham Lincoln ordered the printing of "greenbacks", the *London Times* wrote: 'If this mischievous financial policy, which has its origin in the North American Republic, shall become endurated down to a fixture, then that Government will furnish its own money without cost. It will pay off its debts and be without debt. It will have all the money necessary to carry on its commerce. It will become prosperous without precedent in the history of the world.... That government must be destroyed or it will destroy every monarchy on the globe.'

For 'monarchy' then, read money-lending, interest-collecting middle-man now. By the latter 19th century, anyway, Kings and Queens of Europe and empire-builders such as Cecil Rhodes and John D. Rockefeller were borrowing heavily from private Banks.

A memo that was circulated among the American Bankers Association in 1891 anticipates our current, supposed "credit-crisis". Read its calculating plot and devastating aim. 'On Sept. 1st, 1894, we will not renew our loans under any consideration,' this memo says. 'On Sept. 1st we will demand our money. We will foreclose and become mortagees in possession. We can take two-thirds of the frams west of the Mississippi, and thousand of them east of the Mississippi as well, at our own price.... Then the farmers will become tenants as in England.' The memo, in short, urges dispossession of families so that can be returned to feudal servitude.

The plot that led to creation of the Federal Reserve System in 1913 is well-documented in Ellen Hodgson Brown's recent <u>The</u> <u>Web</u> of <u>Debt</u>, G. Edward Griffin's <u>The</u> <u>Creature</u> <u>from</u> <u>Jeykll</u> <u>Island</u>, and in Eustace Mullins' monumental <u>The</u> <u>Secrets</u> <u>of</u> <u>the</u> <u>Federal</u> <u>Reserve</u> (a book so revealing that all 10,000 copies of its first German edition were burned in 1955 with the approval of the then U.S. High Commissioner to Germany, James B. Conant, a future President of Harvard University).

Most succinct and germane to our predicament, now, however, is this stark admission by Sir Josiah Stamp, speaking at the University of Texas in 1927, when he was President of the Bank of England and reputed to be the second-richest person in Britain.

For whatever reason or reasons, Sir Josiah spoke to problems and solutions with a clarity startling as splashes of fresh water. Sir Josiah told his audience: "The modern banking system manufactures money out of nothing. The process is perhaps the most astounding piece of sleight of hand that was ever invented. Banking was conceived in inequity and born in sin . . . . Bankers own the earth. Take it away from them but leave them the power to create money, and, with a flick of a pen, they will create enough money to buy it back again. . . . Take this great power away from them and all great fortunes like mine will disappear, for then this would be a better and happier world to live in. . . . But, if you want to continue to be the slaves of bankers and pay the cost of your own slavery, then let bankers continue to create money and control credit.'

What We Can Do within the U.S. Government

First, I think, we must be rid of the Fed.

Its controlling families, many of them based in Europe, have gorged long enough--gorged for decades on this country's riches and the goods our bodies and minds produce. "Is there no danger to our liberty and independence in a bank that in its nature has so little to bind it to our country?' Andrew Jackson said in 1832 about vetoing a second charter to the privately owned Bank of the United States.

What do we face in this work-week of September 22-26, 2008?

The almost unbelievable arrogance of the still expanding Bailout Bill grants unilateral and 'unreviewable' powers of limitless lending to the Treasury Department, the FRS, and the U. S. President, accomplishing a *coup d'etat* by legislative declaration even more extreme than 2002's similarly headlong USA PATRIOT Act.

What we can see in the Bill's provisions are like the effects of another 9/11 without the pretext of another terrorist incident.

Passage of this Bill will mean the end of even the theater of democracy in this nation.

The Bill also cannot succeed in any of its pitchmen's stated aims. The amount of speculator Corporations' debt through derivatives (commonly called Collectivized Debt Obligations, or CDO's, now) far exceeds even nations' resources.

The Switzerland-based Bank of International Settlements estimates the 2008 total of derivatives' debt to exceed $450 trillion, far more than the staggering heap resting indigestibly inside JP Morgan Chase, Citigroup and the Bank of America circa <u>Facing Our Fascist State</u> 2002.

That is, the fat-with-debt have grown by 2008 immovably gargantuan. They're irredeemably corrupt and beyond saving. They sit like parasitic Jabba the Huts on the Boulevards of Capitols.

Such a fantastical amount as $450 trillion can't be whittled down or attacked.

Rather, it should be left alone. Let it explode on itself, thereby exploding the clearly unfit system that created it. The Earth won't mind any missing credit- or debit-entries, nor will we need them in our abilities to make and share wealth from technology and resources.

Likewise, the imposition of $1.2 trillion more in debt to the U.S. Federal Budget on top of the $480 billion deficit already projected for this nation in 2008 makes no sense as a intended remedy. It makes sense only as an inflationary monster, certain to hasten devaluation of the U. S. dollar and disempowerment of the U. S. public at the same time as the U. S. Military is threatened with more bogging warfare in the Middle East and Central Asia. It makes sense, in short, only if it's intention is to further sap and wreck the U. S. public's ability to resist orders imposed on us.

The Bill must be rejected, I think, as firmly as Andrew Jackson and Thomas Jefferson rejected the first and second Europe-based 'Bank of the United States' in their eras. It must be opposed, I think, as courageously as Abraham Lincoln, Mohandas Gandhi, and Martin Luther King, Jr stood against irrational inequity and for the public's well-being in their places and times.

Article 30 of the U.S. Constitution lets Congress rescind the Federal Reserve Act. If we wish to urge elected Representatives to action, let's urge them to rescind the Fed.

What, then, could we have instead of the Federal Reserve System? Ellen Hodgson Brown's <u>The</u> <u>Web</u> <u>of</u> <u>Debt</u> quotes Richard Russell, an analyst for nearly 50 years, from his April 2005 'Dow Theory Letter.'

'To simplify, when the US Government needs money, it either collects it in taxes or it issues bonds. These bonds are sold to the Fed, and the Fed, in turn, makes book entry deposits. This "debt money" created out of thin air is then made available to the US government. But if the US government can issue Treasury bills, notes and bonds, it can also issue currency, as it did prior to the formation of the Federal Reserve. *If the US issued its own money, that money could cover all the its expenses, and the income tax tax wouldn't be needed.* So what's the objection to getting rid of the Fed and letting the US government issue its own currency? *Easy, it cuts out the bankers and eliminates the income tax.*'

Ellen Hodgon Brown and many others have proposed practical means by which banking of all kinds could be nationalized and middle-men removed from public works. The American Monetary Institute, headed by Stephen Zarlenga, is one source of alternatives. The A.M.I.'s Momentary Reform Conference happens to be taking place in Chicago next weekend.

What We Can Do to Create Our Own Sustainable Worlds, Both Local and Global

'Every one shaded / By dat Mountain of Debt / Waiting to fall / On our children's heads' from the year 2000 song "Money Don't Care"

'We're gonna fight-fight-fight for this century / Now we have the tools for all to be free' from the 2008 song "9/11 Is A Big Lie"

We know, of course, that we can't rely on elected Representatives to act for us. The majority of them serve their campaigns' dominant funders, we know--and many of those funders are the speculating Banks and other Corporations that have brought about 2008's " 'crisis' " and " 'bail-out' " and predicaments for us.

For one specific response to free ourselves, we in the United States can consider the refusal to pay Individual Income Tax until such time as our Federal Government funds peoples' needs and children's futures instead of Corporation's bad bets and debts.

That $927 billion or so, mentioned at the start of this piece, can be used for far better purposes than its allocation has previously been employed.

Think what <u>we</u> could do with $927 billion! Imagine!

With health-care. With education. With employment.

With transformations that can make the 21st century sustainable and that can make further centuries sustainable for our descedants.

With wind-farms and wetlands and Internet streaming of Music Festivals.

With "Everyone doing and doing their best!" (Bob Marley, "Jump Nyabinghi", on his album <u>Confrontation</u>).

Taking back control of our food-supply as well as our money-supply or means-of-fiscal-exchange will also be vital for our survival. Please see the Organic Consumers Association website--it's loaded with excellent articles. The 'Local Control and Organic Solutions' pictorial brochure on that site lists many 'Resources'.

One last cautionary. As said above, I think the only rational reasons for the " 'bail-out' " are 1) to temporarily float ships that are going to sink anyway and 2) to more sap the U.S. public's ability to resist orders imposed on us.

Many measures for martial law in a declared 'Emergency', with the U.S. President as effectual dictator, are already waiting, enacted in the seven years since 9/11/01.

And the Bank of International Settlements, the hub of the Western world's Central Bank transactions, waits to substitute a global currency for the wrecked and devalued U.S. dollar and to thereby allow European financiers fulfillment of their centuries-old desire: outright and 'unreviewable' possession of the 'North American Republic'.

They want to steal all of our homes.

Now is the test of our lives.

AGAINST THE THEFT OF A NATION:
FIVE STEPS TO FREEDOM AND SOLVENCY
(October 31, 2008)

BACKGROUND

The first two weeks of October 2008 have seen the most bare-faced and brazen, yet sly and and secretive, theft of a nation proceed, robbing the public of the United States of both rights and posterity.

Never before has so much money and means been taken from a supposedly sovereign country as here in the U.S. since October 3, 2008.

On October 15 mainstream commentators tallied the amounts taken so far, a total that adds more than $1.1 trillion to the national debt for the current fiscal year.

• $700 billion for the original "Bail-out Bill" unveiled by Treasury Secretary Henry Paulson and Federal Reserve System Chairman Ben Bernanke after the failures of bettor/debtor speculators Fannie Mae/Freddie Mac, Lehman Brothers, and the American International Group (AIG) in September;

• $130 billion added on by the U. S. Senate and House of Representatives to the Bill that became law on October 3;

• $200 billion separately devoted to sustaining Fannie Mae and Freddie Mac;

• Over $100 billion already allocated to sustaining AIG.

Beyond this $1.130-trillion total are unknowable and 'unlimited' expenditures that the powers given to the Treasury and to the Fed by the vote on October 3 have opened up:

• Lending and credit without check, cap or oversight to the United States' most major, surviving commercial Banks (which now include the former investment-banks Goldman Sachs and Morgan Stanley;

• Lending and credit without check, cap or oversight to "foreign" commercial <u>and</u> central Banks.

That last new means and power given to the Treasury and Fed deserves an exclamatory pause, then scrutiny, then it deserves any resort to rejection that we can raise against it.

Now, you see, the Treasury Department (headed by "Hank" Paulson, former $37-million-a-year CEO of Goldman Sachs) and the Federal Reserve System (that private consortium of Banks that allies and/or relatives of the Rothschild and Rockefeller families manipulated into control of the U.S. money-supply just before World War I, its majority ownership and subsequent hundreds of billions in profits held by European financial interests, most of them based in the City of London) can give unlimited amounts of fiat money and credit to Germany's Deustche Bank, to Holland's Fortis Bank, to the Bank of England, to the Bank of France, to the Hong Kong and Shanghai Corporation, ...

How?

Well, now, you see, the Fed, whose "war-chest" of $800 billion for ailing Banks and other Corporations is essentially tapped out by 2008's failures, can receive bonds from the U.S. Treasury, (bonds whose fiat value is created simply by computer key-stroke, please remember, though U.S. tax-papers remain ultimately liable for every penny of their nominal value) and then count them as funds which it can then distribute to any needy Bank or Corporation, regardless of said supplicant's nominal nationality, so long as the supplicant is doing business somewhere in the 50 United States.

And the Federal Reserve System and Treasury Department can exercise this new and marvelous form of charity without check, cap or oversight, thanks to 74 Senators and 263 Representatives, despite the vehement opposition by a vast majority of these politicians' constituents to such obvious devaluation of the U.S. Dollar, impoverishment of our children's futures, and certain bankruptcy of the nation.

Across every map of the United States should now be stamped: Owner, as of October 3, 2008, the City of London.

We can, however, regain control of this nation. We can reject the destructive nonsense that's now imposed on us. We can throw off the vampire/zombie Banks now stuck on our backs and necks. We can simply repudiate the hundreds of trillions of dollars of debt these gamblers have assumed through "derivatives." We can go back to a real economy that produces goods for people's needs and prosper as never before through a true globalism that employs 21-century technology and recognitions.

We can take five direct steps toward rationality and justice, solvency and freedom, personal independence and collective responsibility.

FIVE STEPS

1. Replace the Federal Reserve System with a Publicly Owned National Bank that Issues Interest-Free Funds for Operation of the United States.

The privately owned Fed is now as it has been since its covert creation in 1913: a drain on the nation's resources, a guarantor that no Commercial Bank shall fail despite whatever excesses in speculation that the Bank commits , and a means of yoking people and businesses to unnecessary debt (sometimes called " 'credit' ") that instrinsically produces inflation and consequent, de facto devaluation of the U.S. dollar.

The Fed is the central vampire that allows insolvent or "zombie" Banks to survive, drawing from workers' collective and personal wealth so that obviously bankrupt bettor/debtor Banks and other Corporations live on.

In 2005 $352 billion of the $927 Individual Income Tax paid by workers in the U. S. went to to the Fed's consortium of private Banks as interest.

The FRS and the IRS both violate the U.S. Constitution.

Article 1, Section 8 of the U. S. Constitution states that Congress alone shall have the power 'to coin money'. In 1910, three years prior to legalization of the FRS, the U.S. debt was $1 billion, or $12.40 per citizen, according to Pastor Sheldon Emry's Billions for the Bankers, Debts for the People. By 1920 the amounts were $24 billion and $228 respectively. By October 2008 the amounts are over $10 trillion and over $33,000 respectively (not counting, of course, individual consumers' and home-buyers' debts).

2. Replace all international Commercial Banks with local, cooperative institutions that supply funds to the public without usurious interest and without 'fractional reserve-lending' that allows said Banks to lend at least 7 1/2 times the amount of their assets.

According to the Insurance Information Institute, at the end of 2004 the 'book-value' (assets minus liabilities) of all U.S. Commercial Banks was $850 billion.

In her book The Web of Debt Ellen Hodgson Brown generously gives a double value to these Banks in advancing her solution to them: that 'around $1.7 trillion might be enough to purchase the whole U.S. commercial banking industry.'

Now, how have U.S. Banks with a book-value of $850 billion gotten into a $180-trillion (yes, $180 trillion) total amount of debt from "derivatives" by 2008, so that the largest of them (J.P. Morgan Chase, Citigroup, and Bank of America) have assets whose worth amount to 40, or 50, or more multiples times less than their debt from derivatives?

Well, you see, derivatives are most often "side-bets", as you can register in this excerpt from CBS --60 Minutes-- piece on 'The Shadow Market' from October 5.

> http://60minutes.yahoo.com/segment/197/credit_default_swaps
> or http://crooksandliars.com/nicole-belle/60-minutes-wall-
> streets-shadow-market

Interviewer Steve Kroft asks University of California San Diego professor Frank Partnoy how 2008's stupendous "crisis" and "collapse" could have happened.

Professor Partnoy answers: "It's the side-bets, it's the side-bets."

By "side-bets" the emphatic professor means the unregulated "Credit Default Swaps" through which AIG, Bank of America, Citigroup, JP Morgan Chase et cetera have assumed nominal responsibility for highly risky "sub-prime mortgages" that they themselves previously packaged as "securities" before then treating and trading them as "swaps" at huge and highly leveraged profits (as much as $40 of nominal profit against $1 of nominal investment) among themselves and their global brethren.

In short, a reality staggering to see, much less accept, these Banks have made colossally bad bets that we the public are now supposed to cover so that they, their gambling and lifestyles, can continue.

We should, instead, take them over. We should liquidate them and their liabilites as judiciously as possible. We should replace them with sane system and local, community-governed institutions. We should eschew them as we would a loan-shark who peddles bunco money and as we would a pusher who peddles narcotics to children.

3. After replacing the Federal Reserve System, we the public should assume control of all Institutions that currently owe more to the FRS than they hold in assets.

As you can see in the chart below, Henry Paulson's former firm, Goldman Sachs, began the 21st century with assets of nearly $600 billion against borrowings, or 'Bank Credit', of about $240 billion from

the Federal Reserve System. By end of 2007, however, Goldman
Sachs had assets of about $815 billion against Bank Credit of over
slightly more than $850 billion. That is, the firm accumulated a net
deficit of about $400 billion in the eight years 2000 to 2007.

As you can see, borrowing was especially heavy during Paulson's
term as CEO 2004-2006--when Goldman, Sach borrowed about $230
billion from the Fed and yet grew its assets little more than $20 billion,
a net drain on the nominally Federal agency of more than $200 billion.

The average annual bonus of a Goldman, Sachs partner in the 21st
century is $5 million. Henry Paulson received $37 million in
compensation 2005 as Goldman, Sachs' CEO..

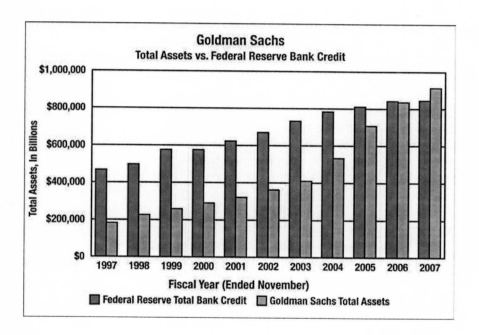

**4. The hundreds of billions that we the public save through replacing
the Fed, substituting local cooperatives and credit-unions for bettor/
debtor Commercial Banks, and assuming control of firms that already
owe more to our Government's nominal lending agency (the Fed) than
they are contributing to our economy, can be spent on society's
urgent needs.**

Rebuilding infrastructure with 21st-century technology is one urgent
need. Remedies and protections against climate-change are other

urgent needs. Health-care and education equal to other nations' and equal for all are also urgent and possible. So too is affordable housing with features of renewable energy that allow net-zero expenditure.

Before and above anything else, however, our savings from being rid of the Fed and its leading bettor/debtor, zombie/vampire Banks should go to assure that those made homeless or threatened with foreclosure by criminally structured loans have the opportunities to regain or keep their homes.

5. At the same time, we should forget about and live apart from Big Government as much as possible.

The great lie of "de-regulation" and a "free market" is now exposed within the U.S., just as it's been exposed for decades in countries that the Western world has exploited throughout the "Third World."

Banks in particular of supranational Corporations favor "deregulation" and a "free market" only when they hold absolute control over access to funds and hence livelihoods and indeed life.

We can can get along very well without such Banks and their like.

We can substitute local cooperatives and credit-unions for supranational loan-sharks that have no connection or commitment to the communities they exploit and under-serve.

We can devise local community-currencies as our own, less corruptible means of exchange.

We can use our 21st-century tools to assure access to needs such as water and to unprecedented modes of global connection. "Now we have the tools for all to be free."

We can grow our own, more reliable food.

The one good thing from the suffering already undergone by people in the "financial crisis" of 2008 is that it can force new and healthy choices and changes.

Crises produce opportunities.

As in the first month after the attacks of September 11, 2001, we need clarity, courage and compassion to face realities and overcome difficulties. (Please see 'Truth Is the Way to Peace, ...'). Although ignored or hidden by mumbo-jumbo of financiers and their politicians, solutions can be as straightforward as the 'Five Steps' set forth above.

News of contemporary Victory Gardens is at
http://www.organicconsumers.org/articles/article_14315.cfm

We need to control our nations' economies to control our destinies.
Exploitative control of society by private bankers can only be
sustained through acts of terror and war. (Please see page 176: 'The
"New World Order" of financiers' Corporate State has nowhere to go
but to terror and war').

The entire history of criminal and elitist financiers over more than
300 years, from founding of the Bank of England forward, proves two
realities. First, the Ruling Few flourish in climates of fear that hide the
cruel unreason of their systems of exploitation. Second, they profit most
from the wars their pretexts produce. " '9/11' " and the current " 'credit
crisis' " are these literal blood-suckers' 21st-century means of terror
and *de facto* war against We Masses' present potential for a world of
freedom and abundance.

We need to turn more from control by any few.

We need to more empower <u>ourselves</u>. We may then advance into
the 'America' of ancestors' and immigrants' dreams and struggles, an
all-world 'America' that releases all of humanity's truly amazing,
benign potentials.

There are many to thank for this book.

First is my main collaborator since 2003 in investigating particulars of the crimes of September 11, 2001, Jim Hoffman. The movement for truth and justice in regard to these crimes is incalculably indebted to JIm's research and critiques, I think. He and this movement have had great help from Victoria Ashley and Gregg Roberts.

Early on, from 2002 into 2004, when exposing demolitions and refuting the Official 9/11 Story was much less widespread an effort than it has since become, the 'Consorts' e-mail list gave me ongoing information and support: contributions from Larry Chin, Shiu Hung, the late Jerry Longspaugh, Kellia Ramirez, Brian and Eric Salter, Jeff Strahl, and Joseph Wanzala I remember now. By 2003 Ken Jenkins and Curtis Charles were active in the San Francisco Bay Area as researchers and documentarians. How lively and concerned were the standing-room-only crowds, how exciting were the revelations and analyses, at showings and discussions in the Bay Area in 2003-04!

Later in 2004 findings from the 'International Inquiries' into 9/11, organized primarily in San Francisco by Carol Broulliet and in Toronto by Barrie Zwicker and Ian Woods, rippled outward. A stream of books, a growing Counterforce of rebellious deliverers of suppressed knowledge (as such are designated in Gravity's Rainbow), and the first Citizens' Grand Jury in Los Angeles, followed.

By 2006, public knowledge that the Official 9/11 Story amounted to a grand structure of lies, built with the care of compartments in a Bank's headquarters. was so widespread that 83% who were polled in the U.S. agreed that their Government was hiding some 'conspiracy' about the attacks that had triggered the Western world's " 'War on Terrorism' ".

Over the past two years, researchers with Doctorates in Physics, Chemistry and Archiecture have added evidence in proof of the demolitions of the Twin Towers and WTC 7. They've advanced in their studies despite losses of position and/or income and graver threats. Representatives among them contributed to the *San Diego Citizens' Grand Jury*--Richard Gage, Steven Jones and Kevin Ryan. Their *Scholars for 9/11 Truth and Justice* and *Architects and Engineers for 9/11 Truth* Websites continue to gain support from other courageous professionals.

In short, we on the side of exposing truths about the events of 9/11/01 have won the battle to inform and persuade a majority of our peers. No amount of lying Reports can hide realities as obvious as two skyscrapers exploding and one imploding, viewed tens of millions of times on the Internet worldwide. Further investigation is needed only as to the Who, How and Why of these epoch-shaping crimes--and such knowledge too has become extensive and profound by 2008.

The opposite page offers more complete lists of workers and allies. To it let me add here one who has become a warm and good friend out of the blue, Bill of puppetgov.com. Please check out "How You Won The War" and "LIes, False Flags, and Nuclear Bombs".

THANKS or THANKS AGAIN
to

Henry Dakin	Vergilia Dakin	Denise Attewell
Richard Gage	Kevin Ryan	Steven Jones
Hummux	*stj911.org*	*ae911truth.org*
Steven Jones *(SFBG)*	Kevin Hammond	Ed Spencer
Shiu Hung	Joe Wanzala	Jerry Duncan
Steve Martinot	Chris Carlisle	Yuri Kochiyama
Bev Conover	Meria Heller	Kathy Guruyawa
Ed Kendrick	Larry Sells	Paragon Radio
Veterans for Peace	9/11 Visibility	Mia Hamel
The Peace Project	Dave Ogle	Paul Berenson
Sofia Shafqat	Kiilu Nyasha	Marcus Books

Denver, Houston, Kansas City, Sacramento, San Diego, ... events

Uptown Theater	Stephen Myers	Grand Lake Theater
San Diego State U.	University of Toronto	Havens Center

Otto Center   Unitarian Universalist Fellowship, Berkley, CA
Portland, OR Downtown Library   Humanist Hall

Lark Theater	Peace Action	Women's International

Global League for Peace and Freedom   Internationalist Books

Ian Johnston	Tracy Larkins	Mark Robinowtiz
Peter B. Collins	Charles Giuliani	Cosmos
Michael Dietrick	Celestine	Michael Castagnola
Tony Brasunas	Dave Heller	Dave Ijams
Matt Everett	Thom Spiedel	Chaim Kupferberg
J. McMichael	James S. Adam	James Richards
Eric Bart	Jeff King	Bob Feldman
Sakura Kone	Dave Berger	John Gannon
Mac McGill	Chris Cardinale	Seth Tobocman

Bork, Sam Jackson, and Ots   Angie, Tsu, Kingman Lim

Abel	Peter Phillips	Michel Chossudovsky
C.A.S.S.	Stop the Spray S.F.	Stop the Spray Marin

Organic Valley Farms   Organic Consumers Association

Ellen Brown	Kevin Danaher	Sue Supriano
Jeannette Armstrong	Aung San Suu Kyi	Mumia Abu Jamal
Richard Levins	Ron Paul	Terbo Ted

Willie and Mary and Maurice and the *San Francisco Bay View*
Jeff, Jonathan, Bob, Matt, Marie, V. Vale, Dave Ratcliff, Betsey Culp

Christine Rose	Karen Johnson	al uh looyah, *911blogger.com*

Ministry of Culture, Venezuela, C.E.N.A.L., and F.I.L.V.E.N. 2008
Cristina and Juan   Hanneke and Pablo and all of *Cacri Jazz*

About *Rebuild Green / New Orleans*

Stanley Covington and O.C. Draughan at the house of Structural
Concrete Integrated Panels built for Robert and Elaine Legier in New
Orleans' Upper 9th Ward, June of 2007. Photo by Jaime Hazard.

Rebuild Green / New Orleans has yet to accomplish what I and others
hoped could be done after the flooding of New Orleans due to
Government's failures in 2005. We have built part of one S.C.I.P. house
and we have installed the first two earth-energy systems in NOLA's Upper
9th Ward. Updates at **rebuildgreen.org** tell the story. Bob and Elaine now
live in the house that should withstand the next Hurricane and flood.

Huge tasks remain, however. Natives of New Orleans still work to reclaim
their city despite serial obstacles. The primary obstacle is City, State and
Federal agencies' frustrations of communication to the displaced. At the
same time, residents of New Orlean face the enduring vulnerability of their
city and all of southern Louisiana to Hurricanes and storm-surges. Two
articles of mine at the puppetgov.com site tell how close New Orleans
came in September 2008 to massive flooding from merely tropical-storm
winds. Our 'Levees, Wetlands and Jobs' working-group has begun a
campaign to raise levees and walls, to restore wetlands through the
planting of spartina grass and cypress trees, and to employ tens of
thousands in this vital public-works project.

Sites with good information include **bioliberty.net, foodmusicjustice.org,
levees.org**, and those for the Gulf Recovery Network and the Gulf Coast
Civic Works Project.

On Waking Up Our Nightmare /
The 9/11/01 Crimes in New York City
(co-authored with Jim Hoffman)

'Don Paul's and Jim Hoffman's *Waking Up* ... does the public a great service by graphically exposing some of the lies regarding the 9/11/01 crimes in New York City and then proposing alternatives to the system that perpetrates such crimes and lies..'
DR. KEVIN DANAHER, co-founder of *Global Exchange*

'Don Paul and Jim Hoffman have performed a feat that the public has waited three years for: solving the 9/11 mystery in a nutshell.'
JOHN LEONARD

'Another great job! It is a really beautifully produced little book. As well as your clear evidence of the deliberate demolitions of the WTC towers, I much liked your final section about cooperative solutions. I think this shows how we can all aim towards a much healthier future.'   MATTHEW EVERETT

'The best of the best of the best ... Waking Up manages to synthesize into less than 80 illustrated pages the contents of a whole stack of books about the crimes of 9/11/01 in New York City and then another stack of books about related subjects whose actual operation and possible transformation are crucial to the future of our world. And you can put it in your pocket!'   BILL KAUTH

On "9/11 Guilt / The Proof Is in Your Hands"
a DVD co-produced with Celestine Star and Jim Hoffman

'This documentary does an excellent job of connecting the dots about 9/11 and the possible political blueprint and financial reasons leading to that momentous event.'   ED ASNER

On " '/9/11' " / Facing Our Fascist State

'A fascinating and breathtaking tour de force through the belly of America's dirty little secrets. Don Paul briliantly recounts the tragic karma of America's corporate greed.... A must-read for anyone who is questioning the media's spoonfed journalism of recent world events and is asking themselves, "What the hell is really going on here?" '   JEFF ADACHI

'Even after spending an entire year devoted almost full-time to consuming every source I could get my hands on concerning 9/11 and the great scam called the "war on terrorism", I was still stunned reading Don Paul's new book. Not only does it offer vivid details and lucid observatons of ruling-class crime, it delivers a much-needed fog-busting WAKE UP! call in just the right way and at the right time.'   BRIAN SALTER

'Don's analysis will remove all doubt from your mind that our government is not the good guy here and that we need to take action now....'   MARIE HARRISON

'David Ray Griffin's The New Pearl Harbor is a great introduction to the truth of 9/11, but Don Paul's earlier " '9/11' " / Facing Our Fascist State gives more depth, especially concerning the forces and people that have created events like 9/11 throughout history.'   KEN JENKINS

On "'9/11' " / Great Crimes, a Greater Cover-up
(co-authored with Jim Hoffman)

'I think the booklet is the most concise, readable and credible piece I have read on the unanswered questions about 9/11.'
RICHARD HEINBERG

Don Paul was the youngest winner of a Wallace Stegner
Fellowship in Creative Writing at Stanford University, age
20 in 1971. He qualified for the 1980 and 1988 U. S. Men's
Olympic Marathon Trial and held the World Best for running 50
kilometers between 1982 and 1994 (2:50:55). He's the author of
more than 20 books and has led or produced more than 20
albums. See wireonfire.com/donpaul .

As Chief Prosecutor for the *San Diego Citizens' Grand
Jury on the Crimes of September 11, 2001 in New York City*
on April 14, 2007 at San Diego State University

'Don Paul has been at the forefront of research into the ultimate
question about the events of September 11th, 2001: Who
benefits? Mr Paul's work begins at Ground Zero and leads right
up to the international elite of finance, weapons, oil, and
narcotics, or as he puts it 'Guns, Oil, Drugs, and Debt' -- the four
pillars of power. Unlike many other 9/11 researchers, Don Paul is
ready to ask the hard questions, and name the names.'

> MIKE COPASS, a convener of the *San Diego Citizens'
> Grand Jury* ... and the Progressive Democrats' 2008
> candidate for Congress in California's District 53.

Printed in the United States
133866LV00003B/2/P